Easter,

Dear Angel!

Wouldn't you know it! They left one beautiful blonde from the 50's out...
You!
(Eva Marie Saint)
Well you'll just have to Fill in!

All my love to you my caring sweetheart
Tom

HOLLYWOOD FASHION

100 YEARS OF HOLLYWOOD ICONS

NANCY J. HAJESKI

© 2019 Moseley Road Inc.

All rights reserved. No part of this publication may be reproduced, stored in a retrieval system, or transmitted, in any form or by any means, electronic, mechanical, photocopying, recording, or otherwise, without prior written permission from the publisher.

President: Sean Moore
Production Director: Adam Moore
Editorial Director: Lisa Purcell
Author: Nancy J. Hajeski
Art Direction: Duncan Youel at OilOften Graphic Design, London. www.oiloften.co.uk
Design: Kate Williams at KatieLoveDesign

Editor: Karen Lawrence

ISBN: 978-1-62669-147-6

Printed and bound in China

10 9 8 7 6 5 4 3 2 1

CONTENTS

The Birth of Hollywood Fashion	8

The Nineteen Twenties

Mary Pickford	12
Lillian Gish	13
Gloria Swanson	14
Clara Bow	15
Fashion Influence:	
The Flapper	16
Vilma Banky	18
Theda Bara	19
Anna May Wong	20
Dolores Del Río	21
Style Maker:	
Adrian	22
Janet Gaynor	24
Louise Brooks	25
Greta Garbo	26
Men of the 1920s:	
From Sheiks to Slapstick	28

The Nineteen Thirties

Jean Harlow	32
Fashion Influence:	
The Bias Cut	34
Mae West	36
Carole Lombard	37
Marlene Dietrich	38
Myrna Loy	40
Claudette Colbert	41
Fashion Influence:	
Shirley Temple	42
Ginger Rogers	44
Jean Arthur	45
Style Maker:	
Travis Banton	46
Norma Shearer	48
Vivien Leigh	49
Album of Trendsetters:	
The Blonde Leading the Blonde	50
Style Maker:	
Orry-Kelly	52
Men of the 1930s: Dapper, Dancing, or Dangerous	54

The Nineteen Forties

Katherine Hepburn	58
Ingrid Bergman	60
Rita Hayworth	61
Album of Trendsetters:	
Queens of Technicolor	62
Barbara Stanwyck	64
Gene Tierney	65
Style Maker:	
Edith Head	66
Loretta Young	68
Lana Turner	69
Bette Davis	70
Fashion Influence:	
Working Women	72
Rosalind Russell	74
Lauren Bacall	75
Joan Crawford	76
Betty Grable	78
Lena Horne	79
Fashion Influence:	
Hollywood Goes to War	80
June Allyson	82
Irene Dunne	83

Judy Garland	84
Men of the 1940s: Heroes and Heartthrobs	86

The Nineteen Fifties

Marilyn Monroe	90
Kim Novak	92
Sophia Loren	93
Style Maker: Helen Rose	94
Grace Kelly	96
Fashion Influence: From Sports to Screen	98
Elizabeth Taylor	100
Style Maker: Walter Plunkett	102
Fashion Influence: Teenage Trends	104
Deborah Kerr	106
Debbie Reynolds	107
Fashion Influence: The Hollywood Musical	108
Judy Holliday	110
Natalie Wood	111
Fashion Influence: Cowboy Couture	112
Sandra Dee	114
Janet Leigh	115
Men of the 1950s: Rebels with a Cause	116

The Nineteen Sixties

Shirley MacLaine	120
Doris Day	121
Album of Trendsetters: Oscar Styles 1930s—1960s	122
Jane Fonda	124
Nancy Kwan	125
Fashion Influence: The Counterculture	126
Audrey Hepburn	128
Fashion Influence: Gangster Chic	130
Goldie Hawn	132
Julie Christie	133
Fashion Influence: The Bikini	134
Julie Andrews	136
Faye Dunaway	137
Fashion Influence: Foreign Films	138
Mia Farrow	140
Ann-Margret	141
Men of the 1960s: The Cinema Antihero	142

The Nineteen Seventies

Barbra Streisand	146
Jill Clayburgh	148
Diana Ross	149
Ali MacGraw	150
Susan Sarandon	152
Diane Keaton	153
Fashion Influence: Annie Hall	154
Bo Derek	156
Liza Minnelli	157
Fashion Influence: Disco	158
Men of the 1970s: Edgy Actors and Men of Action	160

The Nineteen Eighties

Jessica Lange	164
Meryl Streep	165
Melanie Griffith	166
Kathleen Turner	167
Demi Moore	168
Molly Ringwald	169
Fashion Influence: Dudes and Valley Girls	170
Whoopi Goldberg	172

CONTENTS

Jamie Lee Curtis	173
Fashion Influence: Workout Clothes	174
Winona Ryder	176
Sigourney Weaver	177
Michelle Pfeiffer	178
Bette Midler	179
Fashion Influence: Rock and Roll	180
Cher	182
Kim Basinger	183
Men of the 1980s: Decade of Decadence	184

The Nineteen Nineties

Julia Roberts	188
Kate Winslet	189
Fashion Influence: Science Fiction/Fantasy	190
Jennifer Lopez	192
Sharon Stone	193
Sandra Bullock	194
Meg Ryan	195
Style Maker: Ann Roth	196
Cate Blanchett	198
Nicole Kidman	199
Cameron Diaz	200
Halle Berry	201
Album of Trendsetters: Our Favorite Brunettes	202
Drew Barrymore	204
Gwyneth Paltrow	205
Men of the 1990s: Tender-Hearted Tough Guys	206

The New Millennium

Anne Hathaway	210
Catherine Zeta-Jones	211
Charlize Theron	212
Uma Thurman	213
Album of Trendsetters: Oscar Styles 1970s—2000s	214
Angelina Jolie	216
Sarah Jessica Parker	217
Fashion Influence: Horror Films	218
Keira Knightley	220
Natalie Portman	221
Reece Witherspoon	222
Zoe Saldana	224
Style Maker: Patricia Field	225
Lupita Nyong'o	226
Emma Stone	227
Men of the New Millennium: Pirates, Superheroes and Regular Joes	228
Oscars for Costume Design	230
Timeline	232
Author biog & Credits	240

THE BIRTH OF HOLLYWOOD FASHION

The American motion picture industry, arguably the oldest in the world, began in New York and New Jersey in the early 1900s. It was truly under way by 1911, when Nestor Studios opened in Los Angeles, California, on Sunset Boulevard—within view of the "Hollywoodland" real estate sign that would give the film capital its name. In addition to big-name stars and lavish productions, Hollywood films also became known for cutting-edge fashions, including opulent evening wear, stylish sportswear, seductive loungewear, and trendsetting street clothes.

Yet in most early films there were no specific costume designers. Actors and actresses wore clothing from their own closets…or the studios rented costumes for them from a supply house. (This lack of interest in customized wardrobes is ironic considering how many studio heads had backgrounds in the garment trade—Adolph Zukor of Paramount had been a furrier, Samuel Goldwyn was formerly a glover, and Louis B. Mayer worked as a shoemaker.)

It wasn't until 1915 that Clare West, who worked with D.W. Griffith on *Intolerance*, was given the title "studio designer." Up until then, wardrobers had been a division of the drapery department—where costumes would be tacked together for filming and then torn apart hours later. Cecil B. DeMille understood the audience's desire for "cinema" clothing; he hired West in 1918 to create a costume department at Famous Players-Lasky's, where she worked on at least 10 DeMille productions.

It is believed to be 1916 when a costume designer first received a film credit. He was Louis J. Gasnier, a Frenchman who also occasionally directed. He created a black suit with a white blouse and black beret for American actress Pearl White, famous for the *Perils of Pauline* adventure serials. The outfit was an immediate hit with young women, who demanded retail copies, and its success helped boost the role of the studio designer.

Several years earlier across the Atlantic, a 1912 French production of *Queen Elizabeth* starring Sarah Bernhardt—and with costumes by couturier Paul Poiret—had created such a stir that American producers began to import foreign designers like Paul Iribe and Erté to work with their in-house staff. By the early 1920s, studios were focusing more energy and money on costume design, to the point that inventive American designers outshone the Parisians…and the United States took her first steps as an international fashion powerhouse.

The importance of studio-based designers continued into the 1950s, when the taste for lavish musicals created a sort of Renaissance of costume design. With the unraveling of the studio system that shortly followed, however, many design departments felt the axe fall. Of course, Hollywood continues to employ designers, but now they are

BELOW

Intolerance, from 1915, was the first film where a wardrobe person, Clare West, was given the title "studio designer."

THE BIRTH OF HOLLYWOOD FASHION | HOLLYWOOD FASHION

> They gave to their Goddesses... the serenity of perfection and the fabulous appearance of freedom.
>
> ELSA SCHIAPARELLI, ON THE ANCIENT GREEKS

free to move from studio to studio and place to place, perhaps working on a big-budget movie epic one month and a quirky independent film or a TV series or stage play the next.

The Evolution of Movie Costumes

The craft of film costume design quite naturally grew out of theatrical design. Yet the film medium called for something less obvious than "must-see-it-from-the-balcony" stage clothing. The movie camera was intimate with its subjects, so clothing could be more detailed. And unlike stage costumes, which had to allow freedom of movement, film costumes might be so closely fitted that the wearer could not sit down. Studios began using leaning boards between takes so actresses in tight gowns could rest standing upright.

Costume designers typically begin sketching ideas during the pre-production phase of a film. In addition to dressing the stars, a designer might also be responsible for costuming the supporting players, the extras, and even animal actors. They can either create the costumes from scratch, rent from costume suppliers, or order "ready-made" outfits from specialty houses.

In the case of historical films, designers must research the styles of the era, the fabrics and accessories, even the undergarments. Keeping in mind what level of discomfort modern actors will—and won't—tolerate, designers usually try to capture the feel of a period without slavishly copying each nuance or detail.

The ideal design is one that so effortlessly blends with the film character that the audience barely notices it...which makes costume design a sometimes-thankless pursuit.

A Changing Role

Hollywood fashion over the past ten decades has come to serve a dual purpose, reflecting what Americans were wearing while affecting the clothing they chose. The cinema is now as much a mirror of Main Street as it is a style arbiter. Yet one aspect of Hollywood fashion is forever unchanging: from the teenaged girl in the 1930s copying Ginger Rogers's sailor suit to the young boy of modern times improvising Christian Bale's Batman cape, the glorious truth is that when movies showed us how to dress, they also taught us how to dream.

ABOVE

Greer Garson, in 1940's *Pride and Prejudice*, famously rejected the historically accurate high-waisted gowns of the Regency period and insisted on Victorian-style gowns with natural waistlines.

TOP LEFT

1957's *Funny Face*, with Fred Astaire and Audrey Hepburn, was all about Paris haute couture.

9

THE NINETEEN TWENTIES

Hollywood movies grew up during the 1920s. Increasingly, they were sophisticated, full-length productions instead of patched-together two- or three-reelers. Film technology advanced rapidly, and in the middle of the decade, sound made its debut. On screen, more attention was being paid to the subtleties of acting, to lighting, set decoration, and other production values, and, most visibly, to costume design.

Although the tradition of actors raiding their own closets for wardrobe material continued, more and more studios were paying attention to the audience's demands for glamorous clothing that reflected the style of Coco Chanel and other top designers.

There was now also a need for designers to create film-specific costumes, since movies were being marketed by genres based on archetypal story lines—Biblical epics like *Ben-Hur*, Westerns, melodramas, comedies, historical films, swashbucklers, romances, and thrillers. Genre films required costumes that reflected the overall theme and contributed to the story.

By the late 1920s, most studios boasted a bona fide costume department. Many had brilliant innovators at the helm, some had separate designers for male and female actors. Even nightgown and lingerie design mattered, since in this decade before the advent of the morally restrictive Hays Code, couples were filmed in bed together and women were shown in varying states of undress.

HOLLYWOOD FASHION | THE NINETEEN TWENTIES

MARY PICKFORD

America's golden-haired sweetheart, who possessed "luminous tenderness in a steel band of gutter ferocity," was also a skilled businesswoman and one of the founders of United Artists and the Academy of Motion Picture Arts and Sciences.

Mary Pickford (1892–1979), known for her plucky, youthful characters and spill of long glowing curls, was born Gladys Marie Smith in Toronto, Canada. The early 1900s saw Pickford—and her two younger siblings—working the low-end theater circuit in America.

In 1907, Gladys was cast in a Broadway play, *The Warrens of Virginia*—in which producer David Belasco changed her name to Mary Pickford. When she impressed director D. W. Griffith during a screen test, he signed her to a contract at assembly-line studio Biograph, where she made 51 movies in 1909, playing bit parts and leads.

By 1913 she was on the West Coast under contract to Famous Players-Lasky. The film *Tess of the Storm Country* "sent her career into orbit" and made her famous around the world. Pickford used her power to gain more control over her films, and in 1919 she formed United Artists with future husband Douglas Fairbanks, comedian Charlie Chaplin, and director D.W. Griffith.

By the late 1920s, a more mature Pickford, minus her crowning curls, was no longer enthralling audiences, and she retired in 1933. But as one of the first bona fide movie stars, she was a pioneering torchbearer. She tirelessly promoted Liberty bonds, helped found the Motion Picture Relief Fund, and earned the gratitude of future film buffs by convincing Hollywood that motion pictures could be much more than "canned theater."

MOST FASHIONABLE FILMS

REBECCA OF SUNNYBROOK FARM (1917)
THE POOR LITTLE RICH GIRL (1917)
POLLYANNA (1920)
LITTLE LORD FAUNTLEROY (1922)

Pickford Style
Pickford knew how much appearances mattered. Even when "Little Mary" played waifs, she made sure expert seamstresses sewed on her patches in exactly the right places.

Signature Look
- Picture hats
- Waist-length baloney curls
- Frilly dresses and ruffled pinafores

ABOVE
Pickford was known for playing youthful roles in films such as *Rebecca of Sunnybrook Farm* and *Pollyanna* and she was dressed accordingly.

RIGHT
Few of Pickford's attempts to escape her little girl image were successful, but her role in *Coquette* (1929), which earned her an Oscar, saw Pickford playing a flapper, complete with bobbed hair and boyish silhouette.

12 1920s

THE NINETEEN TWENTIES | HOLLYWOOD FASHION

LILLIAN GISH

Gish Style

Gish's angelic features remained well into old age. She never aspired to flapper fame, but kept her hair and clothing simple and her makeup natural. As Gish herself said, "I've never been in style, so I can never go out of style."

Signature Look

- Soft eyes
- Sheer, fluttering gowns
- Pearl chokers

Lillian Gish used her ethereal looks and strength of character to sustain a long and venerable career on stage and screen.

Lillian Gish (1893–1993) excelled at playing imperiled waifs and distraught heroines. Born Lillian Diana de Guiche, she did stage tours as a child to support her family and made her screen debut with sister Dorothy in D.W. Griffith's *An Unseen Enemy* (1912). It was under Griffith that she developed the hauntingly vulnerable persona that matched her physical delicacy.

Gish was especially effective in costume dramas such as *The Birth of a Nation*, *Broken Blossoms* (1919), and *Orphans of the Storm*, the latter with Dorothy. Gish was arguably the first "method" actress, forcing herself to endure starvation and extreme heat and cold to add reality to her performances. Film scholars later dubbed her the "First Lady of the Silent Screen."

Gish continued to act occasionally after the advent of sound—in 1955, she played a courageous farmwoman battling evil preacher Robert Mitchum in the suspense classic, *Night of the Hunter*, directed by actor Charles Laughton. Gish later became an advocate for the preservation of silent films; she received an honorary Academy Award in 1971 and an AFI Life Achievement Award in 1984.

MOST FASHIONABLE FILMS

THE BIRTH OF A NATION (1915)
ORPHANS OF THE STORM (1921)
LA BOHÈME (1926)

ABOVE

In a different turn for Gish, she dressed in tartan for *Annie Laurie* (1927), a story of warring Scottish clans.

LEFT

Gish was usually known for wearing soft, flowing gowns that accentuated her angelic features.

13

HOLLYWOOD FASHION | **THE NINETEEN TWENTIES**

GLORIA SWANSON

By the time I was 15, my mother had turned me into a real clotheshorse
GLORIA SWANSON

ABOVE
With pert spit curls framing her dark-rimmed eyes and well-defined lips, Swanson looked every inch the flapper in *Sadie Thompson*.

RIGHT
Standing barely five feet, Swanson nonetheless often swathed her tiny frame in jewels, feathers, furs, and lace. In the silent film *The Hummingbird* (1924), she wore a delicate gown with graceful points of lace and a raised waistline..

Not only a hugely popular silent film star, Swanson was also one of Hollywood's first fashion icons.

Gloria Swanson (1899–1983) brought her own style to all her roles—comedies or costume dramas. Gloria May Josephine Svensson was born in Chicago, but grew up in Puerto Rico and Key West. After touring a Chicago studio, Swanson found work as an extra, but by 1916 she was headed to Hollywood to work in Mack Sennett's Keystone comedies.

Cecil B. de Mille made her a leading lady in hits like *Don't Change Your Husband* and *Male and Female* (both 1919) and by 1922 she was one of Hollywood's top stars. During the filming of the first French/American co-produced film, *Madame Sans-Gêne*, she met her third husband, Henri de La Falaise, Marquis de La Coudraye. Swanson was now European royalty as well as screen royalty.

Swanson's pet project, 1928's *Sadie Thompson*, could be filmed only because the actress toned down Somerset Maugham's racy story, and it became her most successful independent film. Swanson made several hit talkies in the 1930s, but it wasn't until 1950—and Billy Wilder's *Sunset Boulevard*—that she found the role of a lifetime. Only Swanson possessed the self-confidence to play delusional, faded, silent-era star Norma Desmond. Many critics consider it the best film about Hollywood ever made.

MOST FASHIONABLE FILMS
ZAZA (1923)
MADAME SANS-GÊNE (1925)
SADIE THOMPSON (1928)
SUNSET BOULEVARD (1950)

Swanson Style
Swanson was known for her own couturier clothing and the elaborate period costumes in her films.

Signature Look
- Feathered turbans and exotic furs
- Strings of pearls and beads
- Distinctive dark mouth

14 1920s

THE NINETEEN TWENTIES | HOLLYWOOD FASHION

CLARA BOW

Tomboy Clara Bow rose from the slums of Brooklyn to become America's vivacious Jazz Age heroine.

Clara Bow (1905–1965) epitomized the carefree flapper to millions of filmgoers. She grew up in grim poverty, where watching movies provided her only escape. Determined to improve her life, she entered and won a beauty contest, giving her the confidence to pursue acting roles.

Bow was cast as flappers in films like *Dancing Mothers* and *Mantrap*, but it was her performance as a plucky shop girl in 1927's *It* that made her "The It Girl"—and a genuine star. 1927's *Wings* was rewritten to include a part for her and it went on to win the first Best Picture Oscar.

Bow made an easy transition to talkies, but she was not a fan, complaining that they reduced her "cuteness." In 1936, she retired from the screen to marry cowboy star—and future lieutenant governor of Nevada—Rex Bell. During the late 1940s, Bow suffered from mental illness and underwent shock treatment. She spent her final years in the care of a nurse.

MOST FASHIONABLE FILMS

DANCING MOTHERS (1925)
MANTRAP (1926)
IT (1927)
WINGS (1927)

Bow Style

Bow was never confident about her looks. Casting directors often told her she was too short, too awkward, or too fat. But she truly possessed that "It" factor, an appeal that had little to do with exterior beauty.

Signature Look
- Bobbed hair with side spit curls
- Bee-stung dark lips
- Cloche hats

ABOVE

A publicity still from the lost silent *Rough House Rosie* (1927) shows Bow as the ultimate flapper—feisty and fun-loving in a sexy little boxing outfit and curly bob.

LEFT

Bow became "The It Girl" after starring in *It* where she played a shopgirl with her eyes on the boss. She wore dresses and skirts that were shorter and looser to let the working girl move more easily.

HOLLYWOOD FASHION | THE NINETEEN TWENTIES

FASHION INFLUENCE
THE FLAPPER

> **They were smart and sophisticated, with an air of independence about them, and so casual about their looks and clothes and manners as to be almost slapdash**
> COLLEEN MOORE

Also called the Jazz Baby, the flapper of the 1920s represented easy-going, unrepressed American womanhood in all its glory. The flapper drank and smoked, she danced to wild music, she bobbed her hair into a sleek cap, and rolled her stockings down below the hem of her short, fringed dress.

The rise of the flapper from the late 1910s into the 1920s was due to a number of factors, including a new optimism after the miseries of World War I; increased education for females and new arenas for careers and recreation; women acquiring the vote; and a reaction to the unpopular restrictions of Prohibition. Some scholars believe the flapper was the logical offspring of the free-spirited Gibson girl, who had arisen three decades earlier.

Whatever her origin, the true flapper had to possess one thing—style. As French dressmakers began to establish themselves as worldwide arbiters of taste, Parisian couturier Coco Chanel popularized the unstructured clothing with simple lines that became associated with the flapper. Chanel's boyish "garçonne" look was quickly adopted in Europe and America. And with the availability of paper-template dress patterns, many women found they could duplicate these simpler flapper styles at home.

The flapper's male counterpart was either the fresh-faced College Boy, or the suave Man About Town. The collegiate look consisted of Oxford bag trousers, varsity sweaters, raccoon coats, and straw boaters or beanies—comedian Harold Lloyd made a career of personifying this look—while the man about town lived in dinner jackets or tuxedos and was rarely seen in daylight. In his contemporary screen roles, Rudolph Valentino exemplified the ultimate "lounge lizard."

Hollywood's Own Flappers
It didn't take Hollywood long to embrace the

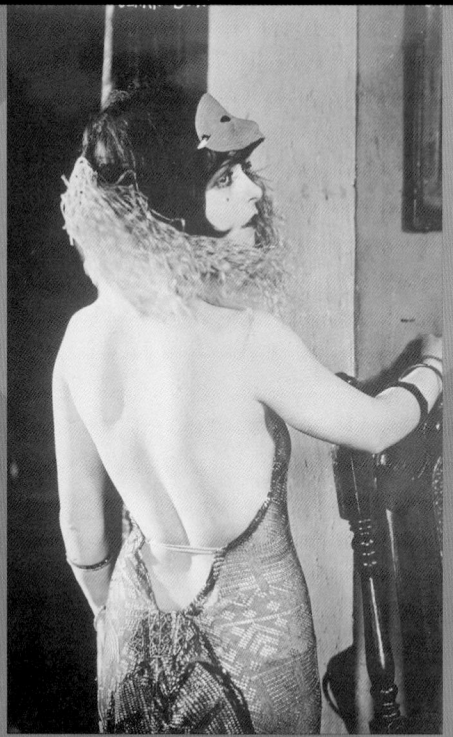

TOP RIGHT
Clara Bow personified the spirit of the roaring twenties in an open-backed flapper dress.

flapper—she was saucy, sexy, and stylish. Olive Thomas played one in 1917 and then again in 1920, in a film aptly entitled *The Flapper*. The film was a hit and the term—and the attitude—rapidly caught on with American audiences. Other notable screen flappers include Clara Bow, Louise Brooks, Colleen Moore, and the young Joan Crawford.

That Fabulous Flapper Face
The advent of portable cosmetics, such as metal lipstick cases and powder and blush compacts with mirrors, aided the flapper in maintaining her well-made-up "look"—the kohl-dark eyes, bee-stung mouth, and rouged cheeks. Now stylish girls on the street could emulate their cinema sisters.

THE NINETEEN TWENTIES | HOLLYWOOD FASHION

TOP

Coco Chanel popularized the unstructured look of the flapper era.

ABOVE

Colleen Moore was one of the most fashionable flappers of the silent film era.

LEFT

The silent film *Our Dancing Daughters* (1928) glamorized flapper fashions while demonizing flapper morality. Against iconic Art Deco sets, Dorothy Sebastian (left), Joan Crawford (center), and Anita Page (right) play Jazz Age moderns. Crawford, with kohl-lined eyes and bee-stung lips, was a star here, before she really hit her stride as a style icon of the 1930s and 1940s.

Where did the word Flapper originate?

The term appeared in a 1903 story about Oxford, *Sandford of Merton*, by Desmond Coke, in the line: "There's a stunning flapper." Originally "flapper" connoted an ingénue, too young to wear long frocks or put her hair up. By 1911, the impudent and flirtatious young flapper was a recognized stage type in Britain. During World War I, however, the word began to refer to pleasureseeking women of any age. By 1920, on both sides of the Atlantic, flapper had evolved to its present-day meaning with its emphasis on both style and attitude—a scantily clad, dance- and cocktail-crazy gadabout with little more on her brain than the latest fashions and the hottest new club.

17

HOLLYWOOD FASHION | **THE NINETEEN TWENTIES**

VILMA BANKY

Banky, a smoldering European import, played opposite legendary actors and became Samuel Goldwyn's biggest money-maker in the late 1920s.

Vilma Banky (1898–1991) was known for her elegant, aristocratic roles. She was born in Hungary and began her film career in Hungarian, Austrian and French films. In 1925, studio chief Samuel Goldwyn put the actress under contract, even though she spoke no English. (Goldwyn supposedly told her to answer all reporters' questions with "lamb chops and pineapple.")

Once in Hollywood, the lovely Banky became known as The Hungarian Rhapsody. She caught the eye of Rudolph Valentino, who cast her as his enemy's daughter in *The Eagle* (with costumes by an uncredited Adrian) and as a dancing girl in what would be his final film, *The Son of the Sheik*. The actress also costarred with matinee idol Ronald Colman in a number of successful romances, including *The Dark Angel* (1926) and *The Winning of Barbara Worth*.

When Banky wed actor Rod La Rocque (1896—1969), Goldwyn bankrolled the event, said to be one of the most extravagant weddings of the era. Banky retired from films shortly thereafter—she said she wanted to spend time with her husband and play golf. The couple remained together until La Rocque's death in 1969.

Banky Style

The delicate beauty looked as good in period costumes as she did in modern dress. As leading lady to two of the screen's most desirable men, Banky inspired many fans to emulate her style.

Signature Look
- Blond Marcel curls
- Ostrich feathers and fur muffs
- Art Deco jewelry

MOST FASHIONABLE FILMS

THE EAGLE (1925)
THE WINNING OF BARBARA WORTH (1926)
THE SON OF THE SHEIK (1926)

ABOVE

Banky was known for looking and dressing like royalty.

RIGHT

As dancing girl Yasmin In *The Son of the Sheik*, Banky smoldered in sheer chiffons and sumptuous brocades.

THE NINETEEN TWENTIES | HOLLYWOOD FASHION

THEDA BARA

The career of the cinema's first screen siren spawned both the Hollywood publicity machine and the press agent.

Theda Bara (1885–1955) created a completely new female character—the predatory sex symbol. Born Theodosia Burr Goodman in Cincinnati, Ohio, the actress's exotic screen name was, famously, an anagram of "Arab Death"...though there was a branch of her family called Barranger.

Bara appeared on Broadway in 1908 and did extra work in films until she won the role of a vampire who destroys men in *A Fool There Was*. She signed with Fox Studios (of Fort Lee, New Jersey) in 1915 and did six films for them, ending with *Carmen*. After she followed Fox to Hollywood in 1917 to make *Cleopatra*, she continued her string of notorious females, starring in *Madame Du Barry*, *Salome*, *The She-Devil*, *La Belle Russe*, *The Unchastened Woman*, and *Madame Mystery*.

Bara's revealing costumes, sultry film persona and a studio bio claiming that she had spent her youth in Egypt, set audiences aflame. The term *vamp* (short for "vampire") was coined for her and soon became associated with any predatory female. Although the actress made more than 40 movies, only six complete films remain—in great part due to a devastating fire at Fox's film storage facility in Little Ferry, New Jersey.

MOST FASHIONABLE FILMS

CLEOPATRA (1917)
SALOME (1918)
LA BELLE RUSSE (1919)
MADAME MYSTERY (1926)

Bara Style

The actress played to her audience even while at home, discussing the occult with reporters, toying with skulls, and making sure even her lounging clothes reflected her sex goddess image.

Signature Look
- Dark, smoky eyes
- Head scarves and fringed shawls
- Bold jewelry with snake and insect motifs

ABOVE

Bara excelled at playing strong women, as in *Cleopatra*, one of her biggest hits, in costumes that matched her supersized personality.

LEFT

Before the 1920s even started, Bara's large, kohl-rimmed eyes and small, pouty mouth presaged the coming flapper's ideal look.

HOLLYWOOD FASHION | **THE NINETEEN TWENTIES**

ANNA MAY WONG

The first Asian-American to become an international star, Wong fought against "Dragon Lady" stereotyping.

Anna May Wong (1905–1961) was considered one of the best-dressed women in Hollywood, even as she fought for roles. A third-generation Chinese-American born in Los Angeles, Wong used to haunt directors shooting in her neighborhood, and they started calling her C.C.C.—Curious Chinese Child.

At 17, she won the lead in *The Toll of the Sea*, based on Puccini's opera, *Madame Butterfly*. Both *Variety* and the *New York Times* called her extraordinary. Sadly, similar roles were hard to find. The law made it illegal for a Chinese actress to kiss a Caucasian actor, and Hollywood had no Asian leading men. Wong was finally cast as a Mongol slave in Douglas Fairbanks' 1924 fantasy *The Thief of Bagdad*. The film became a huge hit and Wong's fame increased.

In 1927, she starred in a Chinese-backed film, *The Silk Bouquet*, but found only supporting roles at the studios. She moved to Europe in 1928, where she was a smash in the German films *Song* and *Pavement Butterfly*, and in the British *Piccadilly*. She returned to America in 1930. Her most famous sound film was 1932's *Shanghai Express* with Marlene Dietrich.

MOST FASHIONABLE FILMS

THE TOLL OF THE SEA (1922)
THE THIEF OF BAGDAD (1924)
PICCADILLY (1929)
SHANGHAI EXPRESS (1932)

Wong Style
In 1934, Wong was voted the Best Dressed Woman in the World by New York's Mayfair Mannequin Society. The yearly Asian Fashion Designers award is named after her.

Signature Look
- Straight bangs with floral hairpieces
- Silk and satin fitted gowns
- Exotic prints

ABOVE

Straight bangs were part of Wong's signature look.

RIGHT

Her influence on fashion wouldn't take full effect until the next decade, but from the time Anna May Wong stepped into the Hollywood scene in the early 1920s, her Asian-inspired sense of style left its mark.

THE NINETEEN TWENTIES | HOLLYWOOD FASHION

DOLORES DEL RÍO

This exotic beauty—the first international Latin-American movie star—wowed Hollywood and later became a fixture of Mexican cinema.

Dolores Del Río (1905–1983) embodied the pampered, exotic, patrician female. She was, in fact, born to a wealthy, upper-class family in Durango, Mexico. She caught the eye of film producer Edwin Carewe, who offered her a Hollywood contract. She quickly gained a following in films like *What Price Glory?*, *The Loves of Carmen*, and *Ramona* and was considered Valentino's smoldering female counterpart.

Even though Del Río fought against studio stereotyping, she was often cast in "Mexicali Rose" roles—or even as a jungle princess in early sound film, *Bird of Paradise*. She is perhaps most famous for 1933's *Flying Down to Rio* (the first Astaire-Rogers film) where she was paired with Gene Raymond, a blond actor who provided a striking contrast to her dark beauty.

After a torrid affair with Orson Welles (he was impressed by her lingerie, which it is said was made by French nuns), Del Río returned to her roots. She became the most famous film star in Mexico and won their Academy Award, the Silver Ariel, four times. 1964 found her back in Hollywood, playing a Native American in John Ford's epic *Cheyenne Autumn*.

MOST FASHIONABLE FILMS
RESURRECTION (1927)
BIRD OF PARADISE (1932)
FLYING DOWN TO RIO (1933)
MARIA CANDELARIA (1943)

Del Río Style
Del Río was a tiny, birdlike woman, with large dark eyes, lustrous hair, and a sensual mouth. Her narrow body was ideal for showcasing bias-cut gowns and clingy lounging outfits.

Signature Look
- White, form-fitting gowns
- Defined, dark lips
- Over-sized sparkling earrings and layered, draped necklaces

ABOVE
Del Río's dark beauty made her an exotic rarity in an age when Hollywood was ruled by blond actresses.

LEFT
In *Bird of Paradise*, set in the south seas, Del Río scandalized audiences by not wearing much and then swimming naked with Joel McCrea. This was before the Hays Code brought censorship to Hollywood.

MOST FASHIONABLE DESIGNS

DINNNER AT EIGHT (1933)
NAUGHTY MARIETTA (1935)
MARIE ANTOINETTE (1938)
THE WOMEN (1939)
THE WIZARD OF OZ (1939)
THE PHILADELPHIA STORY (1940)

THE NINETEEN TWENTIES | HOLLYWOOD FASHION

STYLE MAKER
ADRIAN

Gilbert Adrian (birth name: Adrian Adolph Greenberg) was born in Naugatuck, Connecticut, in 1903. While he was studying art in Paris, Irving Berlin noticed one of his designs at a costume ball and Adrian's career took off.

After working with Berlin in New York on his *Music Box Revue*, Adrian went to Hollywood in the mid-1920s. He designed opulent Russian costumes for *The Eagle* (1925) for Rudolph Valentino, and then did 26 films for Cecil B. DeMille. In 1928, he moved with DeMille to MGM and was made head of their costume department, where he reigned supreme until 1942.

Adrian was a versatile craftsman, who worked on up to 15 films a year, including some memorable classics that required widely differing styles: the classy couture of *Dinner at Eight* (1933), the frothy confections of *Naughty Marietta* (1935) and *Marie Antoinette* (1938), and the storybook costumes of *The Wizard of Oz* (1939).

When the studio assigned him to make the stocky, short-waisted Joan Crawford appear taller and more slender, Adrian widened her shoulders with padding and dressed her in fitted jackets with narrow skirts. The illusion worked like a charm—and broad shoulders became the rage for ladies' daytime and evening wear. Adrian had also been responsible for crafting the unique looks of Jean Harlow and Greta Garbo—the latter's retirement marked the end of his sojourn at MGM.

Adrian is credited with many fashion innovations and was responsible for the evolution of a distinct American style. He was also a savvy and enterprising businessman—he had been one of the first Hollywood designers to merchandise cinema-based clothing. His layered, organza gown from the Crawford film *Letty Lynton* (1932) was successfully mass-produced in the early 1930s and reportedly sold 500,000 pieces at Macy's. In 1948, he opened salons in New York and Los Angeles to market his couture designs and soon also had ready-to-wear lines in department stores.

When the designer suffered a heart attack in 1952, he left film work and retired to his Brazilian ranch with wife, actress Janet Gaynor. He did not return to costume design until 1957, when he worked on the musical *Grand Hotel*. Adrian was collaborating with Tony Duquette on costumes for the play *Camelot* in 1959 when he died of a heart attack. He won a posthumous Tony Award in 1961 for this work.

LEFT

The Women featured Norma Shearer, Joan Crawford, and Rosalind Russell, along with an all-female cast. It was set in New York and Reno and was full of high fashion and high society hijinks.

FULL PAGE

Here, Adrian sits surrounded by some of his sketches. In the course of his Hollywood career he designed costumes for over 250 films; his screen credits usually read as "Gowns by Adrian."

23

HOLLYWOOD FASHION | THE NINETEEN TWENTIES

JANET GAYNOR

Winner of the first Academy Award for Best Actress, Gaynor was one of the silent era's most versatile stars.

Janet Gaynor (1906–1984) played the plucky, aspiring ingénue or the noble, long-suffering wife. She was born Laura Augusta Gainor in Philadelphia, PA, and not long after, her family moved to San Francisco. When teen-aged Gaynor decided on an acting career, she headed to Los Angeles. After struggling with bit parts for two years, she was cast in the 1926 hit *The Johnstown Flood*. By early 1928 she was the new queen of Hollywood, with roles in three major films: *Seventh Heaven*, *Sunrise*, and *Street Angel*. She was twenty-two.

Gaynor was paired with Charles Farrell, her *Seventh Heaven* costar, in more than a dozen films, earning them the nickname "world's favorite sweethearts." Gaynor made an easy transition to sound films, but insisted on taking voice lessons. Though not glamorous and barely five feet tall, Gaynor possessed a gamine charm that helped her establish empathy with audiences in a number of melodramatics, including the first version of *A Star is Born* in 1937.

Gaynor retired from films in 1939 to marry her second husband, legendary costume designer Adrian. The couple had one son, Robert Gaynor Adrian, and remained together until the designer's death in 1959.

MOST FASHIONABLE FILMS
SEVENTH HEAVEN (1927)
SUNRISE (1927)
STREET ANGEL (1927)
A STAR IS BORN (1937)

Gaynor Style
Gaynor was petite and slender, with large eyes, curly auburn hair, and a distinctive dimple in her chin. She often played youthful innocents in films, so her wardrobes were appropriately girlish.

Signature Look
• Sweet organdy gowns
• Pale blouses with ruffles or bows
• Tam O'Shanter hats

ABOVE
The actress was often costumed in feminine gowns embellished with bows and flowers that underscored her innocent charm.

RIGHT
In *Street Angel*, the airy, down-trimmed costume of a circus performer was the perfect foil for Gaynor's gamine good looks.

24 1920s

THE NINETEEN TWENTIES | HOLLYWOOD FASHION

LOUISE BROOKS

This independent-minded actress became one of the first stars whose look and style women copied.

Mary Louise Brooks (1906–1985) embodied the modern, emancipated woman of the 1920s. She was born in Cherryvale, Kansas, and began her stage career with the Denishawn Dancers before appearing in *George White's Scandals* and the *Ziegfeld Follies* on Broadway. After several years of playing lighthearted flappers for Paramount, Brooks traveled to Germany and found her breakthrough role: Lulu, the tragic temptress, in G.W. Pabst's *Pandora's Box*. The film was shockingly sexual by American standards but it became a global hit.

Never one to bow to authority, Brooks alienated many influential people in Hollywood. She refused to return to America to do sound retakes for *The Canary Murder Case*, and was blacklisted. When she did come back to Hollywood, and was offered the role in *The Public Enemy* that made Jean Harlow a star, she turned it down to visit her lover.

Brooks retired from films in 1938 and lapsed into obscurity. In the 1950s, French critics rediscovered Brooks' films and proclaimed her superior to Garbo and Dietrich. She found recognition as a film writer for her 1982 collection, *Lulu in Hollywood*.

MOST FASHIONABLE FILMS

A GIRL IN EVERY PORT (1928)
BEGGARS OF LIFE (1928)
THE CANARY MURDER CASE (1929)
PANDORA'S BOX (1929)

Brooks Style
Brooks' distinctive hair style created a sensation and had women all over America bobbing their long locks. Brooks was also the inspiration for two comic books, John H. Striebel's *Dixie Dugan* and Guido Crepax's erotic *Valentina*.

Signature Look
- Pearls against a dark neckline
- Lush fur wraps
- Sleek, blunt-cut "helmet" bob and dark lipstick

ABOVE

Brooks' bob haircut started a trend in the 1920s and is still closely associated with her look.

LEFT

In *The Canary Murder Case*, Brooks plays a showgirl dressed in swanky outfits with feathers and jewels.

25

HOLLYWOOD FASHION | THE NINETEEN TWENTIES

GRETA GARBO

ABOVE
The camera loved Garbo's face. Skillful lighting was often used to bring attention to her Nordic bone structure and graceful neck and to disguise her somewhat clumsy arms.

RIGHT
Garbo received an Oscar nomination for *Anna Christie*, her first talkie. It helped that famed designer Adrian created her exquisite period costumes.

FULL PAGE
In her own time, women copied her, and even now Garbo's classic style lives on. Menswear fabrics added to the androgynous style that has become her fashion legacy.

Few women compelled audiences like Garbo, with her physical beauty and with the wistful melancholy in her eyes.

Greta Garbo (1905–1990) brought a powerful presence to the screen and exhibited a relaxed informality away from it. Greta Lovisa Gustafsson was born in Stockholm, Sweden, to a working-class family. A job in the PUB department store's millinery department led to work as a hat model, which led to appearing in store commercials. After studying at the Royal Dramatic Theater, Garbo was chosen for a stage production of *The Saga of Gösta Berling* by director Mauritz Stiller. He would become her mentor and manager, and the man who included her in his film contract with Louis B. Mayer.

Garbo and Stiller arrived in America in 1925. Initially cast as a temptress in *The Torrent*, she struck a chord with filmgoers and received top billing in her second movie. Eight more silent films followed, including three with matinée idol, John Gilbert. In their first film together, *Flesh and the Devil*, they apparently continued their steamy love scenes off the set—and were soon living together.

The actress's Swedish accent proved no impediment to sound recording and her first talkie, *Anna Christie*, was hyped by two words, "Garbo Talks!" The film was the top draw in 1930 and earned Garbo her first Academy Award nomination. The early 1930s saw two hits, *Mata Hari* and *Grand Hotel*, resulting in the spread of "Garbomania" across the country. Women copied her hair, her brows, her clothing, and her Swedish pout.

Garbo, who often wore pants, now embarked on a "trouser" role, playing the breeches-and-boots-wearing Queen Christina of Norway. Garbo's lover, Gilbert, had trouble making the transition to sound, but she insisted on including him in the film. Their scenes together are remarkably tender, and the film was another triumph. She continued her streak of hits with *Anna Karenina* and *Camille*.

The Wrong Film
She displayed a skillful shift to comedy in *Ninotchka*, this time with the tagline "Garbo Laughs!" and was immediately given another comedy, *Two-Faced Woman*. The studio, which now wanted her portrayed as a "regular" woman, completely misread her mystique, and the film was panned. Garbo referred to it as "her grave" and it truly was. She never made another film. (Another factor in this decision was the loss of her extensive European market during World War II.)

Garbo never really fell in love with Hollywood. A woman of enormous dignity, she found the demands of the studio publicists demeaning. She loathed fame, banned visitors from her sets, and had barriers erected to screen her from the crew. Although she kept her life very private during her retirement—as she explained it, she did not want to be alone, she wanted to be left alone—she had many friends and traveled the world to visit them.

26 1920s

> **I don't want to be a silly temptress. I cannot see any sense in getting dressed up and doing nothing but tempting men in pictures.**
> GRETA GARBO

MOST FASHIONABLE FILMS
ANNA CHRISTIE (1930)
ANNA KARENINA (1935)
CAMILLE (1937)
NINOTCHKA (1939)

Garbo Style
On screen, Garbo appeared to best advantage in close-ups and long shots; mid-range shots revealed a slight slouch and clumsy limbs. Designer Adrian accentuated her exquisite features with upturned collars and brimmed hats, drawing attention away from her torso.

Signature Look
- Simple, finger-waved hairdos
- Small, chic hats or berets
- Classic, unfussy dresses or suits

HOLLYWOOD FASHION | THE NINETEEN TWENTIES

MEN OF THE 1920s
FROM SHEIKS TO SLAPSTICK

> **I am begining to look more and more like my miserable imitators.**
> RUDOLPH VALENTINO

The male stars of the 1920s covered a wide spectrum of "types."
On one end were the smoldering sex gods—Rudolph Valentino, John Barrymore, John Gilbert, and Fredric March—and the dashing adventurers like Douglas Fairbanks and Tom Mix. On the other end were a trio of nimble comedians—Charlie Chaplin, Buster Keaton, and Harold Lloyd—who were often more involved in battling fate than in getting the girl. In the middle were a few stalwart leading men, the "steady guys" like Richard Barthelmess, who won the day through good deeds and fair play. And there was one more actor of note who enriched the decade, the genius of horror films known as "The Man of a Thousand Faces": Lon Chaney.

TOP RIGHT

In 1921, Charlie Chaplin debuted the Little Tramp, complete with Derby hat, baggy pants, and cane, in *The Kid* with Jackie Coogan. Comedians over the next nine decades would seek similarly effective costume props.

RIGHT

The Thief of Baghdad (1924), starring Douglas Fairbanks and featuring towering sets by William Cameron Menzies and exotic costumes by Mitchell Leisen, set off a craze for the Arabian Nights—harem pants, gauze scarves, Moorish lamps, glazed tiles, and opulent Oriental carpets.

BOTTOM RIGHT

In *The Four Horsemen of the Apocalypse*, Rudolph Valentino introduces the exotic Gaucho look—and the sultry tango—to America. Women would later adopt the gaucho pants as culottes.

28 1920s

THE NINETEEN TWENTIES | HOLLYWOOD FASHION

Men's clothing changed considerably during the Jazz Age compared to the decade before—men's suits became more relaxed and sporty. In fact, the construction of the modern suit is, for the most part, still based on patterns from the late 1920s. For casual occasions men wore tweed jackets with "Oxford bag" trousers or jodhpur riding breeches. For relaxing at home, the brocade smoking jacket was a stylish choice. These new trends were incorporated into contemporary films where they became part of 1920s' iconography.

Men of Seduction and Action
Needless to say, fashion choices were critical for Valentino and his seductive brethren, who required an arsenal of evening wear, lounging outfits, and sporty resort wear. Likewise for the adventurers...for what was Doug Fairbanks without his mask of Zorro or his dashing musketeer uniform? Where was Tom Mix without his bandana or white Stetson?

Make 'Em Laugh
Costuming options were not so critical for the comedians, who had each developed—and stuck to—a film persona with a signature look. Chaplin's Little Tramp had his Derby hat, baggy pants, and cane; Keaton's Great Stone Face wore a pork-pie hat and homespun garb; and Lloyd's "Glasses Character" was rarely without a natty suit and boater hat.

Master of Disguise
Lon Chaney was, in a sense, his own costume designer—he could transform the Hunchback of Notre Dame's rags into a Fool King's regalia and make the Phantom of the Opera's dark, severe evening coat look both elegant and sinister. And while Chaney himself created his monstrous facial transformations with makeup and wigs, his wardrobe staff (uncredited in most films) certainly added to the chilling effect.

Signature Menswear Looks of the 1920s
- Shorter suit jackets
- High-waisted jackets, often with belts
- Narrower lapels
- Straight, narrow trousers, sometimes cuffed
- Double-breasted suit vests
- Oxford bags
- Knickers and tweed jackets
- Top hats, homburgs, fedoras, and straw boaters
- Short tuxedo jackets (rather than tails) for evening
- Brocade smoking jackets with ascots

ABOVE
Heartthrob John Gilbert dressed to impress in finely tailored classic suits and elegant dinner jackets and tuxedos.

LEFT
Lon Chaney's cape was hand-tinted red in the Bal Masqué scene of The Phantom of the Opera (1925).

THE NINETEEN THIRTIES | HOLLYWOOD FASHION

THE NINETEEN THIRTIES

The Depression sent beleaguered citizens to the cinema in record numbers, and studios produced in excess of 400 movies per year. It didn't matter whether theaters were showing comedies, dramas, Westerns, adventures, or mysteries, Americans couldn't get enough. With the advent of sound came a new, wildly popular genre—the movie musical. Al Jolson and Rudy Vallee sang, Fred Astaire and Ginger Rogers danced, and hundreds of chorus girls in feathers contorted under mirrors for choreographer Busby Berkeley.

To the audiences devouring these film fantasies, the costuming was nearly as important as the stories. Costume designers were suddenly in demand—and three legends rose to prominence in this decade, Orry-Kelly, Travis Banton, and Adrian. Stars—or their fans—demanded signature "looks" and the studios complied. With musicals, especially, the costumes had to dazzle, with the result that they influenced what couples wore to the Saturday night dance or the local supper club.

In 1939, so many classic films were released it became known as the Golden Year. To wit, *The Wizard of Oz, Mr. Smith Goes to Washington, Ninotchka, Destry Rides Again, Stagecoach, Wuthering Heights, The Hunchback of Notre Dame, Dark Victory, Gunga Din,* and a host of other favorites. The year was capped by the premiere of the first true blockbuster—*Gone with the Wind,* a Civil War epic that won ten Academy Awards, featured hundreds of costumes, and remained the box office champ until 1966.

HOLLYWOOD FASHION | THE NINETEEN THIRTIES

JEAN HARLOW

America's first platinum blonde reigned as the standard of beauty and sexuality—until her untimely death.

Jean Harlow (1911–1937) virtually minted the concept of the sassy, freewheeling blonde bombshell. Born Harlean Harlow Carpenter in Kansas City, Missouri, she was called "The Baby" as a child, a nickname that stuck. When her parents divorced, she and her overly possessive mother briefly moved to Hollywood. When they returned to Missouri, her mother married a man called Marino Bello. Eight months later, 16-year-old Harlean eloped with 20-year-old Charles "Chuck" McGrew, the heir to a fortune. The couple moved to Beverly Hills in 1928, partly to get away from Mother Jean.

While waiting to pick up a female friend at Fox Studios, Harlean caught the eye of a film executive who offered her an introduction to central casting. Harlean's friend bet her she didn't have the nerve to take him up on his offer, so Harlean drove back to the studio and signed in using her mother's maiden name, Jean Harlow. She refused the studio's early offers, but her mother and Bello—now in LA—encouraged her to try acting. She signed with Hal Roach, but quit when the demands of her career interfered with her marriage. It was too late, however. Harlow eventually left McGrew and moved in with her mother.

When Howard Hughes needed an actress for a talkie reshoot of *Hell's Angels*, Harlow tested and got the role. Though her reviews for the film were less than flattering, she made an impression with audiences. Next she was cast in the Loretta Young vehicle, *Gallagher*; Hughes insisted the title be changed to *Platinum Blonde* to cash in on Harlow's silvery-white hair.

Harlow was dating William Powell—and filming *Saratoga* with Gable—when she fell gravely ill. Doctors initially diagnosed a gall bladder attack, but they soon realized it was something much more

MOST FASHIONABLE FILMS

PLATINUM BLONDE (1931)
RED DUST (1932)
DINNER AT EIGHT (1933)
LIBELED LADY (1936)

Harlow Style
In addition to her platinum hair, Jean Harlow was famous for her scandalously tight bias-cut gowns, satin lounging pajamas, and for often leaving off her underwear.

Signature Look
- Blond, bobbed hair in Marcel curls
- Clinging white gowns
- Ermine fur accessories

serious. Harlow lapsed into a coma on June 6 and died a day later. She was 26.

Speculation has continued over the cause of her death—sunstroke, alcoholism, a botched abortion, poisoning from hair dye—but recent examination of the medical evidence indicates she was—and had been—suffering from kidney disease, possibly the result of a childhood bout of scarlet fever.

The inscription on her grave reads, simply: Our Baby.

ABOVE
Platinum Blonde was renamed to capitalize on Harlow's iconic look. Women across the country dyed their hair to look like her.

RIGHT
Harlow was buried wearing one of her gowns from *Libeled Lady*.

FULL PAGE
Frothy feathers top off a flowing lamé boudoir set designed by Adrian. The designer created Harlow's revealing costumes for *Dinner at Eight*, which came before the Hays Code was enforced.

32 1930s

> **Must I always wear a low-cut dress to be important?**
> JEAN HARLOW

HOLLYWOOD FASHION | THE NINETEEN THIRTIES

FASHION INFLUENCE
THE BIAS CUT

Every so often, some clever individual rethinks how an item is made or how a material is utilized—vulcanized rubber being one example—and the results can be startling. This was the case with the bias-cut fabrics that became so synonymous with 1930s' style.

Woven fabrics typically have threads that go in two, perpendicular directions: the warp and the weft. Prior to the 1920s, most fabric used for garments was cut in the same direction as the warp or weft threads. But when a designer named Madeleine Vionnet, who was inspired by the flowing tunics of Grecian statues, began cutting fabric for clothing at an angle of 45 degrees from the warp and weft threads, it created a radical new look. Bias-cut fabric draped differently; it became clingier and more elastic. Vionnet did not invent the bias cut, however—as far back as the Middle Ages, before the advent of knitting, men's woven hose were cut on the bias to make them fit better—but she certainly put her stamp on the process.

Mme. Vionnet (1876—1975) was born to a poor family in the French province of Loiret and was apprenticed as a seamstress at the age of eleven. As an adult, she trained in Paris with the House of Callot Soeurs and with Jacques Doucet before starting her own fashion house in 1912. Vionnet was noted for sensual clothing that glorified the female form—and for discarding corsets, padding, or anything else that distorted the figure. When she introduced the bias cut in 1927, it shot her to worldwide fame. In addition to silk and chiffon, Vionnet also used fabrics not typically seen in the couture of her day—crepe de chine, gabardine, and satin. Today, she is viewed as one of the most influential designers of the 20th century.

By the early 1930s, Hollywood had adopted the bias cut—Jean Harlow was photographed so often in bias-cut gowns and lounging pajamas, they

became her trademark look. And the style wasn't only for outfitting sexy sirens—its flowing lines could make even an ingénue appear more curvy.

There was another reason Hollywood "clung" to the bias-cut gown: After the restrictive Hays Code had been imposed, censors began banning women's clothing that featured low bodices or revealing cleavage. Costume designers quickly realized that bias-cut gowns could be incredibly seductive—especially if an actress left off her underwear—without having to be scandalously low cut.

ABOVE

Vionnet, in her workshop, simplified women's clothing by letting fabric drape their figures.

RIGHT

A slinky gown of bias-cut black charmeuse silk provided a sensuous flowing movement that wouldn't restrict Gingers Rogers as she took to the dance floor with Fred Astaire in *Shall We Dance?* (1937).

34 1930s

The dress must not hang on the body but follow its lines. When a woman smiles the dress must smile with her.

MADELEINE VIONNET

FULL PAGE
Harlow models one of her signature white gowns—this version by Adrian features a crossover bodice and halter top—in a sultry publicity still from 1933's *Bombshell*.

TOP RIGHT INSERT
Carole Lombard, here with Clark Gable, in 1932's *No Man of Her Own* strikes a pose in a Travis Banton bias-cut gown with a looped sash waist and opulent fur sleeves that hug her curves as well as Gable does.

BOTTOM RIGHT INSERT
Looking like a glittering goddess from a futuristic fantasy, Katharine Hepburn arrives at a costume party in 1933's *Christopher Strong*. Howard Greer designed the breathtaking moth costume.

HOLLYWOOD FASHION | THE NINETEEN THIRTIES

MAE WEST

Voluptuous, bawdy, and shrewd, this former vaudeville performer was the original red-hot mama.

Mae West (1893–1980), the queen of double entendre, easily brought men to their knees... and made them like it. Born Mary Jane West in Brooklyn, she graduated from childhood stardom in vaudeville to writing her own plays, including one entitled *SEX*, which got her arrested. Her first hit film, 1933's comedy *She Done Him Wrong*, costarred Cary Grant (costumes by an uncredited Edith Head) and set the tone for her next seven movies, where West plays a savvy woman of the world intent on getting whatever she wants: *I'm No Angel* with Grant; *Belle of the Nineties* (costumes by Travis Banton); *Goin' to Town* (Banton); *Klondike Annie: Go West Young Man* with Randolph Scott (costumes by Irene Jones); *Every Day's a Holiday* (gowns by Schiaparelli); and *My Little Chickadee* with W.C. Fields (gowns by Vera West).

Ironically, West has gained respect as a proto feminist— her confident, slyly amourous portrayals of women paved the way not only for future cinematic bombshells but for sexually explicit female comics as well.

MOST FASHIONABLE FILMS
I'M NO ANGEL (1933)
SHE DONE HIM WRONG (1933)
BELLE OF THE NINETIES (1935)
GO WEST YOUNG MAN (1936)
MY LITTLE CHICKADEE (1940)

West Style
Her lavish costumes made the most of assets that needed little amplification and high platform shoes worn under her long gowns elevated her diminutive five-foot frame.

Signature Look
- Corset-waisted gowns in lush, ornamented fabrics
- Lots of sparkling jewels
- Big picture hats with feathers and furs

> Cultivate your curves—they may be dangerous but they won't be avoided.
> —MAE WEST

ABOVE
Showing off the assets "God gave her" in a revealing corset gown by Edith Head, West set the bar for smoldering sexuality in 1933's *She Done Him Wrong*.

RIGHT
By combining sheer, embroidered "illusion" fabric in her gown and luxurious ermine in her robe, West becomes a study in contrasts in 1936's *Go West Young Man* (Irene Jones).

THE NINETEEN THIRTIES | HOLLYWOOD FASHION

CAROLE LOMBARD

Lombard Style
The actress, who was happy ranching in khakis and flannel, also shone in the Hollywood spotlight in sophisticated gowns.

Signature Look
- Lamé gowns
- Classic daywear with silk scarves
- Tams and berets

The queen of screwball comedies had leading lady looks …and the salty tongue of a sailor.

Carole Lombard (1908–1942) was the quintessential 1930s' heroine—eccentric, frenetic, and ultimately lovable. She was born Jane Alice Peters in Fort Wayne, Indiana, but her family later moved to Los Angeles. At age 12, Jane was the ideal choice to play a tomboy in *A Perfect Crime* (1921), and by the 1920s she was acting in minor films as Carole Lombard.

When Howard Hughes cast her opposite John Barrymore in 1934's *Twentieth Century* (gowns by Robert Kalloch), the film's success earned Lombard starring roles in a series of "screwball" comedies—*Hands Across the Table*, *My Man Godfrey* (costumes by an uncredited Brymer), and *Nothing Sacred* (T. Banton/W. Plunkett). The latter film established her as one of the highest paid stars in Hollywood. After a few lackluster dramas, the actress returned to comedies with *Mr. and Mrs. Smith* and *To Be or Not to Be* (her costumes by Irene), a great success—and her final film.

In 1936 Lombard fell in love with married man Clark Gable, but the brewing scandal threatened to prevent Gable from taking the coveted role of Rhett Butler in *Gone with the Wind*. After Louis B. Mayer gave Gable enough money to settle with his wife, he and Lombard were wed and bought a ranch in Encino complete with chickens and horses. Sadly, in 1942, while flying home from an Indiana war bond rally, Lombard was killed when her DC-3 crashed into a mountain. A grief-stricken Gable joined the Army Air Force.

MOST FASHIONABLE FILMS
NO MAN OF HER OWN (1932)
TWENTIETH CENTURY (1934)
RUMBA (1935)
MY MAN GODFREY (1936)
NOTHING SACRED (1937)

ABOVE
Travis Banton paired a wide Art Deco belt with the draped bodice of a lamé gown to show off Lombard's figure in 1932's *No Man of Her Own*.

LEFT
Lombard evokes a Greek goddess in a satin tunic gown with crisscross bodice in a publicity still for *Rumba*, a 1935 dance film costarring George Raft.

HOLLYWOOD FASHION | THE NINETEEN THIRTIES

MARLENE DIETRICH

MOST FASHIONABLE FILMS
BLONDE VENUS (1932)
THE SCARLET EMPRESS (1934)
THE GARDEN OF ALLAH (1936)
DESIRE (1936)
DESTRY RIDES AGAIN (1939)

No one was better at reinventing herself—or reinvigorating her career—than this sultry-eyed, smoky-voiced German import.

Marlene Dietrich (1901–1992) symbolized the captivating blonde who was beyond the reach of most mortal men. Marie Magdalene Dietrich was born to a prosperous Berlin family. She studied the violin as a child, but a wrist injury ended her hopes for a career as a musician. Instead, she began performing on stage, first as a chorus girl and then in minor stage and screen roles.

Dietrich worked with director—and mentor—Joseph von Sternberg for the first time in 1929, when she was cast as seductive cabaret singer Lola Lola in the hit film, *The Blue Angel*. (The song, "Falling in Love Again," became Dietrich's theme.) Von Sternberg brought Dietrich to America, where she signed with Paramount; they planned to market her as their answer to MGM's superstar, Garbo.

Von Sternberg often boasted that he'd discovered Dietrich, but he can take credit for her transformation in America. His skill in lighting (and some advice that she lose weight) turned the slightly doughy dishwater blonde into a divine, sculpted, golden-haired temptress in films like *Morocco*, *Dishonored*, *Blonde Venus*, *Shanghai Express*, *The Scarlet Empress*, and *The Devil Is a Woman*.

After Paramount fired von Sternberg, Dietrich and the studio parted ways. She made *The Garden of Allah* (costumes by Ernest Dryden) for David O. Selznick in 1936 and *Knight Without Armor* for Alexander Korda in 1937. When both films fizzled, movie exhibitors declared her "box office poison." Not long after, Dietrich was approached in London by several Nazi officials who offered her a fortune to return to Germany as the premier star of the Third Reich. Dietrich flatly refused—and soon applied for U.S. citizenship.

Dietrich took a cut in pay in 1939 to play saloon hostess Frenchy in the comic Western *Destry Rides Again* opposite James Stewart (with gowns by Vera West). The wry performance restored her luster and resulted in a hit record, "The Boys in the Backroom."

While Dietrich's postwar films never attained the glory of her Paramount years, she was effective in Alfred Hitchcock's *Stage Fright*, Orson Welles's *Touch of Evil*, and Billy Wilder's *Witness for the Prosecution* (with outfits by Edith Head).

In 1953 Dietrich was offered a startling $30,000 a week to do a live show at the Sahara Hotel in Las Vegas. She accepted…and took the stage in a "nude" beaded dress designed by Jean Louis. The Sahara show was a smash—and a new career was born. With composer Burt Bacharach, she created a one-woman cabaret combining songs from her films with popular music. Dietrich spent her final years in Paris, writing to friends and penning an autobiography, which was published in 1979.

Dietrich Style
Hollywood groomed Dietrich to highlight her sexuality, including, occasionally, her more androgynous side.

Signature Look
- Sheer fabrics with the illusion of transparency
- Opulent furs
- Relaxed menswear, satin tuxedoes

ABOVE
Here, from 1936's *Desire*, Dietrich strikes a pensive pose in a simple, pale silk blouse, proving her glamour was not dependent on lavish costumes.

FULL PAGE
Designed by Travis Banton, a mannish suit set off with a cascade of feminine lace ruffles reflects both sides of the actress's nature in 1937's *Angel*.

38 1930s

I dress for myself. Not for the image, not for the public, not for the fashion, not for men.
MARLENE DIETRICH

HOLLYWOOD FASHION | **THE NINETEEN THIRTIES**

MYRNA LOY

Delicate and steely, Loy possessed an exotic appeal but was also believable playing a mother or a housewife.

Myrna Loy (1905–1993) first played Eurasian bad girls, but soon switched to sensible, bemused wives. Myrna Adele Williams was born in Radersburg, Montana, and named after a train station her father liked. After being widowed, her mother settled the family in Culver City, California. Loy studied dancing and by age 15 was appearing in stage plays. In 1928 she was cast as a vamp in *What Price Beauty?* Although the exotic role landed her a contract with Warner Bros., the studio then typecast her as shady dames or Eurasian characters.

Her breakthrough movie was the notorious *Manhattan Melodrama*—the film gangster John Dillinger was exiting when police gunned him down—starring Clark Gable and William Powell (costumes by Dolly Tree). Loy finally shook her bad-girl image and switched to comedy, playing Nora, the wealthy, wisecracking wife of William Powell's detective Nick Charles in the popular *Thin Man* series (costumes by Dolly Tree, Robert Kalloch, and others).

More significant pictures came her way, including *The Great Ziegfeld* (Adrian), *The Rains Came* with Tyrone Power (costumes by Gwen Wakeling), *Mr. Blandings Builds His Dream House* with Cary Grant, and Oscar-winner *The Best Years of Our Lives*.

In 1991, the actress received her own special Oscar for "Lifetime Achievement."

MOST FASHIONABLE FILMS

MANHATTAN MELODRAMA (1934)
THE THIN MAN (1934)
THE GREAT ZIEGFELD (1936)
THE RAINS CAME (1939)

Loy Style
Loy's look was simple and unfussy; she was truly a case of "seeing the woman first and the clothing second."

Signature Look
- Capes and elegant gowns for evening
- Stylish suits or tailored dresses for day
- Chic, angular hats

ABOVE
Although *When Ladies Meet* (1933) wasn't one of Loy's most important films, it featured 1930s' fashions at their best with long and lean lines, such as in this light and airy day dress with polka-dot trim.

RIGHT
The ruched, bias-cut satin gown worn by Loy in *Manhattan Melodrama*—shown here in a scene with Clark Gable—manages to be both elegant and flamboyant.

40 1930s

THE NINETEEN THIRTIES | HOLLYWOOD FASHION

CLAUDETTE COLBERT

With her wide-set eyes, rounded features, and slender shape, this French-born American actress made the most of her unusual looks.

Claudette Colbert (1903–1996) was adept at playing intelligent, upper-class beauties. She was born Émilie Claudette Chauchoin in Paris, but in 1906 her family emigrated to New York City. After a speech teacher encouraged her to perform, she found stage work while still a teen. She played ingénues on Broadway until the late 1920s, when she signed a contract with Paramount.

Colbert's remarkable film career encompassed widely different genres—from historical epics, such as Cecil B. DeMille's *The Sign of the Cross* (costumes by Mitchell Leisen) and *Cleopatra* (costumes by uncredited Vicky Williams) to frothy romances like Leisen's *Midnight* (gowns by Irene) to melodramas like *So Proudly We Hail*, a tale of battlefield nurses.

Her most acclaimed role was in 1934's *It Happened One Night* (an uncredited Robert Kalloch). The Frank Capra comedy featured Colbert as a runaway heiress being trailed—and protected—by newspaperman Clark Gable. Not only did the film sweep the Academy Awards: Best Picture, Director, Actor, Actress and Screenplay, it made Colbert a major star. (It also depressed the men's undershirt industry when Gable revealed in the motel scene that he didn't wear one!)

Colbert Style
Early in her career, Colbert wore provocative costumes (or nothing at all as in the bath scene from *The Sign of the Cross*), but once her stature increased, she refused such roles. On screen or at home she could stylishly carry off bias-cut gowns or sporty twin sets.

Signature Look
- Short, curly bob
- Thin, arching eyebrows
- Tailored outfits

MOST FASHIONABLE FILMS

THE SIGN OF THE CROSS (1932)
CLEOPATRA (1934)
IT HAPPENED ONE NIGHT (1934)
MIDNIGHT (1939)

ABOVE

Even though in 1939's *Midnight* she played a baroness down on her luck, Colbert's gowns, like this form-fitting satin example by Irene, were all top drawer.

LEFT

As Nero's wife, Poppaea, Colbert displays a provocatively draped gown designed by Mitchell Leisen for Cecil B. DeMille's Biblical epic, *The Sign of the Cross*.

HOLLYWOOD FASHION | THE NINETEEN THIRTIES

FASHION INFLUENCE
SHIRLEY TEMPLE

Child star Shirley Temple (1928–2014) is unique in the history of show business. Not only was she the top box office draw in America for four years (from ages 6–9), her management team virtually invented celebrity merchandising. And if that were not enough, after retiring from movies, Temple went on to host her own TV show and to become a respected American diplomat.

Temple was born just outside Hollywood in Santa Monica. Her mother, Gertrude, enrolled her in a Los Angeles dance school soon after she learned to walk. In 1932, after winning a talent search, the child was signed by Educational Pictures and made a series of one- and two-reelers for them. Fox then offered her a film contract, and in 1934 she appeared in *Stand Up and Cheer!*

Depression audiences instantly fell in love with the wholesome cherub with the dark blonde ringlets. Her salary increased and she was loaned out to Paramount for *Little Miss Marker* (1934), another success. The film *Bright Eyes* was made specifically to highlight her talent—it introduced her signature song "On the Good Ship Lollipop"—and her name appeared above the title. It was also the film that furnished a template for the typical Shirley Temple plot—a gruff, old curmudgeon eventually melts when confronted with the child's cheerfulness, pluck, and charm.

In 1935, Temple received a Special Juvenile Oscar from the Motion Picture Academy, recognizing her film accomplishments. She wasn't yet seven years old.

Of course every mother wanted to dress her own daughter like this cinema darling; other fans wanted her image in their homes ...and American retailing complied. There was soon a line of dresses and accessories, soap, china, paper dolls, sheet music, and even breakfast dishes inside boxes of Wheaties. Perhaps the most iconic offering was the Shirley Temple doll manufactured by the Ideal Toy and Novelty Company of New York. In addition to the polka-dot dress from *Stand Up and Cheer!*, the doll featured Temple's gleaming ringlets, her dimples, and even her two adorably visible front teeth. By 1941, the dolls had tallied up more than $45 million in sales.

By the end of 1935, Temple's income from licensed merchandise was $100,000, more than twice her movie salary. The following year that income doubled, partially due to endorsements for Postal Telegraph, Drifted Snow Flour, Quaker Puffed Wheat, General Electric, and Packard automobiles.

Temple starred in more than fifteen classics as a child. She made several fine films as a teenager, but retired from movies in 1949. As an adult, she

ABOVE

Temple was often photographed holding dolls, which is fitting since her own look-alike doll became an international bestseller.

ABOVE RIGHT

1934's *Stand up and Cheer!* was Temple's breakout role; here, she poses in one of the short, high-waisted, flounced dresses that became her trademark.

42 1930s

THE NINETEEN THIRTIES | HOLLYWOOD FASHION

> When I was 14, I was the oldest I ever was... I've been getting younger ever since.
> SHIRLEY TEMPLE

entered politics and was appointed US ambassador to Ghana and Czechoslovakia. After undergoing a mastectomy, she discussed her treatment in a February 1973 article for the magazine *McCall's*—becoming one of the first prominent women to speak openly about breast cancer. She died at home in Woodside, California, in 2014.

ABOVE

For 1934's *Little Miss Marker* Fox loaned Temple, seen here with her trademark curls, to Paramount after the popularity of *Bright Eyes* (1934).

LEFT

In this scene from *Poor Little Rich Girl* (1936), Temple dons a band uniform to perform with costars Jack Haley and Gloria Stuart.

FAR LEFT

With its Chinese-influenced neckline and charming floral embellishments, this pleated dress from *Rebecca of Sunnybrook Farm* (1938) became a fan favorite.

43

HOLLYWOOD FASHION | THE NINETEEN THIRTIES

GINGER ROGERS

MOST FASHIONABLE FILMS
THE GAY DIVORCEE (1934)
TOP HAT (1935)
SHALL WE DANCE (1937)
KITTY FOYLE (1940)
LADY IN THE DARK (1944)

Initially known as Fred Astaire's dance partner in nine groundbreaking RKO musicals, Rogers was also a gifted comedian and dramatic actress.

Ginger Rogers (1911–1995) could play the freckle-faced girl next door or a vision of loveliness in a gossamer gown. She was born Virginia Katherine McMath in Independence, Missouri, and embarked on a stage career abetted by her scriptwriter mother. By 1930 she was on Broadway in *Girl Crazy* and afterward went to Hollywood and worked for a number of studios.

Her breakout film was *Gold Diggers of 1933* for Warner Bros., but when RKO paired her with Broadway star Fred Astaire for *Flying Down to Rio*, her career took off. Astaire never had a better partner—in Rogers he found a malleable dancer, a fine singer, and a natural mimic. Their hugely popular films redefined movie musicals and helped keep RKO Studio solvent.

The actress also excelled in non-musical films such as *Stage Door*, *Bachelor Mother*, *Tom, Dick and Harry*, and *Kitty Foyle*, for which she won the Oscar (wearing gowns by Renié). With her appealing youthful quality, Rogers believably played a young girl in *The Major and the Minor* and *Lady in the Dark* (both with designs by Edith Head).

Though she made fewer films as she aged, Rogers continued to be a presence on the stage and on television.

Rogers Style
Rogers often displayed a sense of fun, from her monocle and Pekingese in *42nd Street* to the roller-skating parties she popularized. Her dance numbers featured a series of delicious gowns—the ostrich-feather dress from *Top Hat*... the lamé gown with the weighted hem from *Follow the Fleet*—many of which were copied by retailers.

Signature Look
- Blonde hair braided or woven into a chignon
- Backless gowns with swirling skirts
- Tailored, feminine daywear

ABOVE
Rogers collaborated with costume designer Bernard Newman to create the divine—and infamous—feathered confection she wore for the "Cheek to Cheek" dance scene in *Top Hat* (1935).

RIGHT
Rogers strikes a provocative pose in 1937's *Shall We Dance* while wearing a shimmering lamé gown with a slightly raised waistline and dark sash by designer Irene.

> I believe in dressing for the occasion. There's a time for sweater, sneakers, and Levis, and a time for the full-dress jazz.
> GINGER ROGERS

44 1930s

THE NINETEEN THIRTIES | HOLLYWOOD FASHION

JEAN ARTHUR

This versatile comedian with the raspy, oddly endearing, voice was a mainstay of Frank Capra's Depression-era film fables.

Jean Arthur (1900–1991) played the "everywoman" role in screwball comedies opposite some of Hollywood's biggest stars. Born Gladys Greene in upstate New York, Arthur made silent films for seven years as a brunette and then went blonde for talkies and became a star. Her first hit was the Capra classic *Mr. Deeds Goes to Town* with Gary Cooper (costumes by Samuel Lange), followed by Howard Hawks' melodrama *Only Angels Have Wings* (gowns by Kalloch) with Cary Grant, and Capra's masterpiece, *Mr. Smith Goes to Washington*, with James Stewart (costumes by Ray Howell).

In 1942, she starred in *The Talk of the Town* with Grant and Ronald Colman (gowns by Irene). 1943's *The More the Merrier* with Joel McCrea, earned Arthur a Best Actress Oscar nomination, while costar Charles Coburn won for Best Supporting Actor.

Arthur also made several Westerns—*The Plainsman* in 1937 with Gary Cooper, *Arizona* with William Holden in 1940, and her final screen role in 1953, the mythic *Shane*, with Alan Ladd and Van Heflin.

Arthur Style
While rarely showy on screen, Arthur, unlike many glamour girls, was still playing romantic leads well into her forties.

Signature Look
- Classic, tailored tweed suits
- Rakish little hats
- Flower worn over one ear

MOST FASHIONABLE FILMS

MR. DEEDS GOES TO TOWN (1936)
ONLY ANGELS HAVE WINGS (1939)
THE MORE THE MERRIER (1943)

ABOVE

With jaunty little hats and sleek, no-nonsense suits, Arthur made a name for herself portraying wise-cracking working girls.

LEFT

Even though Arthur often appeared in sporty separates and spectator shoes, as seen here in this still from 1935's *Party Wire*, she also had the willowy figure to do justice to clingy 1930s gowns.

MOST FASHIONABLE DESIGNS

IT and WINGS (1927)
I'M NO ANGEL (1933)
THE SCARLET EMPRESS (1934)
MY MAN GODFREY (1936)
NOTHING SACRED (1937)

> He was a god there...nobody [would] dare oppose him about anything, including the budgets.
>
> EDITH HEAD,
> BANTON'S ASSISTANT AT PARAMOUNT

FULL PAGE
The daring use of crisscrossed satin ribbons gives this gown from 1935's *The Gilded Lily* a classic silhouette with a very modern edge.

TOP RIGHT INSERT
Ida Lupino, playing a British aristocrat opposite Arthur Treacher in *Anything Goes* (1936), finds her white, fur-edged cape is the perfect lure for a high-seas romance with Bing Crosby.

BOTTOM RIGHT INSERT
1939's *Intermezzo, A Love Story*, cast a young Swedish actress named Ingrid Bergman, seen here in a simple white evening frock, opposite British matinee idol Leslie Howard.

THE NINETEEN THIRTIES | HOLLYWOOD FASHION

STYLE MAKER
TRAVIS BANTON

Although he started out in the wild and wooly town of Waco, Texas, Travis Banton would one day epitomize the height of Hollywood elegance and glamour.

After serving on a submarine in WWI, Banton attended Columbia University and then studied fashion at the Art Students' League in NYC. His apprenticeship to society dressmakers Madame Frances and Lucile led to some early fame, which was then cemented when one of his dresses was chosen for Mary Pickford's highly publicized wedding to Douglas Fairbanks. Banton opened his own salon in New York and was soon designing costumes for the Ziegfeld Follies.

Hollywood beckoned in 1924, and he headed for the West Coast to work on Paramount's *The Dressmaker from Paris*. Although his designs were worn by major stars such as Norma Talmadge, Pola Negri, Clara Bow, Kay Francis, Miriam Hopkins, and Claudette Colbert, Banton was also known for creating the signature looks of Carole Lombard, Mae West, and Marlene Dietrich. While his costumes for Dietrich in *The Scarlet Empress* were far from authentic, they were quite spectacular. In other films, he swathed her in sheer fabrics, lush fur stoles, and miles of pearls...and set a new benchmark for screen glamour.

Among the classic films Banton worked on are *Wings* from 1927; *The Wild Party* in 1929; *Morocco* in 1930; *Dr. Jekyll and Mr. Hyde* in 1932; *Blonde Venus*, *A Farewell to Arms*, *No Man of Her Own*, and *The Sign of the Cross* in 1932; *Design for Living*, *I'm No Angel*, and *Death Takes A Holiday* in 1934; *Ruggles of Red Gap* and *The Gilded Lily* in 1935; *The Devil is A Woman*, *The Crusades*, and *Anything Goes* in 1936; *Desire* and *My Man Godfrey* in 1936; *Maid of Salem* and *Nothing Sacred* in 1937; *Intermezzo* in 1939; *The Mark of Zorro* in 1940; 1941's *Charley's Aunt*; 1946's *Sister Kenny*; 1947's *Mourning Becomes Electra*; and 1948's *Letter from an Unknown Woman*.

In the 1950s, Banton worked for a time as a freelancer on various films and TV shows. As his career waned, many of his female stars remained faithful to him. He died in Los Angeles in 1958, leaving behind an extensive collection of drawings that are now housed in the Brooklyn Museum.

Unfortunately, Banton did his strongest work before the Academy Award for Costume Design was established in 1948. But his peers were not backward in their praise. Norman Norell claimed Banton had been underrated and insisted that his costumes were timeless. Cecil Beaton singled out his creations for *Angel* (1937) and called Banton one of the "most important designers of Hollywood's Golden Age."

Signature Looks
- Sleek, streamlined silhouettes
- Bias-cut gowns
- Satin and lamé fabrics
- Beads, furs, and feathers

Legacy
Every drag queen wearing a sequined gown, big hair, platform shoes, and a feather boa owes his thanks to Banton for creating the iconic Mae West look.

TOP

Marlene Dietrich, here in *Morocco* (1930), often dressed in men's suits and tuxedoes, including during her hit Las Vegas stage shows.

ABOVE

Clara Bow in Banton's natty version of a World War I ambulance driver's uniform sends off pilot Charles "Buddy" Farrell in *Wings*, the first Best Picture winner.

47

HOLLYWOOD FASHION | THE NINETEEN THIRTIES

NORMA SHEARER

Wed to "boy wonder" film producer, Irving Thalberg, she overcame several physical flaws before being hailed as the first lady of MGM.

Norma Shearer (1902–1983) was best known for her woman-of-the-world roles.

She was born in Montreal, Canada, and decided on an acting career after attending a vaudeville show. Undeterred by her own shortcomings—a stocky figure, thick legs, and a cast in one eye—Shearer moved to New York, made the rounds of theaters and studios, exercised her bad eye, and did some modeling, which opened the door to film roles.

She made six films in eight months for Irving Thalberg, production head of MGM. She and Thalberg were wed in 1927, a week before *The Jazz Singer* debuted. Determined to make the transition to talkies, Shearer was aided by her brother, Douglas, who helped develop MGM's sound technology.

Shearer's screen persona, a sexually liberated sophisticate, was showcased in *The Divorcée*, which earned her an Oscar, *A Free Soul*, and *Private Lives*. With the advent of the morally rigid Hays Code in 1934, Shearer switched to period films like *The Barretts of Wimpole Street* and *Marie Antoinette*, and melodramas like *The Women*.

When Thalberg—who had a congenital heart condition— died of pneumonia in September of 1936, all of Hollywood mourned. Shearer continued to work until 1942, when she retired.

MOST FASHIONABLE FILMS

THE DIVORCEE (1930)
MARIE ANTOINETTE (1938)
THE WOMEN (1939)

Shearer Style
Portrait photographer George Hurrell helped Shearer disguise her flaws and she refused to be photographed by anyone else. By focusing on her throat and shoulders, designer Adrian was able to mask her long torso.

Signature Look
- Softly upswept hair
- Eye-catching collars and necklines
- Small-brimmed hats

ABOVE
For her role in 1938's *Marie Antoinette*, Adrian garbed Shearer in taffetas, velvets, and sumptuous furs, like this enveloping hooded cape in silver fox.

RIGHT
Shearer wears another Adrian creation, a voluptuously ruffled organdy gown with a velvet bodice, in the 1932 tragic melodrama *Smilin' Through*.

48 1930s

THE NINETEEN THIRTIES | HOLLYWOOD FASHION

VIVIEN LEIGH

Leigh Style
Green-eyed Leigh was a favorite with fashion photographers, and enjoyed wearing couturier clothing. As Vogue editor Diana Vreeland wrote, "She had such an exquisite unreality about her."

Signature Look
- Bright blouses and quiet tweeds
- Stylish accessories—gloves, pearls, brooches
- Wide-brimmed hats

MOST FASHIONABLE FILMS
FIRE OVER ENGLAND (1937)
GONE WITH THE WIND (1939)
ANNA KARENINA (1948)

The screen's beloved Scarlett won two Academy Awards, but endured illness and breakdowns in her private life.

Vivien Leigh (1913–1967) was known for playing delicate women with enormous resolve. Born in Darjeeling, India, the daughter of a cavalry officer, Leigh had one success on the London stage in 1935, before she was signed by producer Alexander Korda. She fell in love with husband, Laurence Olivier, while filming Korda's *Fire Over England*.

After reading *Gone with the Wind*, Leigh told a journalist, "I've cast myself as Scarlett O'Hara." She wanted the part, but so did every actress in Hollywood. Producer David O. Selznick thought her too British—until his brother Myron, Leigh's agent, brought her to the set during the burning of Atlanta scene. "Hey, genius," said Myron, "meet your Scarlett." Leigh embodied the role—a scheming Southern vixen in costumes by Walter Plunkett—and won the 1939 Academy Award for Best Actress.

Leigh won another Oscar in 1951 for playing faded belle Blanche DuBois in Tennessee Williams' *A Streetcar Named Desire*. But the grueling role took a toll on the already-frail actress, who suffered from tuberculosis and bipolar disorder. She divorced Olivier in 1960 and continued to act on the stage—winning a Tony for *Tovarich* in 1963—but in 1967 the tuberculosis resurfaced while she was rehearsing *A Delicate Balance*. She took time off to rest, but several weeks later collapsed and died in London.

ABOVE
Leigh's luminous beauty made her a favorite of fashion editors, as well as film directors. Here, the scarflike sash of her chiffon lounging costume shows off the tiny waist that was one of her trademarks.

LEFT
Walter Plunkett designed a magnificent array of costumes for Leigh in 1939's *Gone with the Wind*, including a green sprig muslin dress Scarlett O'Hara wears to the barbecue at Twelve Oaks. Restored by Plunkett in 1976, the iconic dress has become the most visited item in the Costume Department of the Los Angeles County Museum of Art.

HOLLYWOOD FASHION | THE NINETEEN THIRTIES

ALBUM OF TRENDSETTERS
THE BLONDE LEADING THE BLONDE

BLONDE BOMBSHELLS
While Harlow and Monroe set the gold standard for smoking-hot blondes, there were plenty of other actresses who earned the term "bombshell."

- Mamie Van Doren
- Jayne Mansfield
- Alice Faye
- Carol Baker
- Simone Signoret
- Betty Hutton
- Scarlett Johansson
- Dolly Parton

RIGHT

Draped in luxurious velvet, Alice Faye blends into her Art Deco backdrop. Before her lovely singing voice made her a huge box-office draw in her own right, Faye began her career as Jean Harlow look-alike, with the same platinum waves and pencil eyebrows.

ABOVE RIGHT

In a press shot for *The Girl Can't Help It* (1956), fur trim adds a luxurious finish to a figure-hugging satin gown with a midriff-baring inset that shows off Jayne Mansfield's bombshell curves.

BOTTOM RIGHT

Scarlett Johansson's creamy skin was a fixture of Sofia Coppola's *Lost in Translation* (2003); here, in Woody Allen's 2005 *Match Point*, she shows off her curves in a simple white wrap dress.

BLONDE GODDESSES

Cool and collected, like their muse Grace Kelly, these serene actresses were ice queens just waiting for a steamy encounter.

- Joanne Woodward
- Constance Bennett
- Jody Foster
- Claire Danes
- Kirsten Dunst
- Diane Lane
- Vanessa Redgrave
- Naomi Watts
- Laura Linney

FAR LEFT
In 1960's *From the Terrace*, the usually demure Joanne Woodward poses seductively in a strapless black lace gown by Travilla.

LEFT
2005's *King Kong* allowed Naomi Watts to channel the ghost of Fay Wray in this 1930s'-style bias-cut lamé gown from Terry Ryan.

THE HITCHCOCK BLONDES

Suspense director Alfred Hitchcock felt blondes made the perfect victims, perhaps because blood created such a contrast against their pale hair. In addition to his favorite, Grace Kelly, he also favored these actresses.

- Tippi Hedren in *The Birds*
- Kim Novak in *Vertigo* (1958)
- Eva Marie Saint in *North by Northwest* (1959)
- Janet Leigh in *Psycho* (1960)
- Madeleine Carroll in *The Thirty-Nine Steps* (1935)
- Priscilla Lane in *Saboteur* (1942)
- Doris Day in *The Man Who Knew Too Much* (1956)

> Hitchcock said, 'The audience wants to see their leading ladies dressed up.' He saw me as others didn't.
>
> EVA MARIE SAINT

ABOVE
Tippi Hedren, posing with one of her crow foes from 1963's *The Birds*, looks poised and polished in a spaghetti-strap sheath gown.

LEFT
Cool and sophisticated in a striking red roses on black patterned A-line dress with wide bateau neckline, Eva Marie Saint is the epitome of a Hitchcock blonde.

HOLLYWOOD FASHION | **THE NINETEEN THIRTIES**

MOST FASHIONABLE DESIGNS

- 42ND STREET (1933)
- JEZEBEL (1938)
- CASABLANCA (1942)
- AN AMERICAN IN PARIS (1951)
- SOME LIKE IT HOT (1959)

> **I wish I had a dime for every time that's been copied.**
>
> ORRY-KELLY ON INGRID BERGMAN'S JUMPER DRESS FROM CASABLANCA

ABOVE RIGHT

Jazz dance meets ballet in 1951's remarkable *An American in Paris* from Gene Kelly and Stanley Donen. It seems the postwar world craved anything French, including the delicious Leslie Caron in her gamine dance costumes. Orry-Kelly received his first Oscar for the film, sharing the honor with Irene Sharaff and Walter Plunkett

ABOVE

Billy Wilder's *Some Like It Hot* allowed the designer to not only costume the luscious Marilyn Monroe, but to put Tony Curtis and Jack Lemmon into flapper dresses. It resulted in his final Oscar win.

RIGHT

In 1942's *Casablanca*, Ingrid Bergman, shown here with costars Sydney Greenstreet and Paul Henreid, wears a jumper dress that Orry-Kelly designed with war rationing in mind— it was short and did not require a lot of material.

THE NINETEEN THIRTIES | HOLLYWOOD FASHION

STYLE MAKER
ORRY-KELLY

During a career that spanned four decades, Orry-Kelly designed clothing for all the top actresses—including Bette Davis, Katharine Hepburn, Olivia de Havilland, Ingrid Bergman, Ava Gardner, Barbara Stanwyck, and Merle Oberon.

Orry-Kelly (real name Orry George Kelly) was born in New South Wales, Australia, the son of a tailor from the Isle of Man. His unusual name, Orry, was taken from an ancient Manx king. After studying art in Sydney, Orry-Kelly decided to try acting. In 1921 he relocated to New York City, where one of his roommates was a young actor named Archibald Leach. A job painting nightclub murals got him work as a title designer for Fox Films, which then led to Broadway and designing sets and costumes for the Schubert Revues and George White's Scandals.

Hollywood lured him west in 1931, where he quickly became a favorite at the major studios—Universal, 20th Century-Fox, and MGM—but mainly at Warner Bros., where he was hailed as one of Hollywood's top three designers, along with Adrian at MGM and Travis Banton at Paramount. Among the many classic films Orry-Kelly worked on are *42nd Street*; *The Maltese Falcon*; *Now, Voyager*; *Casablanca*; *Arsenic and Old Lace* (starring his former roommate, now known as Cary Grant); *Pat and Mike*; *Oklahoma!*; *Auntie Mame*; and *Some Like it Hot*. His most memorable creation was, arguably, the "red" ball gown Bette Davis wore in the film *Jezebel*.

Orry-Kelly was known as a hot-tempered perfectionist in the film industry, but no one ever questioned his brilliance. His period costumes were remarkable for their rich fabrics and historical accuracy—actors noted the clothing frequently helped them get into the proper character—and even in his contemporary designs, he used only the finest fabrics. Walter Plunkett, himself a legendary stylist, considered his colleague "the greatest of all Hollywood designers."

During the war years, Orry-Kelly wrote a syndicated column "Hollywood Fashion Parade" for the Hearst International News Service. His autobiography, *Women I've Undressed*, was never completed.

In 1944, Orry-Kelly's problems with alcohol put an end to his uneasy relationship with studio head, Jack Warner, and the designer moved to Fox, where he was engaged to dress Betty Grable. After 1950, he freelanced with a number of studios and despite his ill-health, managed to keep designing well into the 1960s. He was working on the Dean Martin film *Kiss Me, Stupid* in 1964, when he succumbed to liver cancer. The pallbearers at his Forest Lawn funeral included Cary Grant, Tony Curtis, and directors Billy Wilder, and George Cukor. Jack Warner gave the eulogy.

ABOVE

Bette Davis shows off her shoulders in the scandalous red ball gown from 1938's *Jezebel*.

HOLLYWOOD FASHION | THE NINETEEN THIRTIES

MEN OF THE 1930s
DAPPER, DANCING, OR DANGEROUS

Several reliable film genres evolved during the 1930s—screwball comedies with debonair heroes and dizzy heroines; rousing, inspirational tales of men and women fighting uphill battles; and gangster melodramas following the fate of good men gone wrong. There was also a wildly popular new genre, courtesy of the new sound technology: movie musicals.

Good Sports

Cary Grant, James Stewart, Henry Fonda, and William Powell all appeared in screwball comedies, often paired with Katharine Hepburn, Carole Lombard, Barbara Stanwyck, or Jean Arthur in films like *My Man Godfrey*, *Bringing Up Baby*, *The Lady Eve*, and *You Can't Take it With You*. The men in these comedies typically dressed in dinner clothes or sports clothes or, occasionally, in a lady's frilly dressing gown.

Nice Guys

Reformer heroes became increasingly popular during this hardscrabble decade, and many films featuring idealists became classics—including Henry Fonda in *The Grapes of Wrath*, Gary Cooper in *Meet John Doe*, and James Stewart in *It's a Wonderful Life* and *Mr. Smith Goes to*

THE NINETEEN THIRTIES | HOLLYWOOD FASHION

Washington. Costume design was critical in these films because the protagonists had to be marked somehow as rubes, misfits, or outsiders.

Bad Boys

On the dark side of the street, Clark Gable, Paul Muni, George Raft, and James Cagney were frequently lost souls at risk of going bad, unless saintly Pat O'Brien or Spencer Tracy influenced them for the better. These films introduced the gangster look to men's fashion—boldly tailored pin-striped, double-breasted suits, often worn with spats and a rakish fedora hat.

Cowboys

Westerns grew in popularity, and many former B-Western actors like John Wayne finally got their shot at stardom. His collaboration with director John Ford—*Stagecoach*, released in the Golden Year 1939—became a screen classic. Gary Cooper appeared in sagebrush sagas like *The Virginian*, and *The Plainsman*. James Stewart fought for justice in *Destry Rides Again*, while Henry Fonda played an infamous bank robber in *Jesse James*. Western styles such as buckskin jackets, fringed shirts, denim pants, and cowboy boots all eventually evolved into the weekend garb worn by Americans of both sexes.

Song and Dance Men

Musicals were a novel treat for moviegoers, especially those with extravagant production numbers like *42nd Street*. Fred Astaire was the preeminent song-and-dance man—popularizing "white tie and tails" for evening—but musicals also featured former hoofers like James Cagney and dance legends like Bill "Bojangles" Robinson. Popular actor-singers included Al Jolson, Eddy Cantor, Bing Crosby, Maurice Chevalier, Dick Powell, and Paul Robeson. Strapping baritone Nelson Eddy appeared with Jeannette MacDonald in a series of enormously popular costume operettas, including *Rose-Marie*, *Naughty Marietta*, and *New Moon*.

Signature Menswear Looks of the 1930s

- Herringbone or stippled suit fabrics
- Glen and other plaids
- London cut or London drape suits
- Windsor or Kent double-breasted suit
- "Palm Beach" suit (made of seersucker, silk, or linen)
- Suntans
- Blazers
- Fedoras

ABOVE

Gary Cooper appears quite debonair in his tuxedo but also typically befuddled by Claudette Colbert's amused vamp in *Bluebeard's Eighth Wife* (1938).

FAR LEFT

Fred Astaire, shown here with Ginger Rogers in their breakout film, *Flying Down to Rio* (1933), managed to make up-tight dinner clothes into fancy-free dancing clothes.

FAR TOP LEFT

Cary Grant as a tweedy professor seems to have taken a pratfall in 1938's *Bringing Up Baby* and still manages to look dapper.

55

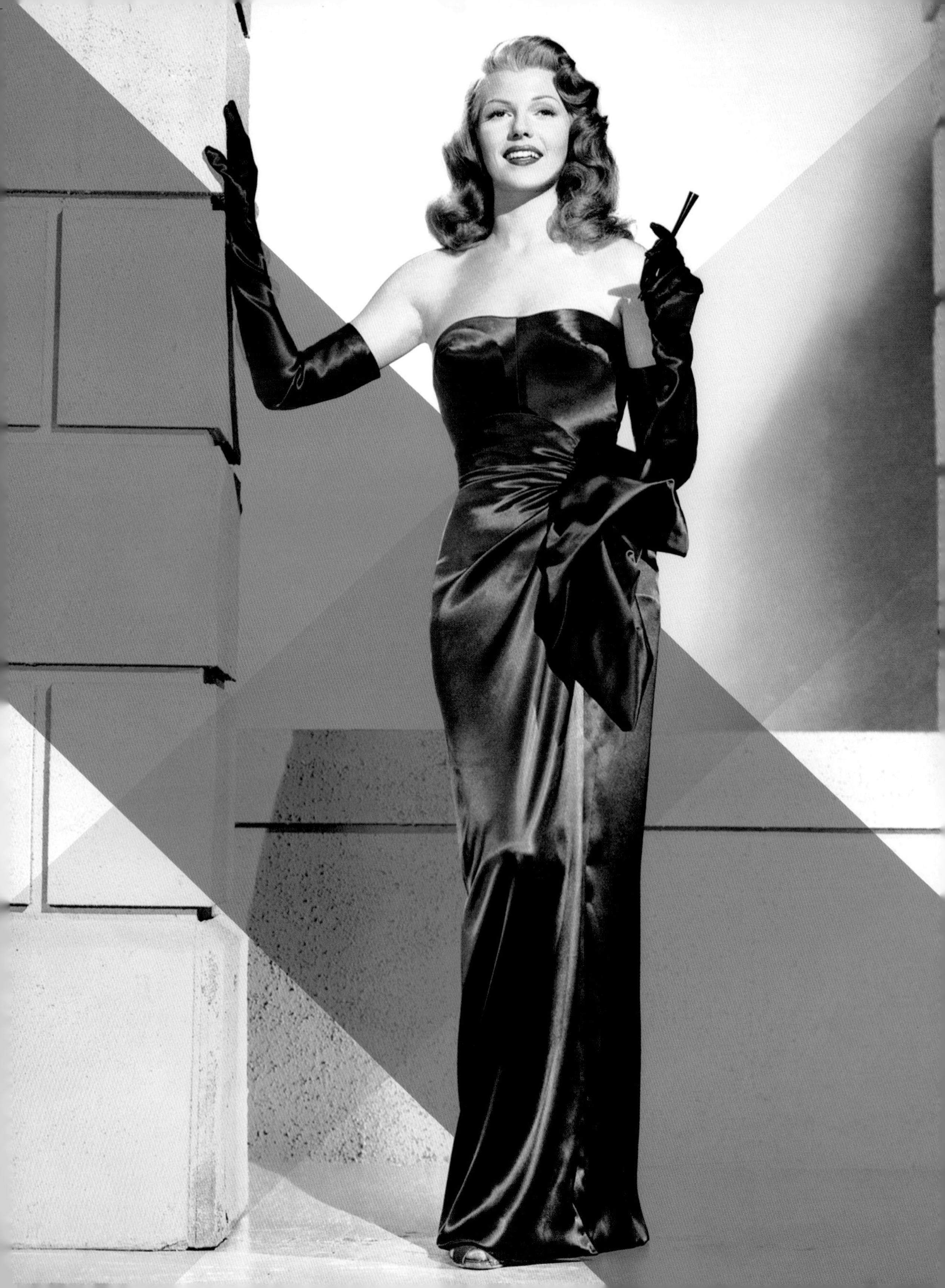

THE NINETEEN FORTIES

America faced great challenges during the 1940s, and Hollywood was not exempt. With the advent of World War II, the film industry lost much of its revenue from foreign markets. Rationing curbed a lot of activities, but Americans flocked to theaters in record numbers—to watch their screen heroes win battles single-handedly while their favorite actresses raised morale on the home front.

In addition to giving audiences gung-ho war movies and stress-relieving comedies or musicals, the 1940s introduced a new genre of film—dark, moody melodramas known as "cine noir." These films featured modern, edgy protagonists—the scheming, streetwise female and the amoral males she preyed upon.

Fashions in Hollywood, as elsewhere, were affected by war shortages—hemlines rose, skirts and trousers narrowed, but the shoulder-padded, belted-waist silhouette Adrian had created for Joan Crawford in the 1930s still reigned supreme. Military-influenced styles were in vogue and jitterbug dance attire often replaced gowns and tuxedoes for an evening out. Women began working in jobs of every description, filling in for the men at the front, and their wardrobes now reflected the need for comfort and convenience.

HOLLYWOOD FASHION | THE NINETEEN FORTIES

KATHARINE HEPBURN

Though Hepburn's popularity fluctuated during her early career, by its end she was possibly the most highly regarded actress on earth.

Katharine Hepburn (1907–2003) was born in Hartford, Connecticut. She attended Bryn Mawr College and after graduation sought any New York theater roles she could find, including understudy. She was hired by and then fired from a number of shows and took voice lessons to improve her range. Her confidence may have faltered, but she drove herself onward.

After playing the lead in *The Warrior's Husband* on Broadway, Hepburn finally achieved critical success. When she tested for the film *A Bill of Divorcement* with John Barrymore, director George Cukor was intrigued by what he saw. He wrote, "There was this odd creature, unlike anybody I'd ever heard." Although not glamorous by Hollywood's standards, Hepburn was tall, brisk, clear-eyed, and frank. So Cukor took a chance with the unknown actress, and the film—and Hepburn—earned rave reviews.

In 1933 she starred in *Morning Glory,* which earned her an Oscar, and in *Little Women,* another top draw. But Hepburn would not play the Hollywood game or "do herself up" for fans, and her next group of films, including current favorite *Bringing Up Baby,* flopped at the box office. She returned to Broadway to star in *The Philadelphia Story* and optioned the rights when it became a hit—and the resulting comedy put Hepburn back on top. She was next paired with Spencer Tracy in *Pat and Mike*, sparking a romance that would last 25 years and produce nine films.

As she aged, Hepburn continued to find quality roles, unlike many actresses of her era. She played lonely spinsters in *The African Queen, Summertime,* and *The Rainmaker* and later scored as toxic mothers in *Suddenly, Last Summer, A Long Day's Journey into Night,* and *The Lion in Winter*. Her last film with Spencer Tracy—*Guess Who's Coming to Dinner?*—was completed eight weeks before his death. Her own final films were *Rooster Cogburn, On Golden Pond,* and *Love Affair.*

During her long career, Hepburn won four Academy Awards and was nominated 12 times, but she attended the ceremony only once, in 1974, to present the Irving Thalberg Award to her friend, producer Lawrence Weingarten. An audience of her peers gave her a standing ovation.

ABOVE
As a high society divorcée in 1940's *The Philadelphia Story,* Hepburn looks ultra feminine in Adrian's delicious chiffon peignoir.

TOP RIGHT
Hepburn models what would come to be part of her on-screen "uniform"—a stylish, man-tailored jacket and open-throated white blouse.

FULL PAGE
Hepburn, who plays an ambitious reporter in 1942's *Woman of the Year,* here models a Grecian-inspired pleated gown with a corded waist.

Hepburn Style
Although Hepburn easily carried off elegant gowns, she often played roles in male clothing—in *Sylvia Scarlett* she travels with a theater troupe dressed as a boy, while in *Christopher Strong* she is an aviatrix who favors flight suits. She first introduced women's trousers to film in 1938's *Bringing Up Baby*. When the producers balked at the idea, Hepburn walked around the set in her underwear until they agreed.

Signature Look
- Pale evening gowns with simple lines
- Khaki pants, cardigans, and loafers
- Quirky but stylish hats

> Dressing up is a bore...At a certain age you decorate yourself to attract the opposite sex and at a certain age I did that. But I'm past that age now.
> KATHARINE HEPBURN

MOST FASHIONABLE FILMS

BRINGING UP BABY (1938)
THE PHILADELPHIA STORY (1940)
WOMAN OF THE YEAR (1942)
PAT AND MIKE (1952)

HOLLYWOOD FASHION | THE NINETEEN FORTIES

INGRID BERGMAN

Though she never actually said, "Play it again, Sam," no one will ever forget Bergman's poignant performance in Casablanca.

After the success of Garbo and Dietrich, studios continued combing Europe for other actresses with style and charisma. Ingrid Bergman (1915–1982) was a prominent Swedish actress brought to America in 1939 by producer David O. Selznick. He featured her in *Intermezzo* (costumes by Travis Banton and Irene), *Gaslight*—earning her an Academy Award, *The Bells of St. Mary's*, *For Whom the Bell Tolls*, and *Notorious* and *Spellbound* for director Alfred Hitchcock—all major hits.

But Bergman ascended to the cinema pantheon when she appeared with Humphrey Bogart in Michael Curtiz's 1942 film, *Casablanca*. This tale of love lost and found and lost again is frequently voted the best movie ever made. Bergman never looked lovelier in outfits by Orry-Kelly.

In the 1956 film, *Anastasia* (costumes by René Hubert), which earned her a second Best Actress Oscar. Her third was for a supporting role in *Murder on the Orient Express* in 1974.

> **Be yourself. The world worships the original.**
> INGRID BERGMAN

Bergman Style
Bergman was a true Nordic beauty, but with her simple hair, understated gowns, and natural-looking makeup, there was nothing flashy about her. She became a style setter precisely because the average woman could relate to her look—and easily emulate it.

Signature Look
- A-line dresses
- Tailored suits
- Picture hats

MOST FASHIONABLE FILMS
INTERMEZZO, A LOVE STORY (1939)
CASABLANCA (1942)
GASLIGHT (1944)
NOTORIOUS (1946)
ANASTASIA (1956)

ABOVE
As the wife of a political refugee in 1942's *Casablanca*, Bergman still managed to look unruffled in this tailored white evening ensemble from Orry-Kelly.

RIGHT
The actress strikes a pensive mood pose in Hitchcock's 1946 thriller, *Notorious*. Her oatmeal tweed suit is accessorized with long black gloves and a self-tie silk blouse.

THE NINETEEN FORTIES | HOLLYWOOD FASHION

RITA HAYWORTH

This popular pin-up girl went from dancer to accomplished actress ...and ended up as Hollywood's first princess.

Rita Hayworth (1918—1987) was known for playing both fresh-faced ingénues and fiery temptresses. Born Margarita Cansino in Brooklyn, she was a third-generation entertainer who performed a touring dance act with her father. She was originally cast as an "exotic" type in minor films, but her career took off in 1937, when Columbia came calling after she had her hairline reshaped by electrolysis and dyed her brown hair a russet red.

Her role as a siren in the hit film, *Only Angels Have Wings* led to *Blood and Sand* with Tyrone Power, *You Were Never Lovelier* with Fred Astaire, and *Cover Girl* in 1944 with Gene Kelly (wardrobe by Travis Banton, Muriel King and Gwen Wakeling, respectively), which established Hayworth as Columbia's top draw. She then made a splash in *Gilda* in 1946, doing her famous striptease in Jean Louis' provocative strapless gown.

In 1943 she married actor-director Orson Welles. When he had her hair cut and dyed blond for 1948's *The Lady from Shanghai*, fans were outraged. After her divorce from Welles, she married Prince Aly Khan, son of Shia Muslim leader the Agha Khan. It was their daughter, Yasmin Khan, who was caring for Hayworth in the 1980s when Alzheimer's disease—first misdiagnosed as alcoholic dementia—claimed her life.

MOST FASHIONABLE FILMS

COVER GIRL (1944)
GILDA (1946)
THE LADY FROM SHANGHAI (1948)
THE LOVES OF CARMEN (1948)

Hayworth Style
When not on set, Hayworth preferred casual clothing—trousers with loafers and a simple sweater. Her favorite feature was her elegant hands.

Signature Look
- Strapless gowns with long gloves
- Masses of wavy hair
- V-necks and sweetheart necklines

ABOVE

The famous redhead went blond at the request of then-husband Orson Welles for his 1947 suspense film, *The Lady from Shanghai*. Here she models a white evening robe with dolman sleeves and a belted waist worn with a knotted gold scarf and ankle-strap sandals.

LEFT

Hayworth, who let a bit of her Latin roots show in 1948's *The Loves of Carmen*, reclines gracefully in a peasant blouse and skirt accented with an ethnic fabric wrap belt, turquoise and carnelian beads, and gypsy earrings.

61

HOLLYWOOD FASHION | THE NINETEEN FORTIES

ALBUM OF TRENDSETTERS
QUEENS OF TECHNICOLOR

REDHEADS
Color movie film seems to have been invented expressly to exalt the coloring of redheaded actresses.

While their fair complexions and light-colored eyes could appear pale and washed out in black-and-white films, redheads were brought to glorious life by the color film process. The term "Queen of Technicolor" was applied to Rhonda Fleming and Maureen O'Hara (and sometime redhead Maria Montez), but it would be appropriate for any of the stars featured here whose pride and joy was a fiery mane of auburn or strawberry-blonde hair.

RIGHT
As Satine, the ill-fated courtesan in 2001's *Moulin Rouge!*, Nicole Kidman wore a number of delectable costumes, among them this boned-bodice, corset-backed red satin gown with an oversize back bow and chapel-length train, which is named "the smoldering temptress."

ABOVE RIGHT
Green-eyed Rhonda Fleming dons a green velvet gown with blue slashed sleeves to win privateer Sterling Hayden in 1952's *The Golden Hawk*.

BELOW RIGHT
Classic comedian Lucille Ball, wearing a wide-collared white lace blouse, appears uncharacteristically demure in this still from 1946's *Lover Come Back*.

THE NINETEEN FORTIES | HOLLYWOOD FASHION

TOP LEFT

Julianne Moore received rave reviews for her portrayal of a mature 1960's "party girl" in Tom Ford's 2009 film, *A Single Man*. Here she models a color-blocked dinner dress and large bauble earrings, both typical of the decade.

TOP RIGHT

Amy Adams, seen here admiring New York in a fairy tale frock with oversized puffed sleeves, makes the perfect storybook princess in the animated/live action hit, *Enchanted*, from 2007.

LEFT

The tempestuous Maureen O'Hara looks convincing as an Arabian Nights' damsel wearing a brocade taffeta robe over a bronze satin harem ensemble in 1947's *Sinbad the Sailor*.

63

HOLLYWOOD FASHION | THE NINETEEN FORTIES

BARBARA STANWYCK

Stanwyck was Hollywood's workhorse—yet during a 60-year career starring in comedies, dramas, and thrillers she always kept her breezy attitude.

Barbara Stanwyck (1907–1990) was born to play shrewd, sassy women who usually landed on their feet. She started life as Ruby Catherine Stevens of Brooklyn and lead a hard-knock life—her mother died when a drunk pushed her off a streetcar—rotating through foster homes. By 16, she was performing as a chorus girl, most notably in the Ziegfeld Follies of 1922 and 1923. After a brief stage career, she headed for Hollywood.

Stanwyck soon became a directors' darling, working for King Vidor in *Stella Dallas*, Rouben Mamoulian in *Golden Boy*, Preston Sturges in *The Lady Eve* (costumes by Edith Head), Frank Capra in *Meet John Doe*, and Billy Wilder in *Double Indemnity*. In Howard Hawks' *Ball of Fire* she played a stripper (costumes by Head) and reportedly based her slinky walk on that of a panther. She scored as a magazine columnist in 1945's *Christmas in Connecticut* (gowns by Milo Anderson) and as a helpless murder victim in 1948's *Sorry Wrong Number*.

The actress went on to a successful TV career, earning three Emmys. Throughout her time in Hollywood, she was known for her kindness and relaxed attitude off camera. Capra said she was, "destined to be beloved by all directors, actors, crews and extras."

MOST FASHIONABLE FILMS

THE LADY EVE (1941)
DOUBLE INDEMNITY (1944)
CHRISTMAS IN CONNECTICUT (1945)

Stanwyck style
With her wide shoulders and slender waist, Stanwyck had the ideal figure to showcase the 1940s' silhouette.

Signature look
- Less-is-more gowns
- Ankle bracelet (from *Double Indemnity*)
- Dress trousers with silk shirts

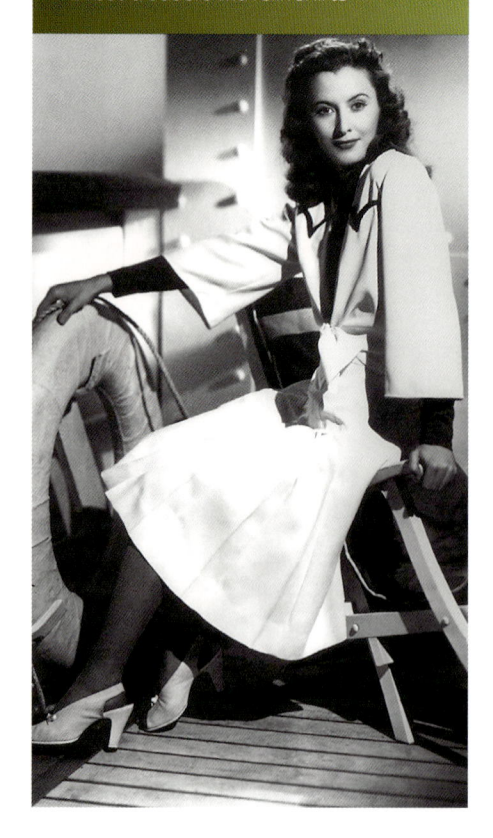

ABOVE
Although not voluptuous, while playing a nightclub singer in 1942's *Ball of Fire*, Stanwyck made the most of her attributes in this clinging, copper-colored, high-cut stage costume.

RIGHT
Stanwyck plays the ultimate con woman in the 1941 comedy, *The Lady Eve*, and every outfit, including this nautical ensemble worn with slingback shoes, is designed to attract her unsuspecting prey.

64 1940s

THE NINETEEN FORTIES | HOLLYWOOD FASHION

GENE TIERNEY

The always-impeccable wife of designer Oleg Cassini had the face of a heartbreaker and the aura of a saint.

Gene Tierney (1920–1991) possessed a wide-eyed innocence that worked effectively in both contemporary and period films. Born in Brooklyn to a life of privilege, her wealthy family even sent her to a Swiss finishing school, but Tierney had her eye on the theater. By the late 1930s, she was appearing on Broadway and in 1940 was signed by Darryl F. Zanuck of 20th Century-Fox. She appeared in five films in 1941 and was nominated for an Academy Award in 1945 for *Leave Her to Heaven* (costumes by Kay Nelson). 1946 brought another notable performance in *The Razor's Edge* and in 1947 she did a charming period piece, *The Ghost and Mrs. Muir*.

To most filmgoers, Tierney will always be associated with Otto Preminger's 1944 classic, *Laura*. As the "murdered" advertising executive, Tierney won the heart of tough detective Dana Andrews—and the admiration of audiences everywhere. Designer Bonnie Cashin created Laura's career-girl wardrobe, including her famous "floppy" hat.

Sadly, Tierney had many problems in her private life— her first daughter with husband Oleg Cassini was born with multiple birth defects, putting a strain on their marriage. The couple finally divorced in 1952. Tierney also suffered from bipolar disorder and in the 1950s underwent 27 shock treatments, which she later denounced in her autobiography, *Self-Portrait*.

Tierney Style
Tierney's baby doll features were tempered by her high cheekbones and a slight overbite.

Signature Look
- Draped evening gowns in solid fabrics
- Sporty separates
- Large, interesting hats

MOST FASHIONABLE FILMS

LAURA (1944)
DRAGONWYCK (1946)
THE GHOST AND MRS. MUIR (1947)

ABOVE

Although Tierney wore a number of charming outfits in the 1944 romantic mystery, *Laura*, her soft brimmed poplin rain hat became a crowd favorite and was designer Bonnie Cashin's attempt to revive the 1920s' cloche.

LEFT

In *On the Riviera*, with Danny Kaye in a double role, Tierney portrays a wealthy industrialist's wife and gets to model a series of alluring outfits like this off-the-shoulder crimson gown by Travilla.

65

Academy Awards:
Head received eight Academy Awards for Best Costume Design from a total of 35 nominations.
- 1950: The Heiress
- 1951: Samson and Delilah
- 1951: All About Eve
- 1952: A Place in the Sun
- 1954: Roman Holiday
- 1955: Sabrina
- 1961: The Facts of Life
- 1974: The Sting

MOST FASHIONABLE DESIGNS

THE HEIRESS (1949)
ALL ABOUT EVE (1950)
ROMAN HOLIDAY (1953)

THE NINETEEN FORTIES | HOLLYWOOD FASHION

STYLE MAKER
EDITH HEAD

Even though Hollywood produced some of the best costume designers of the twentieth century, Edith Head rose...head and shoulders...above her industry peers, collecting eight Oscars and 35 nominations and maintaining a productive career that lasted decades.

Her designs were never ostentatious or trendy. Rather, she grounded them in timeless styles and structured them on the needs of each film. Plus, she was one of the few costumers to consult with her actress clients prior to beginning her sketches.

A Change of Direction

Edith Head (1897–1981) was born Edith Claire Posener in San Bernardino, California. She received her master's degree in romance languages from Stanford, and became a French teacher. When offered the chance to teach art—and increase her salary—she honed her weak drawing skills with evening classes at Chouinard Art College. In 1923, she married a classmate's brother, Charles Head, but the marriage lasted barely a decade.

In 1924—after borrowing another art student's sketchbook for her interview—Head was hired by Paramount as a costume sketch artist. The first film to showcase her designs was 1925's *The Wanderer*. Five years later, she had become one of Hollywood's go-to designers. Initially, she remained in the shadow of bosses Howard Greer and Travis Banton, but when Banton left the studio in 1938, Head was ready to take the spotlight.

She gained the approval of the public for the sexy sarongs she created for Dorothy Lamour in *The Hurricane* (1937), and later generated buzz for the mink-lined dress she designed in 1944 for Ginger Rogers' *Lady in the Dark*—a most extravagant ensemble for wartime America. In 1940, she wed set designer, Wiard Ihnen—who would himself win two Academy Awards—a marriage that lasted until his death in 1979.

In the 1950s, Head's critics dubbed her the "queen of the shirtwaisters" because her designs tended to be restrained rather than flashy. One positive result of avoiding fads, however, was that her films aged well and rarely evoked the "I can't believe women wore that back then!" reaction from modern audiences.

Head's "low-drama mama" approach to design was so popular with the major actresses of the era—Bette Davis, Barbara Stanwyck, Grace Kelly, Sophia Loren, Audrey Hepburn, and Elizabeth Taylor—that Paramount was often required to "loan" her out to other studios. She left Paramount for good—after 43 years—in 1967, when she moved to Universal. Many believe this shift was necessary because she was working so closely with Universal's star director, Alfred Hitchcock.

> You can have anything you want in life if you dress for it.
> — EDITH HEAD

ABOVE
Edith Head, with her signature bangs and owlish glasses, was a Hollywood fixture for decades.

LEFT
Veronica Lake, in a press shot from *Sullivan's Travels* (1942), gets cozy in a sprigged organdy peignoir with a soft lapel collar and bishop sleeves.

FULL PAGE
Grace Kelly epitomized the word "princess" in *Rear Window*'s (1953) oft-copied tulle ballerina-skirted gown with its dramatic black bodice.

67

HOLLYWOOD FASHION | THE NINETEEN FORTIES

LORETTA YOUNG

One of Hollywood's best-dressed actresses, Young was the picture of poise and serenity on screen.

Loretta Young (1913–2000) played gracious, wholesome characters for most of her career. Born Gretchen Young in Salt Lake City, Utah, Young's family moved to Hollywood when she was three. As a teenager Young accidentally intercepted a phone call offering an acting job meant for her older sister, and Young got the part.

In 1935, after a string of minor movies, she starred in the hit adventure film, *Call of the Wild*, with Clark Gable.

Young went on to star in a number of successful films—*Suez* in 1938, *Along Came Jones* in 1945 with Gary Cooper, *The Bishop's Wife* with Cary Grant and David Niven in 1947, *Rachel and the Stranger* with William Holden and Robert Mitchum in 1948, *Come to the Stable* in 1949, as a nun with Celeste Holm, and *Key to the City* in 1950, again with Gable. She won the 1947 Academy Award for *The Farmer's Daughter*—with costumes by Edith Head.

From 1953 to 1961, Young hosted an Emmy-winning dramatic series on TV. Throughout her life, she remained a devout Catholic known for working with many charities.

Young Style
Young remained a glamour icon during her TV years—making a dramatic entrance in an elegant gown to open each episode of her show.

Signature Look
- Soft, face-framing hair
- Wide-shouldered dresses with draped panels
- Gowns with sweeping, wide skirts

MOST FASHIONABLE FILMS
HE STAYED FOR BREAKFAST (1940)
THE MEN IN HER LIFE (1941)
THE FARMER'S DAUGHTER (1947)
THE BISHOP'S WIFE (1947)
KEY TO THE CITY (1950)

> "Glamour is something you can't bear to be without once you're used to it."
> — LORETTA YOUNG

ABOVE
Even though the mood is dramatic as Young poses in an alluring black lace gown with a peek-a-boo bodice, the 1940 film she was promoting, *He Stayed for Breakfast*, was a comedic romp.

RIGHT
In 1941's *The Men in Her Life*, Young played a talented ballerina—seen here in a dance costume with a tulle skirt and bejeweled bodice—torn between career and family.

68 1940s

THE NINETEEN FORTIES | HOLLYWOOD FASHION

LANA TURNER

Hollywood legend said the "Sweater Girl" was discovered at a drugstore counter; the real Turner barely survived an equally tabloid-worthy life.

Well-endowed Lana Turner (1921–1995) played provocative roles throughout her career. After the murder of her father, young Turner moved to California with her family. As she matured—and her beauty increased—she believed she could ensure a more stable life by working in motion pictures.

She wasn't "discovered" as legend says, however. She diligently went from studio to studio seeking work until she made her mark in 1938's *Love Finds Andy Hardy*...and promptly became the "Sweater Girl" to millions of men and boys. By the early 1940s she was getting solid roles—*Johnny Eager*, *Dr. Jekyll and Mr. Hyde*, and her explosively sexual breakout film with John Garfield, *The Postman Always Rings Twice* (costumes by Irene). She continued to make well-received dramas into the 1950s—*The Bad and the Beautiful* (costumes by Helen Rose), *Peyton Place* (1957), and *Imitation of Life*.

Turner's private life, however, was more lurid than any film melodrama. The actress married seven times, battled alcoholism, and dated gangsters. Perhaps the worst scandal came in 1958 when her only child, Cheryl Crane, killed Turner's lover, mobster Johnny Stompanato, in what was later termed self-defense.

Turner Style
Turner, who owned nearly 700 pairs of shoes, preferred white outfits worn with lots of fur. She liked high-waisted dresses and shorts that accentuated her bust. Her sultry style inspired Argentinean first lady, Eva Peron.

Signature Look
- White satin gowns
- High-waisted shorts worn with tight sweaters
- Draped fur stoles

MOST FASHIONABLE FILMS
THE THREE MUSKETEERS (1948)
THE BAD AND THE BEAUTIFUL (1952)
IMITATION OF LIFE (1959)

ABOVE
In 1946's *The Postman Always Rings Twice*, Turner wears a white sports outfit that could have been taken from her private wardrobe—a midriff-baring top that highlights her bust and short-shorts that accentuate her shapely legs.

LEFT
Turner was eye-catching in this lavish white gown in 1959's *Imitation of Life*, one of her greatest movie successes.

HOLLYWOOD FASHION | **THE NINETEEN FORTIES**

BETTE DAVIS

Davis tackled a variety of roles—from spinster to spitfire, Southern belle to saintly schoolteacher—with equal aplomb.

Bette Davis (1908—1989) was a true Hollywood original—tart and edgy, she often played scheming, even ruthless women—and audiences loved her for it. She debuted on Broadway in 1929 and by the early 1930s had a contract with Warner Bros.

After impressing audiences in *Of Human Bondage* (1934), Davis won two Oscars—for 1935's *Dangerous* and 1938's *Jezebel*, both with costumes by Orry-Kelly. But when Warner's kept forcing her into mediocre movies, Davis sailed to England and sued the studio. She lost her case, yet returned to worthier fare, including *The Letter*, *Dark Victory*, *The Little Foxes*, *The Man Who Came to Dinner*, and the classic makeover movie, *Now, Voyager*. As the dowdy, browbeaten daughter of a Boston matriarch, Davis was heartrending; her post-makeover appearance on a cruise ship in a rakish white hat, chic black suit, and white, open-collared shirt (by Orry-Kelly) created cinema magic. The film was also famous for the scene where Paul Henreid lights two cigarettes and hands one to Davis, a courtesy the actor was often asked to repeat.

In the mid-1940s Davis became known for making "women's" films, including *Old Acquaintance* and *Mrs. Skeffington*. During World War II, she cofounded the Hollywood Canteen for servicemen—"one of her proudest moments"—and also performed for black regiments beside Hattie McDaniel, Lena Horne, and Ethel Waters. After giving birth to a daughter, Davis made several unremarkable films—and in 1949 parted ways with Warner's.

In 1950, Davis was offered the lead in *All About Eve* after its original star, Claudette Colbert, suffered a back injury. The film, about a mature stage actress fending off an ambitious newcomer, went on to win the Academy Award and provided Davis with a career-defining role—and Oscar-winning costumes by Edith Head and Charles LeMaire.

As stellar parts waned for the aging Davis, she reinvented herself as queen of the macabre in Gothic horror films like *Whatever Happened to Baby Jane?* (1962) with Joan Crawford (her longtime rival) and *Hush, Hush, Sweet Charlotte* (1964).

Davis received the American Film Institute's Lifetime Achievement Award, the first woman to be so honored. She suffered a stroke in 1983, but continued to act in films and on television until her death.

MOST FASHIONABLE FILMS

JEZEBEL (1938)
DARK VICTORY (1939)
THE LITTLE FOXES (1941)
NOW, VOYAGER (1942)
ALL ABOUT EVE (1950)

Davis Style
Orry-Kelly observed that Davis had no specific personal style in her films because her "character always came before her clothing." Yet Davis had the assured presence to carry off any ensemble...from the brazen red ball gown in *Jezebel* to Dior's New Look in *June Bride*.

Signature Look
- Short, sleek bobs
- Boxy fur coats or jackets
- Stylish, brimmed hats

ABOVE
Primed for action, Davis shows off her nip-waisted riding habit and jaunty feathered cap in 1938's *Jezebel*.

FULL PAGE
Davis, here wearing a luxe silver fox shrug and matching hat, plays a willful socialite who discovers she is dying in 1939's "weepie," *Dark Victory*.

> I often think that a slightly exposed shoulder emerging from a long satin nightgown packed more sex than two naked bodies in bed.
> BETTE DAVIS

HOLLYWOOD FASHION | THE NINETEEN FORTIES

FASHION INFLUENCE
WORKING WOMEN

During the early 1940s, films like *His Girl Friday* and *Woman of the Year* began to portray women as "career girls," not simply as shop girls, typists, or waitresses, but as women with real, challenging, bring-home-the-bacon jobs.

This mirrored what was actually happening in the country—more women were completing high school or college and entering the workforce on a career track. Some desired the challenges and rewards of a profession, while others wanted to explore options other than marriage and motherhood.

After America entered World War II, women from all backgrounds and aspirations were drawn into the vacuum left behind by the departing servicemen. They worked in factories and on construction sites, they brought in the harvest, and delivered the milk. In 1940, the number of working women was 11,970,000; in 1945, it was 18,610,000. And whether the workplace was a corporate office, an art department, or an urban newspaper working women required a new type of attire—something that struck a balance between traditional femininity and professional capability. Most secretaries and assistants wore classic, tailored dresses to

RIGHT

Joan Crawford, playing a restaurateur and aggrieved mother in 1945's *Mildred Pierce*, is all business in a severe, man-tailored pinstripe suit that is barely relieved by a hint of white collar and a necklace.

72 1940s

THE NINETEEN FORTIES | HOLLYWOOD FASHION

work, but initially clothing for female executives followed mannish lines—structured gabardine or tweed suits, blouses worn with string ties or ascots, and walking shoes or spectators. The big-shouldered silhouette of the 1940s made these styles even more oppressively masculine. (This look was revived in the 1980s; the exaggerated shoulder pads worn by Melanie Griffith in *Working Girl* and Diane Keaton in *Baby Boom* were typical of the power suit.)

While movies first acknowledged the career girl phenomenon in the 1940s, Hollywood continued to find something compelling about a plucky heroine battling an unfair boss or trying to make it up the corporate ladder on her own. Here are some outstanding films that lauded the working woman over the past seven decades.

ABOVE LEFT

"Black is the new black." Assistants Anne Hathaway and Emily Blunt try to coach boss Meryl Streep—all attired in ebony couture gowns—at her annual publishing bash in 2006's *The Devil Wears Prada*.

ABOVE

Julia Roberts made push-up bras and low-cut tops part of her work ensemble in her Oscar-winning turn as an environmental crusader in 2000's *Erin Brockovich*.

LEFT

Ginger Rogers, wearing a side-buttoned dress with a white collar and polka-dot bow, stood up for working girls everywhere as the lucky young lady who marries the boss but then learns to follow her own path in 1940's *Kitty Foyle*.

73

HOLLYWOOD FASHION | THE NINETEEN FORTIES

ROSALIND RUSSELL

This versatile powerhouse—and four-time Oscar nominee—seemed to burst off the screen in her many physical roles.

Rosalind Russell (1907–1976) was known for playing sharp-witted, fast-talking, sometimes eccentric characters. She was born in Connecticut (and named after a ship by her father) and studied at the American Academy of Dramatic Art to become an acting teacher. After gaining some stage experience, she wriggled out of a contract with Universal to sign a more lucrative deal with MGM.

Her first success came with the 1939 hit, *The Women*, followed by her breakout film, *His Girl Friday*, where she played a wise-cracking newspaperwoman opposite Cary Grant (gowns by Robert Kalloch). She went on to score not only in comedies like *Take a Letter, Darling* and *My Sister Eileen*, but in dramas such as *Mourning Becomes Electra*, and "message" films like *Sister Kenny*, the last three earning her Oscar nominations.

In the 1950s, Russell continued to find major roles—in *Gypsy*, *Picnic*, and her signature film, 1958's *Auntie Mame*, with playful, bohemian costumes by Orry-Kelly.

MOST FASHIONABLE FILMS

HIS GIRL FRIDAY (1940)
MY SISTER EILEEN (1942)
TAKE A LETTER, DARLING (1942)
AUNTIE MAME (1958)

Russell style
By no means a glamour girl, Russell had her own look—a mannish-but-feminine chic that combined tailored suits, stylish walking shoes, and sporty hats.

Signature look
- Tweed, tailored suits
- Wide-shouldered gowns
- Capri pants and beaded tops

ABOVE
In 1942's *Take a Letter, Darling*, Russell, here glamming it up in a tiered satin halter gown and fur stole, is a powerful ad executive to Fred McMurray's erstwhile male secretary.

RIGHT
One of Russell's most beloved performances came in 1940 when she played Hildy Johnson, a fast-talking ace reporter who is about to desert her former husband—and boss—Cary Grant in *His Girl Friday*. Russell's sleekly tailored woven suit and chic hat bespoke a woman of style who was also a successful professional.

THE NINETEEN FORTIES | HOLLYWOOD FASHION

LAUREN BACALL

Bogey's whisky-voiced "Baby" combined acting ability with the honed style sense of a high-fashion model.

Lauren Bacall (1924–2014) was known for playing seductively intelligent women. She was born Betty Joan Perske in New York City in 1924 and took her mother's maiden name of Bacall when her parents divorced. While still a teen, she became a fashion model; director Howard Hawks's wife, Nancy, saw her on a *Harper's Bazaar* and suggested he offer Bacall a screen test for his upcoming film, *To Have and Have Not*. Hawks liked what he saw and signed her to a seven-year contract. He even gave her his wife's nickname, Slim, in the film.

Before shooting commenced on the Hemingway-based adventure, Humphrey Bogart was already smitten with his young costar, whom he called Baby. Bogart and Bacall were married in 1945—and the film that brought them together became a classic. They were again paired in *The Big Sleep* (costumes by Leah Rhodes), *Dark Passage*, and *Key Largo* (Rhodes). Bacall also scored during the 1950s in *How to Marry a Millionaire*, *Written on the Wind*, and *Designing Woman*. The latter opened only months after Bogart's death from cancer.

Bacall focused mainly on the theater during the 1960s and won two Tony Awards—for *Applause* and *Woman of the Year*. Though she continued to act in movies, it was usually in character roles. *The Mirror Has Two Faces* from 1996 earned her an Oscar nomination for Best Supporting Actress.

Bacall Style
Bacall's way of putting an outfit together was nearly timeless—in some of her films or photo shoots she could easily hail from the 1960s, the 1980s, or even today.

Signature Look
- Golden-blond pageboy
- Form-fitting tweed suits
- Ethnic skirts, blouses, and espadrille shoes

MOST FASHIONABLE FILMS
TO HAVE AND HAVE NOT (1944)
THE BIG SLEEP (1946)
KEY LARGO (1948)
DESIGNING WOMAN (1957)

ABOVE
Bacall had the poise to carry off exotic ensembles like this Chinese-influenced vented velvet jacket worn with loose trousers from the 1946 thriller, *The Big Sleep*

LEFT
Bacall made a rip-roaring film debut in 1944's *To Have and Have Not*, where she won over costar Humphrey Bogart wearing this tweed suit with a notched-lapel peplum jacket and straight skirt accessorized with a black beret and a flirty tweed "ball" purse on a cord.

75

HOLLYWOOD FASHION | THE NINETEEN FORTIES

JOAN CRAWFORD

Crawford's unrelenting ambition and iron resolve took her from dancing flapper to Queen Bee of Hollywood.

Joan Crawford (1905–1977) played tough women who went after what they wanted— men, money, or power. Born Lucille Le Sueur in San Antonio, Texas, Crawford was entranced by the vaudeville acts in stepfather Henry Cassin's theater. She vowed to become a dancer and, while still a teen, went from chorus girl in traveling revues to dancing on Broadway. MGM signed her in 1924, but their head of publicity disliked her name— Lucille Le "Sewer." He arranged a contest in *Movie Weekly* magazine for fans to christen the new starlet, and they chose Joan Crawford (which she disliked).

After a series of bit parts, Crawford increased her visibility by entering—and winning—hotel dance contests. She was soon getting better parts, though the plum roles still fell to Norma Shearer, wife of producer Irving Thalberg. "How can I compete with Norma?" Crawford quipped. "She sleeps with the boss."

When she appeared with Lon Chaney—as an armless knife thrower—in 1927's carnival melodrama, *The Unknown*, Crawford said she finally saw what real acting was about. The following year she found a star-making role in *Our Dancing Daughters*. In 1929, as if to cement her new status, she married Douglas Fairbanks, Jr., son and stepson of Hollywood's royal couple, Douglas Fairbanks and Mary Pickford.

When sound movies arrived, Crawford worked to lose her Southwestern accent by reading aloud. After her first talkie, *Untamed*, was a hit, the studio abandoned her flapper image and presented her as sophisticated and worldly. She next starred in *Possessed* with Clark Gable and the ensemble blockbuster, *Grand Hotel*.

Ironically, Crawford's most influential film, fashion-wise, is one nobody ever sees—*Letty Lynton*. It was released in 1932 and then quickly pulled when MGM lost a plagiarism suit. One of her dresses, a white organdy gown with short, lavishly ruffled sleeves, was the first appearance of Adrian's wide-shouldered look—created to slenderize Crawford—which would reshape the silhouette of the American woman for the next decade.

Crawford's films remained profitable until 1938, when the *Independent Film Journal* declared her "box office poison." The next year she was back in form as a home-wrecker in *The Women*. She moved to Warner Bros. in 1943 and cemented her place among the Hollywood greats as *Mildred Pierce*, a mother who sacrifices for her undeserving daughter. Crawford, not the studio's first choice, wanted the role so badly she agreed to a screen test. It paid off—she got the part and won an Oscar. During the 1950s and 60s, the actress appeared in some decent films and occasional TV shows. After the death of her fourth husband, Pepsi-Cola Chairman Alfred Steele, Crawford was elected to their board of directors, but was forcibly retired in 1973.

ABOVE
Crawford, here dripping with dark fur and black lace, always manages to look dressed to the nines whether she is playing for melodramatic effect or, in the case of 1942's *They All Kissed the Bride*, for laughs.

ABOVE RIGHT
For the dramatic love triangle, 1934's *Sadie McKee*, Crawford dons a simple fitted black halter gown with startling sequined panels descending from the collar.

FULL PAGE
In 1941's *A Woman's Face*, Crawford plays a blackmailer whose life is changed when a terrible facial scar is surgically repaired. Here—scar free—she models a stunning Adrian robe worked in gilt embroidery.

76 1940s

MOST FASHIONABLE FILMS
OUR DANCING DAUGHTERS (1928)
LETTY LYNTON (1932)
SADIE McKEE (1934)
THE WOMEN (1939)
A WOMAN'S FACE (1941)
MILDRED PIERCE (1945)

Crawford Style
Whether playing flappers, rags-to-riches heroines, or a real-life corporate dragon, Crawford's look was always distinctly her own. Though her obsessive personality was skewered in *Mommie Dearest*, costume designer Irene Sharaff did justice to her iconic style.

Signature Look
- Wide-shouldered suits or dresses with narrow, belted waists
- Platform wedge shoes
- Extended, heavily penciled eyebrows

HOLLYWOOD FASHION | THE NINETEEN FORTIES

BETTY GRABLE

The "quicksilver blonde" went from minor parts as a dance specialist to become the highest-grossing star in Hollywood.

Betty Grable (1916–1973) played amiable go-getters in a series of big budget musicals. Born Elizabeth Ruth Grable in St. Louis, Missouri, she was the daughter of a driven stage mother. She studied ballet and tap, and at the age of 13 was already playing minor roles in Hollywood films. But Grable did not get her big break until 1940—in 20th Century-Fox's *Down Argentine Way* starring Don Ameche (with festive Latin-American costumes by Travis Banton). She strengthened her popularity with musical comedies like 1941's *Moon Over Miami*, again with Ameche (Banton), *Springtime in the Rockies* (1942), with bandleader Harry James, and *Coney Island* and *Sweet Rosie O'Grady*, both from 1943, the same year she married James.

Grable was arguably the most popular pin-up girl of World War II and, according to Hollywood legend, Fox had her famous legs insured with Lloyds of London. By 1947, she was the highest paid star in Hollywood, earning $300,000 a year.

After the war, Grable starred in more hit films, including *Mother Wore Tights* (costumes by Orry-Kelly), *Wabash Avenue* in 1950 (costumes by Charles LeMaire), and *How to Marry a Millionaire* in 1953 (costumes by Travilla). Grable retired from films in 1955, perhaps because the movies she was being offered were often lackluster remakes.

Grable Style
Grable knew how to work a tight sweater and shorts better than anyone. With her dancer's legs and hourglass figure, she looked good in both contemporary and period clothing.

Signature Look
- Tropical-print playsuits
- Satin lounging pajamas and tap pants
- Form-fitting sweaters with silk scarves

MOST FASHIONABLE FILMS
DOWN ARGENTINE WAY (1940)
MOON OVER MIAMI (1941)
HOW TO MARRY A MILLIONAIRE (1953)

ABOVE
This shot from 1943's *Coney Island* features Grable's famous legs, which were reportedly insured for a million dollars by Lloyds of London and helped to make her the most popular pin-up girl with American GIs. Grable remade the film as *Wabash Avenue* in 1950.

RIGHT
Grable, in a satin halter top and billowing chiffon skirt with satin panels, commands center stage during the "Kindergarten Conga" dance number in 1941's romantic comedy, *Moon over Miami*.

78 1940s

THE NINETEEN FORTIES | HOLLYWOOD FASHION

LENA HORNE

In a movie career constrained by studio stereotyping, Horne still managed to impress filmgoers with her talent, beauty, and style.

Lena Horne (1917–2010) rarely stretched her acting wings and was often reduced to cameo singing roles. She was born in Brooklyn, NY, and raised by her grandparents. By age 16, she was dancing and singing at Harlem's famous Cotton Club, where she fell under the watchful eyes of big band legends Cab Calloway and Duke Ellington. By 1942, Horne had signed with MGM and was featured as a nightclub singer in *Panama Hattie*. (The studio filmed her scenes so they could be deleted when the movie was shown in the American South—where black people could only be shown in subservient roles.)

Horne went on to star in two successful all-black productions—*Cabin in the Sky* (gowns by Irene), and *Stormy Weather* (costumes by Helen Rose), which furnished her with a hit recording of the title song. Horne then returned to "performer" roles in a series of Broadway-based musical films—*Broadway Rhythm*, *Zeigfeld Follies*, *Till the Clouds Roll By*, and *Words and Music*. Horne was considered to play Julie LaVerne, the racially mixed singer, in the 1951 remake of *Showboat*, but the role went to Ava Gardner.

From the mid 1950s into the 1980s, Horne concentrated on her singing career—she appeared on numerous television variety shows, and also continued campaigning for civil rights.

MOST FASHIONABLE FILMS

STORMY WEATHER (1943)
BROADWAY RHYTHM (1944)
ZIEGFELD FOLLIES (1946)

Horne Style
Horne, with her timeless fashion sense and strong political views, became a role model to many young black women.

Signature Look
- Strapless sheath "mermaid" gowns
- Sundresses with halter tops
- Short hair with wispy tendrils

ABOVE
The singer, here striking a sultry pose in a draped, one-shouldered white gown, became a fashion trendsetter for women the world over and in the early 1970s help popularize ethnic-influenced designer Giorgio di Sant'Angelo

LEFT
Horne, here wearing a glittering sequined gown with an illusion neckline, shared the screen with dancer Bill "Bojangles" Robinson in 1943's hit musical, *Stormy Weather*.

HOLLYWOOD FASHION | THE NINETEEN FORTIES

FASHION INFLUENCE
HOLLYWOOD GOES TO WAR

Even before the attack on Pearl Harbor, Hollywood had gone to war. In films such as *A Yank in the RAF*, *Watch on the Rhine*, and Chaplin's *The Great Dictator*, the American movie industry acknowledged that there was a war going on elsewhere. Still, in an effort to maintain audiences in Europe, most studios shied away from directly vilifying any specific country.

After Pearl Harbor and America's entry into the war, when President Franklin D. Roosevelt announced that the film industry could make "a very useful contribution" to the war effort, Hollywood geared up to do its part. The industry would now begin supplying morale-building films that would raise patriotism to new heights.

Though most of these movies focused on combat—*Air Force*, *Destination Tokyo*, *Objective Burma!*, *They Were Expendable*—others portrayed an individual's gradual evolution toward taking an active part in the war, as with Humphrey Bogart's Rick Blaine in *Casablanca*. Women played key roles in many war films—the combat nurses portrayed in *So Proudly We Hail*, Victory workers, USO hostesses, or simply as dedicated mothers, wives, and girlfriends supporting their fighting men from home.

Outside the studios, movie stars mobilized to sell war bonds, lead recruitment and recycling drives, and entertain soldiers stateside at USO bases and Hollywood canteens as well as in foreign combat zones. Established directors like Frank Capra, John Ford, and John Huston filmed propaganda documentaries on "why we are fighting." Twelve percent of the film industry entered the armed forces, including box office giants like Clark Gable, James Stewart, and Henry Fonda.

In spite of the many hardships Americans endured during the war, audiences still made time for the movies. Attendance averaged 90 million people a week! Hollywood's ability to furnish a stirring catharsis or a brief, stress-free haven was never greater. And what audiences saw the actors wearing on screen was not so different from the clothing they wore at home.

The Cost of Rationing

Wartime rationing had not only led to a reduction in the amount of clothing people purchased—one slogan advised "make do and mend!"—the scarcity of fabric caused dress hemlines to rise and silhouettes for women and men to become leaner. Circle skirts narrowed to become sheaths or A-lines. Silk hose gave way to nylons, and when nylon was needed for parachutes, ladies sported bare legs with a seam penciled down the back. Women were advised to "mix and match" separates

ABOVE
Fighter pilot John Wayne shares a moment with nurse Anna Lee in 1942's *Flying Tigers*. Wayne is wearing the leather "bomber" jacket that would soon become a mainstay of men's casual fashion.

TOP RIGHT
1943's *Cry Havoc* had a cast of mostly women and starred Margaret Sullavan, Ann Southern, and Joan Blondell.

BELOW RIGHT
Although Clark Gable is seen here playing a brigadier general with John Hodiak in 1948's *Command Decision*, he was actually a major in the Air Force during the war and flew in five combat missions.

THE NINETEEN FORTIES | HOLLYWOOD FASHION

and to adapt outfits for multiple seasons. Clothing might have become simpler, but women's hairdos now boasted elaborate curls, waves, pompadours, poufs, and even peek-a-boo bangs, courtesy of Veronica Lake. Women working in factories and military plants adopted trousers or overalls as practical, comfortable daytime wear—a radical departure from the norm that never quite went away. Reports indicate that between 1944 and 1945, women's trouser sales quintupled.

Even for non-combatants the military look—frogs, epaulets, braiding, and patriotic red and blue fabrics—influenced everything from evening gowns to pajamas. The short jacket worn by General Eisenhower, bloused at the midriff and tabbed at the hip, became popular for both sexes.

The jitterbug and big-band music were now the national craze, so eveningwear for actresses was often a short, belted dress worn with pumps and a boxy jacket, while men not in uniform sported narrow pants and double-breasted jackets. Not that Hollywood ever forgot about glamour; for major film events and openings, the lavish gowns and elegant tuxedos were again on parade. After all, part of a star's patriotic duty was to furnish a bright spot among the somber deprivations of the war.

ABOVE

The harmonizing Andrews Sisters, Maxene, Patty, and LaVerne, who appeared in 17 films, entertained the troops during World War II and performed in patriotic films like *Buck Privates* in 1941 and *Hollywood Canteen* in 1944.

LEFT

So Proudly We Hail from 1943 starred Claudette Colbert, Paulette Goddard, and Veronica Lake and honored the U.S. Army combat nurses of the South Pacific battle theater.

HOLLYWOOD FASHION | **THE NINETEEN FORTIES**

JUNE ALLYSON

Everyone's favorite girl-next-door, this singer shone bright in energetic musicals, light comedies, and postwar biographies.

June Allyson (1917–2006) played plucky, upbeat females for most of her film career.

Born Eleanor Geisman in the Bronx, the child was abandoned by her father and shunted between relatives while her mother worked. When she was eight, the hapless girl was struck by a falling tree limb and told she would never walk again. She wore a steel brace for four years and eventually did regain the use of her legs. Allyson hid her background from her fans, yet the truth was much more compelling than any bio concocted by a studio.

Dazzled by Ginger Rogers and other Hollywood dancers, Allyson began to compete in dance contests. She went from the Copacabana to Broadway chorus lines and minor film parts. While filling in for ailing Betty Hutton in *Panama Hattie*, she caught the eye of director George Abbott. He cast her in his military school musical, *Best Foot Forward*—which led to a role in the film version and a contract with MGM.

Allyson earned positive notices in *Two Girls and a Sailor* (costumes by Irene), *Good News* (gowns by Helen Rose), and the period film, *Little Women*. In addition to making five films with pal Van Johnson, Allyson played James Stewart's wife in three biographies: *The Stratton Story*, *The Glenn Miller Story*, and *Strategic Air Command*.

Allyson married screen idol Dick Powell in 1945. After his death in 1963, she retired from acting and was only occasionally seen in films or on TV.

MOST FASHIONABLE FILMS

BEST FOOT FORWARD (1943)
TWO GIRLS AND A SAILOR (1944)
GOOD NEWS (1947)
THE STRATTON STORY (1949)
THE GLEN MILLER STORY (1954)

Allyson Style
The studios dressed Allyson to accentuate her youth, with pale colors and lots of bows, frills, and ruffles, so her style was sweet rather than sophisticated.

Signature look
- White blouses with Peter Pan collars
- Frothy prom-type gowns
- Short, curly bangs

ABOVE
In 1949's *The Stratton Story* with James Stewart, Allyson wears a fitted jacket with a white blouse, a wide skirt, and her signature tight pageboy.

RIGHT
In *Two Girls and a Sailor* from 1944, June Allyson and Gloria DeHaven woo Van Johnson wearing the decade's popular supper club gowns—long, feminine, a bit sparkly, and perfect for dancing.

82 1940s

THE NINETEEN FORTIES | HOLLYWOOD FASHION

IRENE DUNNE

As the star of comedies, musicals, and melodramas, this five-time Oscar nominee's appeal to audiences rarely faltered.

Irene Dunne (1898–1990) was known for playing poised, amusing heroines. Born into a musical household in Louisville, Kentucky, the trained mezzo-soprano hoped for a career in opera but ended up on Broadway. She won the female lead in Jerome Kern's groundbreaking show, Showboat, and was discovered by a Hollywood scout during the musical's Chicago run. (Her father had been a steamboat inspector and Dunne had a great love for the Mississippi.) In 1936 she recreated Magnolia Hawks in the acclaimed film version of Showboat, which also featured legends Helen Morgan and Paul Robeson.

Dunne was equally at home in singing roles—Roberta with Astaire and Rogers in 1935 (gowns by Bernard Newman) and Love Affair in 1939; light comedies—The Awful Truth in 1937 and My Favorite Wife from 1940 (with costumes by Howard Greer); and dramatic "weepers"—Penny Serenade in 1941 and The White Cliffs of Dover in 1944. She also excelled at historical films, such as 1931's Cimarron, 1946's Anna and the King of Siam (costumes by Bonnie Cashin), 1947's Life with Father, and 1948's I Remember Mama—perhaps her most beloved role.

In 1957 Dunne was appointed special delegate to the United Nations and she spent the remainder of her life working for civic causes.

Dunne Style
Dunne was elected to the International Best Dressed List Hall of Fame in 1958. The actress attributed her chic style to keeping up with her dentist husband—who was so well groomed he "always looked like a soap ad."

Signature Look
- Elegant, classic gowns
- Tweed ensembles with perky hats
- Simple, upswept hair

MOST FASHIONABLE FILMS
ROBERTA (1935)
MY FAVORITE WIFE (1940)
PENNY SERENADE (1941)
ANNA AND THE KING OF SIAM (1946)

ABOVE
Dunne is swathed in clouds of white fur in a still from 1940's My Favorite Wife, a love triangle comedy with Cary Grant and Randolph Scott.

LEFT
In 1941's Penny Serenade Dunne, seen here in a softly draped jacket over a matching blouse accessorized with a bold brooch, costarred with Cary Grant as a couple who long for a child.

83

HOLLYWOOD FASHION | THE NINETEEN FORTIES

JUDY GARLAND

Hollywood's darling Dorothy—and America's favorite heartbreak kid—would reach the heights only to find it was "lonely and cold on the top."

Judy Garland (1922–1969) typically played either dreamers or wide-eyed idealists. Born Frances Gumm in Grand Rapids, Minnesota, Garland began singing before the age of three. Initially part of a sister act, she eventually toured solo with her mother. In 1935, she was signed by Louis B. Mayer of MGM and rechristened Judy Garland. Mayer had no idea what to do with the little girl with the big voice. But then she sang "You Made Me Love You" at Clark Gable's birthday party. It was such a hit that Mayer included the song in *Broadway Melody of 1938* and prepared several musical projects for her. To control her fluctuating weight, the studio supplied her with diet pills, marking the start of Garland's lifelong battle with narcotics.

Garland was the surprise hit of the 1939 musical fantasy, *The Wizard of Oz*, especially her rendition of "Over the Rainbow." The studio had wanted Shirley Temple for the role, but modern audiences find it hard to imagine anyone but Garland playing Dorothy.

Garland had several musical mentors who honed her skills. Arranger Roger Edens toned down the theatrical gestures she'd learned from her vaudeville-trained mother, guided her to age-appropriate songs, and showed her how to dress with elegance. For *Meet Me in St. Louis*, composer Hugh Martin encouraged Garland not to belt out every song, but to embrace a more intimate style. Vocal arranger Kay Thompson taught her to "sell" a song by incorporating physicality or humor—as she did in both *The Harvey Girls* and *The Pirate* (1948).

Garland's personal life had always been chaotic. Besides her many affairs, she married five times and had three children—Liza with director Vincente Minnelli, and Lorna and Joey with manager Sid Luft. In 1947 she suffered a nervous breakdown, but was soon back at MGM filming *Easter Parade*, *In the Good Old Summertime*, and *Summer Stock*. When her problems with drugs and alcohol slowed production, she had to be released from three films. In 1950, after her third suspension, MGM fired her; she was only 28.

Garland took to the concert stage for a 19-week engagement at New York's Palace Theater—a smash hit that won her a special Tony. Live performance seemed to furnish her with something vital that her film work could not. In 1954 she signed with Warner Bros. to do a remake of *A Star Is Born*. For her bravura performance she won a Golden Globe and an Oscar nomination. She was again nominated for 1961's powerful *Judgment at Nuremburg*.

Concerts, recording, and TV work were her chief outlets during the 1960s. She was living in London in 1969 when she accidentally overdosed on barbiturates. *Oz* costar Ray Bolger said at Garland's funeral, "She just plain wore out." After her death she became an enduring cult figure.

MOST FASHIONABLE FILMS

MEET ME IN ST. LOUIS (1944)
THE HARVEY GIRLS (1946)
EASTER PARADE (1948)
IN THE GOOD OLD SUMMERTIME (1949)
A STAR IS BORN (1954)

ABOVE
Garland showed off her legs in a slit tuxedo dress during the "You Gotta Have Me Go with You" number from 1954's *A Star Is Born*.

ABOVE RIGHT
In 1939's *The Wizard of Oz*, Garland hits the Yellow Brick Road with the Scarecrow (Ray Bolger), the Tin Man (Jack Haley), and the Cowardly Lion (Bert Lahr) in what is arguably the best children's fantasy film ever made.

FULL PAGE
Garland, in a turn-of-the-century tiered, frilled party frock, dances a cakewalk with her little sister Margaret O'Brien in 1944's sentimental classic, *Meet Me in St. Louis*.

Garland Style

Garland's costume designers were skilled at disguising her figure flaws—a short neck and high waist. As a result, she became a fashion icon in every incarnation of her career—as a musical prodigy, a dramatic actress, a TV variety-show host, and a concert diva.

Signature look
- Tea dresses with nipped-in waists and wide skirts
- Evening gowns with beaded tops and narrow skirts
- Capri pants worn with boat-neck tops

HOLLYWOOD FASHION | THE NINETEEN FORTIES

MEN OF THE 1940s
HEROES AND HEARTTHROBS

> **Style is knowing who you are, what you want to say, and not giving a damn.**
> — ORSON WELLES

World War II was the defining event of the 1940s, and Hollywood got on board in such a big way, they continued to make war movies even after the conflict was over.

John Wayne fought in the Pacific front in *The Fighting Seabees*, *Back to Bataan*, *They Were Expendable*, and *The Sands of Iwo Jima*, while director William Wyler dealt with soldiers returning home in *The Best Years of Our Lives*. As a result of the war—and war movies—military tailoring crept into everyday clothing...where it remains today in the form of epaulets, frogging, and piping. The army greatcoat, the leather flight (or bomber) jacket, and the naval pea coat also became a mainstay of men's fashion.

Movies with a Conscience

Not every film concentrated on combat or politics, however. Hollywood still had its share of idealists and reformers to address society's ills. Anti-Semitism was addressed in *Gentleman's Agreement* with Gregory Peck, and alcoholism was explored in *The Lost Weekend* with Ray Milland. Orson Welles's masterpiece *Citizen Kane* skewered the materialism of the American dream, and Carol Reed's *The Third Man*—starring Welles and Joseph Cotton—exposed the black market after the war. Such serious subjects required subdued wardrobes, and studio designers like Kay Nelson (*Agreement*), Edith Head (*Weekend*), and Edward Stevenson (*Kane*) complied, incorporating thrifty "Victory Suits"

RIGHT
Orson Welles, in pinstripe jacket, ascot, and homburg hat, plays a publishing tycoon in his experimental melodrama from 1941, *Citizen Kane*.

TOP RIGHT
Bing Crosby, in a double-breasted suit and dark fez, appears "captivated" by Dorothy Lamour and her consort Bob Hope in 1942's *Road to Morocco*.

BOTTOM RIGHT
During the 1940s escapist adventures were the rage, and Errol Flynn, here battling Henry Daniell in *The Sea Hawk*, was always ready to don appropriate period costumes and swashbuckling boots.

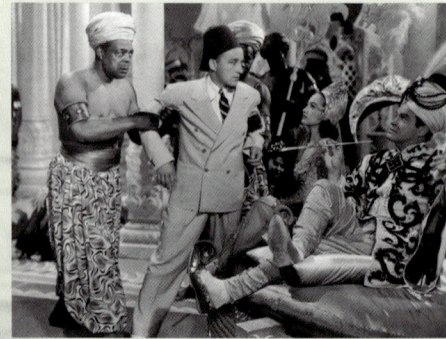

THE NINETEEN FORTIES | HOLLYWOOD FASHION

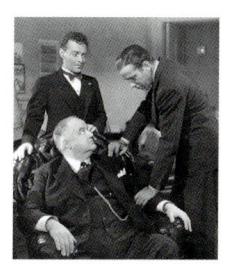

Signature Menswear Looks of the 1940s

Wartime:
- Austere suits without pocket flaps, pleats, or cuffs
- Single-breasted suits with notched lapels
- High-waisted trousers
- Short, colorful, patterned ties worn with Windsor knots
- Decorative tie pins or clips
- Suspenders
- Zoot suits, with high-waisted, baggy-legged trousers and oversized jackets
- Trenchcoats
- Wingtip spectator shoes
- Wide-brimmed fedora hats

Postwar:
- Hand-painted ties with pin-up girls or Western scenes
- Long topcoats
- Hawaiian shirts
- Sports jackets and casual shirts

of synthetic-wool blends with no cuffs, pleats, or patch pockets into their films.

Fun Films
Escapist films were never so popular—Tyrone Power scored in *Zorro*, Errol Flynn dueled his way through *The Sea Hawk* as did Gene Kelly with *The Three Musketeers*. The groundbreaking fantasy, *The Thief of Bagdad* with Sabu, was a hit and, like its 1924 predecessor, put an Arabian Nights' spin on fashion and home décor. Established heroes like Tarzan and Sherlock Holmes also reappeared during the decade, becoming costume party favorites. Bing Crosby and Bob Hope were the top stars of the decade according to many polls. Their comic "Road" movies kept audiences chuckling, and their frequent sidekick, the exotic Dorothy Lamour, became a fashion icon for her sexy sarongs.

Dark Doings
Cine noir offerings included Humphrey Bogart in search of *The Maltese Falcon* and Alan Ladd in *This Gun for Hire* and *The Glass Key*. The trenchcoat became the official emblem of the gumshoe detective, and men all over the country soon adopted this versatile officer's coat from World War I.

ABOVE
Sydney Greenstreet in a staid three-piecer, Humphrey Bogart in a more relaxed suit, and dapper Peter Lorre sporting a bow tie all vie for possession of the black bird in 1942's *The Maltese Falcon*.

TOP LEFT
Sabu and John Justin flank June Duprez in a scene from the classic 1940 Arabian Nights fantasy, *The Thief of Bagdad*. William Cameron Menzies, the film's coproducer, designed the spectacular sets of the Douglas Fairbanks original.

87

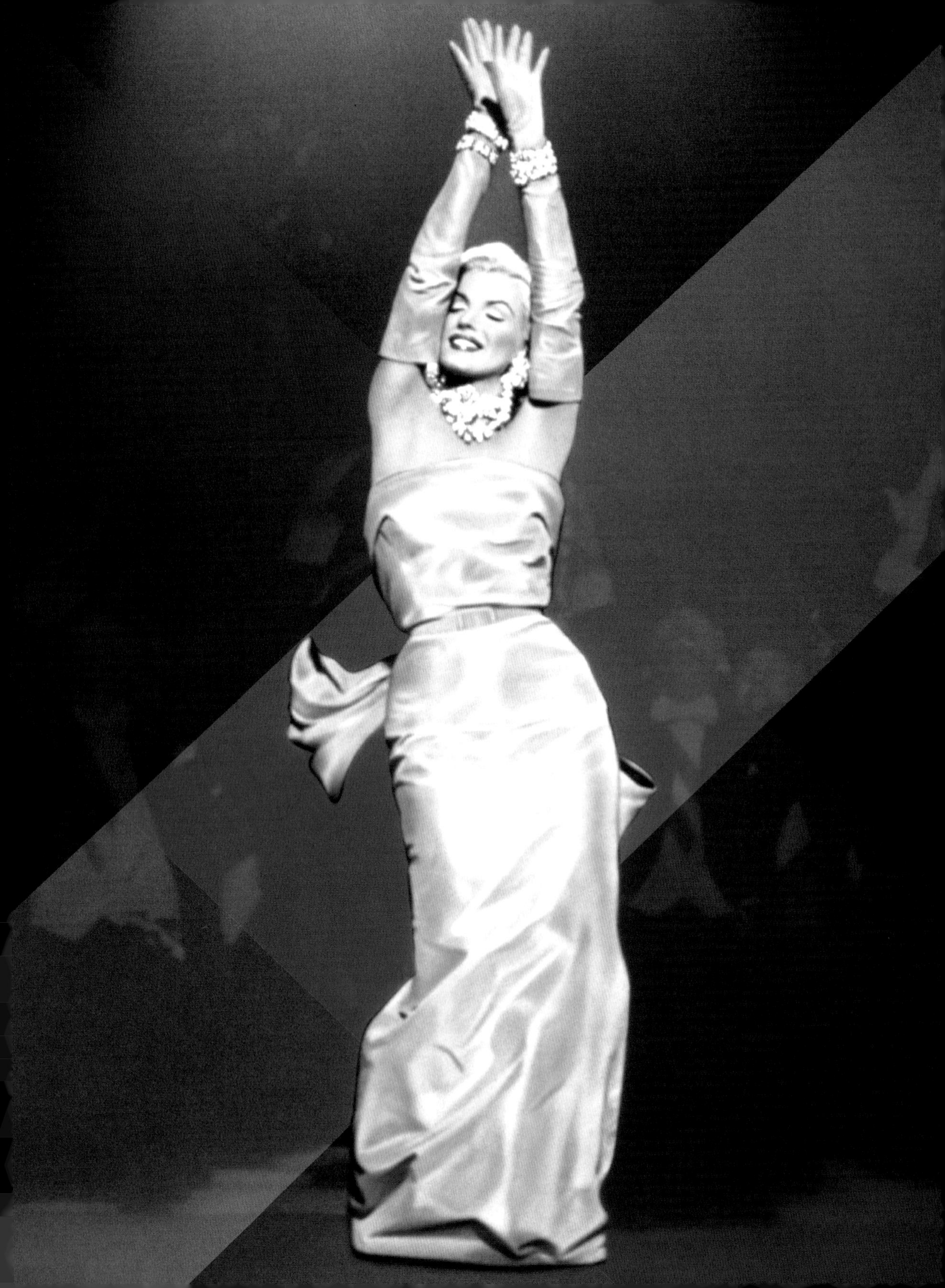

THE NINETEEN FIFTIES

During this decade of national affluence and increased leisure time, teen audiences rejected the nostalgic films produced by the Hollywood establishment and sought symbols of rebellion. They wanted hip, fast-paced, modern films with young stars who reflected their own concerns and style, films like *The Wild One* and *Rebel Without a Cause*. Drive-in theaters, where viewers sat in cars and watched movies on giant outdoor screens, were popular with both teenagers and families.

Meanwhile, old Hollywood still revered the epic—the decade gave viewers a double-dip of Charlton Heston in tunics and sandals in *The Ten Commandments* and *Ben-Hur*— yet a wealth of quality "smaller" films also appeared, character-driven dramas such as *Marty* and *The Quiet Man*; action movies like *The African Queen* and *The Defiant Ones*; edgy Westerns like *Shane*; classic musicals such as *Singin' in the Rain*, *An American in Paris*, and *A Star is Born*; adult dramas such as *A Place in the Sun*, *Sunset Boulevard*, and *From Here to Eternity*; and crowd pleasers like *Rear Window*, *North by Northwest*, and *Some Like it Hot*.

Hollywood adopted Dior's elegant New Look, with its nipped-in waists and wide skirts, proving glamour had not been abandoned during the postwar years, yet a more relaxed attitude toward fashion was evolving. Synthetic fabrics, polo shirts, jeans, loafers, shorts, and sandals, and tropical shirts and casual trousers for men were seen with increasing frequency, onscreen and off.

HOLLYWOOD FASHION | THE NINETEEN FIFTIES

MARILYN MONROE

MOST FASHIONABLE FILMS

GENTLEMEN PREFER BLONDES (1953)
THE SEVEN YEAR ITCH (1955)
SOME LIKE IT HOT (1959)

The voluptuous star was the perfect male fantasy—sensual and vulnerable but ultimately unattainable.

Monroe Style

Monroe's hip-swinging walk—"Like Jello on springs," to quote Jack Lemmon in *Some Like it Hot*—was engineered by alternately wearing a shortened heel on each foot. Her make-up artist Whitey Snyder created the iconic "Marilyn" face on the set of *Niagara* in 1953.

Signature Look

- Gowns with plunging necklines
- Lots of glittering gems
- Softly disarrayed hair

Marilyn Monroe (1926–1962) became one of the most famous women in the world, known for her provocative—some said vulgar—clothing and tousled blonde hair. She was born Norma Jean Mortenson (later Baker) in Los Angeles, California. While enduring the difficult life of a foster child—as a result of her mother's mental illness—she dreamed of finding fame. Modeling work led to a contract with 20th Century-Fox, where she drifted through bit parts in B-movies. Her agent, Johnny Hyde, finally got her noticed by scoring visible roles in two respectable 1950 films, *The Asphalt Jungle* and *All About Eve*.

1953 brought a breakout role, Lorelei Lee in *Gentleman Prefer Blondes*, and a romance with Yankee baseball great, Joe DiMaggio. Her costumes in *Blondes* were by William Travilla, who made eight more films with her, including her next hit, *How to Marry A Millionaire*, with Betty Grable and Lauren Bacall.

Monroe married DiMaggio in January 1954, made *There's No Business Like Show Business*, divorced DiMaggio in November—citing his extreme jealousy—and began filming *The Seven Year Itch*. An already shaky work ethic began to deteriorate at this point, and she was ultimately suspended twice for not reporting to the set.

After taking classes at the Actor's Studio, Monroe requested more challenging parts. She received critical acclaim for the 1956 drama *Bus Stop*, and in keeping with this "newly serious" Marilyn, married playwright Arthur Miller. 1959 brought her Billy Wilder's Jazz-Age romp, *Some Like it Hot*. The tale of two musicians hiding out in an all-girl band required Monroe to be sweetly alluring, but also wistful. "I always get the fuzzy end of the lollipop," she lamented as singer Sugar Kane (in sizzling gowns by Orry-Kelly).

1961's *The Misfits*, with Clark Gable and Montgomery Clift, was a modern Western directed by John Huston from a screenplay by Miller. The heat of the Nevada desert added to the strain on the set; Monroe grew very ill during the shoot, as did many others. Barely a week after filming ended, Monroe filed for divorce from Miller and Gable died of a heart attack.

Monroe was relying heavily on pills when she began working on *Something's Got to Give* and after she delayed filming, the studio fired her. Arrangements were being made, however, to restart production, and Monroe had been "in good spirits" ...when her body was found in her Brentwood home. Few friends were surprised that her death was due to barbiturates, but most assumed it was accidental. So the coroner ruling it a "probable suicide" created an ongoing controversy—murder theorists blamed the CIA or the Mafia, or cited her affairs with John and Bobby Kennedy as the cause.

For 20 years after her death, Joe DiMaggio saw to it that red roses were placed on her crypt. Like James Dean before her, Monroe's physical allure and early death made her into a lasting cult figure.

ABOVE

Monroe strikes a "come hither" pose in Travilla's red-beaded dance-hall costume, which she wore in 1954's Western adventure, *River of No Return*.

FULL PAGE

Monroe was briefly seen in this gold lamé gown in *Gentleman Prefer Blondes* by designer William Travilla. Monroe was sewn back into the gold dress to accept an award at the 1953 Photoplay awards.

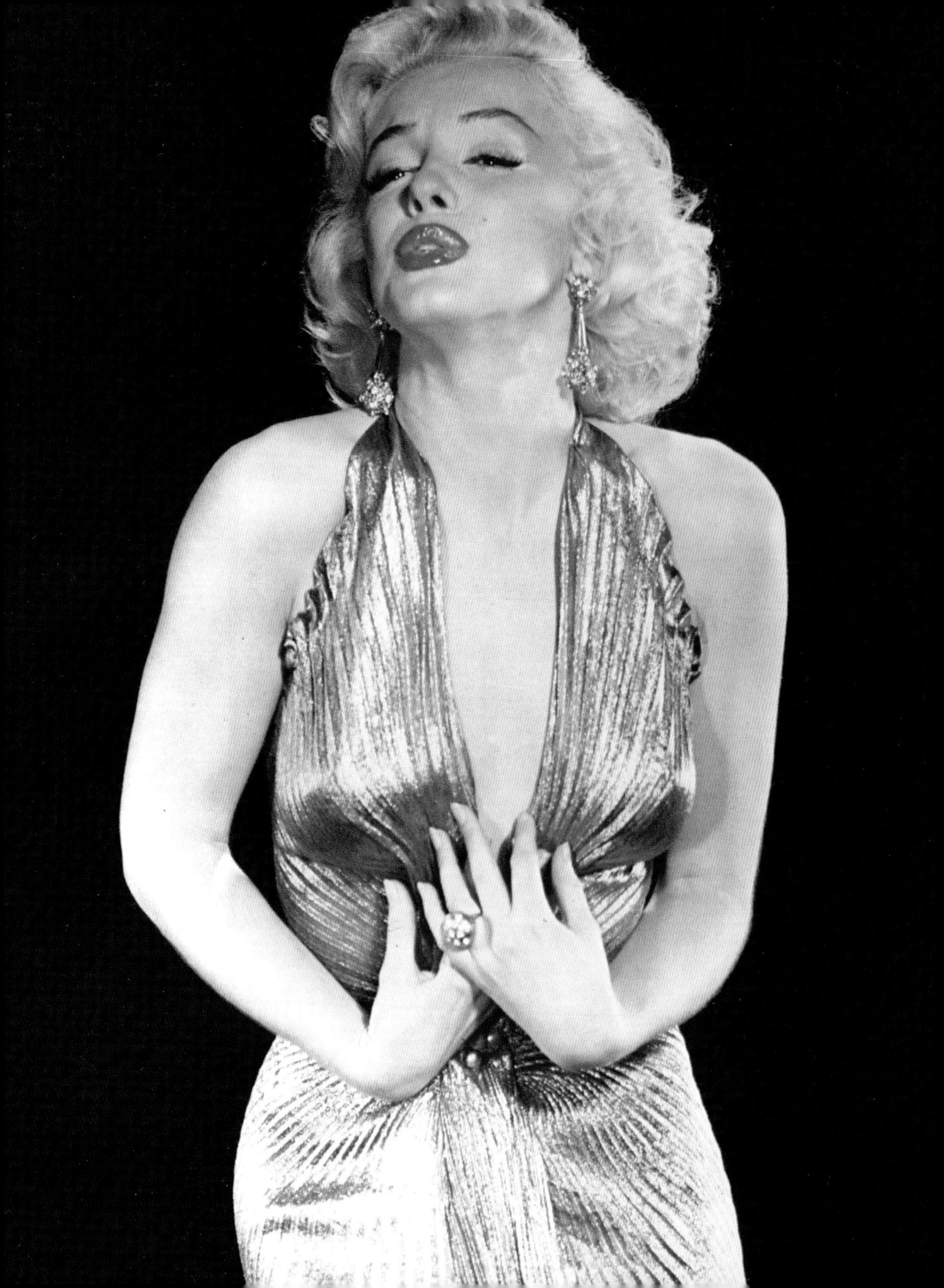

HOLLYWOOD FASHION | THE NINETEEN FIFTIES

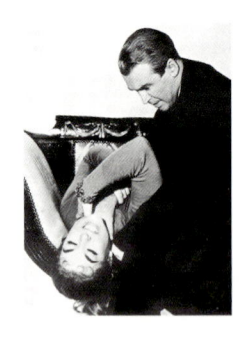

KIM NOVAK

Cat-eyed Kim Novak became one of Hitchcock's iciest blondes but she also had a knack for kooky comedy.

Kim Novak (1933–) was known for playing aloof women whose sex appeal sometimes had to shine through a workaday wardrobe. Chicago-born Marilyn Pauline Novak modeled as a teen and eventually moved to Los Angeles to find work. After appearing in 1954's *The French Line*, Novak was signed by Columbia, who changed her name to Kim and cast her in *Pushover* and *Phffft!* Two breakout films awaited—*Picnic*, which won two Academy Awards, and Otto Preminger's drug exposé, *The Man with the Golden Arm*, with Frank Sinatra.

Audiences were now clamoring for Novak and she offered them her most memorable character, James Stewart's obsession in Alfred Hitchcock's *Vertigo* (with costumes by Edith Head). Novak followed with *Bell, Book and Candle* and *Of Human Bondage*. At this point she knew her career was slipping; she was not getting the hip, edgy roles, perhaps because her look was too "old school." She tried to reestablish herself in *The Legend of Lylah Clare*—which film critics panned so badly that the actress felt she literally had no career left.

Novak did some TV work, and then focused on her home life. She currently resides in Oregon with her veterinarian husband, where she paints, raises llamas, rides horses and skis. She began an autobiography in 2000, but it was destroyed when her house—and computer—caught on fire.

Novak Style
The actress excelled at otherworldly, enigmatic characters, yet her sexual aura and provocative outfits made her equally earthy.

Signature Look
- Pencil skirts
- V-neck sweaters
- Swing coats with wide lapels and long gloves

MOST FASHIONABLE FILMS
PHFFFT! (1954)
BELL, BOOK AND CANDLE (1958)
VERTIGO (1958)
BOYS' NIGHT OUT (1962)

ABOVE
The actress portrays a woman of mystery who drives James Stewart to distraction in Hitchcock's 1958 classic psychological thriller, *Vertigo*.

RIGHT
Novak models Jean-Louis's dramatically embellished black-and-white satin cocktail dress with bronze roses, which she wore in 1954's comic love triangle, *Phffft!* The film also starred Jack Lemmon and Judy Holliday.

92 1950s

THE NINETEEN FIFTIES | HOLLYWOOD FASHION

SOPHIA LOREN

Called "Stuzzicadenti" —or the Toothpick— by her schoolmates, the grown-up Loren's voluptuous curves set the standard for 1950s' screen sirens.

Sophia Loren (1934–) was known for both her youthful earthy roles and mature performances as a savvy woman of style. She was born Sofia Villani Scicolone in Rome and was raised near Naples. After World War II, her grandmother opened a pub for American soldiers and Loren honed her English waiting on the GIs. As a finalist in the Queen of the Sea beauty pageant at age 14 this led to acting classes and work as an extra in *Quo Vadis* (1951). Her first starring role was *Aida* in 1953, followed by a breakthrough role in director Vittorio De Sica's *The Gold of Naples*.

By 1957, she was appearing in Hollywood films like *Boy on a Dolphin* with Alan Ladd and *The Pride and the Passion* with Frank Sinatra and Cary Grant. Paramount Pictures made her an international star in hit vehicles like *Houseboat*, again with Grant (and costumes by Edith Head). In 1961 she worked with De Sica on the gritty Italian war melodrama, *Two Women*, which earned Loren the Best Actress Oscar.

Loren married the much older Carlo Ponti, a film producer, in 1957. When the Italian government refused to recognize his divorce from his wife, he and Loren had the marriage annulled in 1962. They were legitimately remarried in 1966 in France and had two sons together, Carlo Jr. and Edoardo. After the birth of her children, Loren preferred to make films in Italy, often collaborating with De Sica as well as actor Marcello Mastroianni.

MOST FASHIONABLE FILMS

HOUSEBOAT (1958)
YESTERDAY, TODAY & TOMORROW (1963)
LADY L (1965)
ARABESQUE (1966)

Loren Style
The actress still possesses an exotic beauty and continues to turn heads. Her fashion sense evolved from the blatantly obvious to the tastefully sensual, and she has been associated with the House of Dior, Valentino, and Giorgio Armani.

Signature Look
- Low-cut evening gowns with lots of jewels
- Cinch-waisted dresses with wide skirts
- Chic "lampshade"-style hats

> **A woman's dress should be like a barbed-wire fence: serving its purpose without obstructing the view.**
> SOPHIA LOREN

ABOVE

The Alan Ladd adventure film, 1957's *Boy on a Dolphin*, helped introduce the smoldering Italian actress to American audiences. Here, she relaxes in a teal rayon dress with a starburst pattern accessorized with a tomato-red belt.

LEFT

Loren is beyond enticing in the 1966 spy caper, *Arabesque*, as she lounges in her boudoir wearing a whisper-pink, ruffled chiffon peignoir and pink satin mules.

> **If you have a magnificent jewel, you put it in a simple setting—you don't distract from it with a lot of detail.**
> ROSE ON DESIGNING FOR ELIZABETH TAYLOR

MOST FASHIONABLE DESIGNS
LOVE ME OR LEAVE ME (1955)
HIGH SOCIETY (1956)
SILK STOCKINGS (1957)
DESIGNING WOMEN (1957)
CAT ON A HOT TIN ROOF (1958)

Rose Style
- Beaded bodices and chiffon skirts
- Sophisticated luncheon suits
- Emphasis on the silhouette

Legacy
Womanly gowns, dresses, and suits with classic lines that are still being copied today.

THE NINETEEN FIFTIES | HOLLYWOOD FASHION

STYLE MAKER
HELEN ROSE

Helen Rose began her show business career designing costumes for nightclub acts in Chicago. By 1929 she was in Los Angeles, working for the Ice Follies and also creating dance costumes for the brother and sister producing team of Fanchon and Marco. In the early 1940s Rose began working for 20th Century-Fox; she then moved to MGM in 1944—as one of the designers who replaced the illustrious Adrian—where she remained until she retired in 1976.

Rose was known for flattering silhouettes that made the most of a woman's attributes, and she dressed most of the film industry's top actresses, including Judy Garland (*The Harvey Girls*, with Irene), Esther Williams (*Jupiter's Darling*, *The Million Dollar Mermaid*), Lena Horne (*Stormy Weather*), Grace Kelly (*High Society*, *The Swan*), Elizabeth Taylor (*Father of the Bride*, *Butterfield 8*), Lucille Ball (*The Long, Long Trailer*), Deborah Kerr (*Tea and Sympathy*), Lauren Bacall (*Designing Woman*), and Shirley MacClaine (*Ask Any Girl*). She also made a foray into science fiction with Anne Francis' space wardrobe in *Forbidden Planet*. Rose's nightclub experience came in handy when she created dance wardrobes for entertainers like Cyd Charisse in *Silk Stockings* and Doris Day in *Love Me or Leave Me*.

Rose, like Adrian and Irene, modified many of her film designs for the ready-to-wear market—including a cape from the Biblical epic *Quo Vadis*! Her retail version of Elizabeth Taylor's chiffon cocktail dress from *Cat on a Hot Tin Roof* sold in the thousands after the provocative film was released. In fact, Rose's clothing was so wearable—compared to the "stagey" costumes of some other designers—that Taylor often asked her to copy film outfits for her own use. By the 1970s, The House of Helen Rose was selling both custom designs and ready-to-wear lines across the country.

Rose was also famous for her celebrity wedding gowns, most notably the one Grace Kelly wore to marry Prince Rainier of Monaco in 1956. It's not every day a designer gets to clothe a real princess—and the gown was widely copied. It also clearly inspired the Sarah Burton gown worn by Kate Middleton at her 2011 wedding to Prince William.

After retiring, Rose released her autobiography, *Just Make Them Beautiful*.

ABOVE
Rose and Grace Kelly were busy with *High Society* when Kelly asked her to design the gown for Kelly's wedding with Prince Rainier. Rose used one of the ball gowns from *High Society* as a starting point.

LEFT
Doris Day proved her mettle playing real-life jazz-age singer Ruth Etting in 1958's *Love Me or Leave Me*. Here, she struts her stuff in a glittering turquoise stage costume trimmed with ostrich feathers.

FULL PAGE
In 1958's *Cat on a Hot Tin Roof*, Elizabeth Taylor tries to entice husband Paul Newman by donning a series of seductive gowns, including this stunning low-cut white dress with a draped, crossover bodice.

HOLLYWOOD FASHION | THE NINETEEN FIFTIES

GRACE KELLY

Unlike the brassy bombshells of the decade, this star possessed a cool, classy aura that almost disguised her sexual smolder.

Grace Kelly (1929–1982) was known for playing wealthy, self-assured women who wore the latest styles with the relaxed ease of a fashion model. Her family was well-known in Philadelphia society—her wealthy father, among other things, had been a gold-medalist Olympic sculler. As a teen, Kelly did some modeling at social events, and when she was refused entry to Bennington College, she decided to try her luck in the theater. After graduating from the American Academy of Dramatic Arts, she was cast by Gary Cooper as his young bride in *High Noon*.

With the success of the western, Kelly was signed by MGM to a seven-year contract and appeared in *Mogambo* with Clark Gable, and then was chosen by suspense master Alfred Hitchcock to appear in *Dial M for Murder* and *Rear Window* (costumes by Edith Head). When Kelly starred opposite Bing Crosby playing a drab wife in *The Country Girl*, the role won her a Best Actress Oscar and proved that her performances did not depend on a luxe wardrobe.

Kelly became a favorite of Hitchcock, next appearing with Cary Grant in *To Catch a Thief* (costumes again by Edith Head). It was while making this film in Monte Carlo that she met the head of the royal family of Monaco, Prince Rainier III. The two began dating and after Kelly finished her final two films, *The Swan* and *High Society* (costumes by Helen Rose), she and the prince were wed. Her wedding gown, designed by Rose, was widely copied, even serving as inspiration for another royal wedding—Kate Middleton's marriage to Prince William in 2011.

She and the prince had three children, Princess Caroline, Prince Albert and Princess Stéphanie.

ABOVE
Kelly, wearing an aqua frontier-style wedding dress with inset lace neckline and beribboned bonnet by Ann Peck, made the most of her limited screen time in 1952's *High Noon*.

TOP RIGHT
Kelly, whose blonde coloring was the perfect foil for a simple black satin dress and pearl choker, won an Oscar for her portrayal of Bing Crosby's struggling wife in 1954's *The Country Girl*.

FULL PAGE
As a wealthy socialite enjoying the pleasures of the Riviera in *To Catch a Thief*, Kelly wore dazzling gowns created by design legend Edith Head, including this ice blue evening dress with spaghetti straps and a sheer chiffon drape.

Kelly Style
In addition to the chic ensembles captured on film, Kelly left another legacy for fashionistas—the Hermes handbag she often carried in films. Versions of the original bag, christened the "Crocodile Kelly," can sell in the tens of thousands of dollars.

Signature Look
- Ballerina skirts
- Chic little hats
- Lots of tasteful jewelry

Princess Grace died as the result of an automobile accident; she apparently suffered a stroke while driving from their French country home with Stéphanie. The whole world mourned the passing of a member of both Hollywood and Monegasque royalty.

> I don't want to dress up a picture with just my face.
> — GRACE KELLY

MOST FASHIONABLE FILMS

THE COUNTRY GIRL (1954)
REAR WINDOW (1954)
TO CATCH A THIEF (1955)
HIGH SOCIETY (1956)
THE SWAN (1956)

HOLLYWOOD FASHION | THE NINETEEN FIFTIES

FASHION INFLUENCE FROM SPORTS TO SCREEN

With Hollywood's ongoing quest for physical perfection, it was no surprise to anyone when studios began recruiting toned, attractive athletes for film roles.

The Tarzans

Perhaps the most famous example of a film character typically played by an athlete is Edgar Rice Burroughs' *Tarzan*. The most enduring Tarzan, five-time Olympic gold-medal swimmer Johnny Weissmuller, appeared in 12 films as his jungle alter ego. Other athlete Tarzans include Olympic gold-medal swimmer Buster Crabbe and silver-medal shot-putter Herman Brix—later known as Bruce Bennett. Two Olympic gold medalists, decathlete Glenn Morris and swimmer Eleanor Holm made *Tarzan's Revenge* together. UCLA hoops star Denny Miller, and pro football player Ron Ely also donned the loincloth.

The *Tarzan* movies bolstered the fashion trend for safari suits and bush hats, and the films Weissmuller made with Maureen O'Sullivan, which featured them swimming in revealing costumes, banished the prudish bathing suits of the 1920s. Beachwear continued to mimic the loincloths and skimpy tunics worn by Tarzan and his mate well into the 20th century.

Sonja Henie

Even if Norwegian Sonja Henie had never gone to Hollywood, she would have had a remarkable career. She was ten-time World Figure Skating Champion, won three gold medals in three Olympics, and revolutionized women's skating costumes with her short (for that era) skirts. After her final Olympics in 1936, she appeared in an ice show in Los Angeles and was promptly recruited by 20th Century-Fox. In her first picture, *One in a Million* (1937), she played a skater, setting a pattern for subsequent films. The petite blonde with the charming dimples enchanted audiences and, although she was no great actress, comedies like *Thin Ice* (costumes by Royer) and *Sun Valley Serenade* (costumes by Travis Banton) made big money.

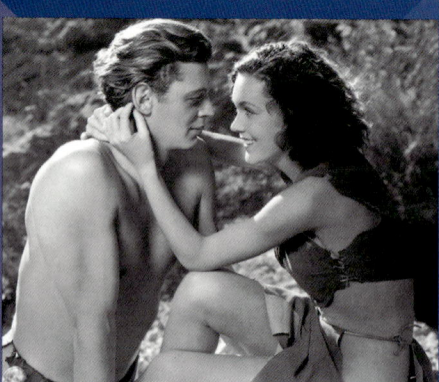

Esther Williams

During the 1940s another swimmer became a Hollywood icon and fashion influence. When Esther Williams was unable to compete in the 1940 Olympics due to the war in Europe, she found work in *Billy Rose's Aquacade* in San Francisco. After appearing in a few MGM shorts, the auburn-haired beauty was given the star treatment—she was to be the studio's answer to Sonja Henie. Her "aquamusicals," where dozens of starlets

ABOVE
Henie was the first female skater to shorten her skirts for competition. By the time she was making movies, her hems had moved from above the knee to mid-thigh—or higher.

TOP RIGHT
Sun Valley Serenade from 1941 was one of a series of light romantic comedies Sonja Henie made that centered around her ice skating abilities. Here, with John Payne, she sports a ski suit with flap pockets accessorized with a Norwegian cap and patterned mittens.

BOTTOM RIGHT
In 1934's *Tarzan and His Mate*, the skimpy costumes Johnny Weissmuller and Maureen O'Sullivan wore scandalized the censors, but heavily influenced bathing suit design right up to the present day, where the "jungle" bikini is still a favorite.

98 1950s

THE NINETEEN FIFTIES | HOLLYWOOD FASHION

> I was the only swimmer in movies. Tarzan was long gone, and he couldn't have done them anyway; he could never have gotten into my bathing suit.
>
> ESTHER WILLIAMS

followed Williams in synchronized-swimming routines, were enormously popular and influenced bathing suit design across America. Her own studio designers were at sea, however, when it came to swimming costumes. One plaid flannel suit got so waterlogged it dragged her to the bottom of the pool! Williams, then spokeswoman for Cole of California sportswear, soon had all her swimmers in Cole's sleek latex suits.

Williams starred in *Bathing Beauty*, *Neptune's Daughter* (costumes by Irene), *Dangerous When Wet*, and *Jupiter's Darling* and also played Australian swimmer Annette Kellerman in *Million Dollar Mermaid*—the title Williams chose for her autobiography. After retiring from films, Williams lent her name to a line of retro-style women's swimwear based on the sexy, one-piece sheath she wore in her films.

TOP LEFT

In 1953's *Dangerous When Wet*, Esther Williams costarred with future husband Fernando Lamas and swam with cartoon characters Tom and Jerry. Here, in a casual mood, she wears a turtleneck jersey top with cap sleeves, while Lamas wears a striped French tee shirt.

LEFT

In 1944's *Bathing Beauties*, Esther Williams shows off a gold version of her signature one-piece sheath suit. After leaving films, she lent her name to a similar line of swimsuits, many of which are still available today.

99

HOLLYWOOD FASHION | THE NINETEEN FIFTIES

ELIZABETH TAYLOR

The "star of stars" enjoyed a long, illustrious career, survived eight marriages, and continued her charitable AIDS work even as she battled pain and illness.

Elizabeth Taylor (1932–2011), known for her fiery performances and lavish lifestyle, was one of the most beautiful women to grace Hollywood or any film capital. No costume, however opulent, stood a chance against her violet eyes and raven hair.

Taylor was born in a London suburb, the child of American parents living abroad. After her family moved to California, their beautiful, young daughter was contracted by MGM and gained fame in *Lassie, Come Home* and *National Velvet*. At 18, Taylor made *Father of the Bride* with Spencer Tracy, but her ingénue roles soon gave way to parts brimming with sexual tension—dissatisfied wives and call girls. She established herself as a force of nature in *A Place in the Sun* (with Academy-Award winning designs by Edith Head), then filmed a number of period films, *Ivanhoe*, the massive 1956 hit *Giant* with Rock Hudson and James Dean, and *Raintree County* with Montgomery Clift. She followed with a series of modern morality tales—*Cat on a Hot Tin Roof*, *Suddenly Last Summer*, and *Butterfield 8*—for which she received the Oscar.

Taylor found out early that movie stars have little privacy, so her many marriages—and divorces—were eagerly followed by the gossip magazines. She wed hotel heir Nicky Hilton, actor Michael Wilding, and her "true love" producer Mike Todd. When Todd was killed in a plane crash, singer and family friend Eddie Fisher consoled the distraught Taylor, who then married him.

While filming the 1963 epic *Cleopatra* in Rome, Taylor fell in love with Welsh actor Richard Burton. Soon the two married costars were shocking fans—and the Pope!—with their affair. She divorced Eddie Fisher, whom she had "stolen" from Debbie Reynolds, to marry Burton. They costarred in nine more films, including the brutal *Who's Afraid of Virginia Woolf?*, which earned Taylor her second Oscar. The two were divorced, remarried, and divorced again, while keeping the tabloids buzzing. Taylor then wed U.S. Senator John Warner and construction worker Larry Fortensky, whom she met at the Betty Ford Clinic. Taylor had many gay friends, including Rock Hudson, and made it her personal mission until her death to raise money for AIDS research. She struggled most of her adult life with chronic back pain—caused by a fall from her horse while making *National Velvet*—and also suffered a near-fatal bout of pneumonia, survived brain surgery, and fought addictions to alcohol and prescription drugs. Yet she endured—some would say prevailed—and became one of the last glamour icons of Hollywood's Golden Age.

> **I adore wearing gems, but not because they are mine. You can't possess radiance, you can only admire it.**
> ELIZABETH TAYLOR

ABOVE
In 1954's *Elephant Walk*, Taylor, as the center of a love triangle, was costumed to accentuate her curves; even this soft pink negligee has a fitted bodice and corded waist.

TOP RIGHT
Taylor's costumes, while not necessarily historically accurate, made her the Queen of Style in the 1963 epic, *Cleopatra*. In this scene she wears an iridescent green gown, ornamented braids, and a serpent armband along with her lapis blue eye shadow.

FULL PAGE
This 1955 publicity shot of Taylor posing in a red, beaded off-the-shoulder dress and white fox stole inspired the design team for the Lifetime biography *Liz and Dick* starring Lindsay Lohan.

100 1950s

Taylor Style
Taylor was blessed with a genetic rarity—double eyelashes. For all her beauty, however, La Liz was not without flaws: a slight double chin and short legs. She liked trendy styles, such as mini-dresses and ponchos, which were not always flattering. As she aged, designers kept her legs obscured and focused on what Burton called her "magnificent bosom."

Signature Look
- Low-cut evening gowns worn with furs
- A wealth of jewels
- Heavy applications of eyeliner, and eye shadow

MOST FASHIONABLE FILMS

A PLACE IN THE SUN (1951)
ELEPHANT WALK (1954)
GIANT (1956)
CLEOPATRA (1963)
THE SANDPIPER (1965)

Plunkett's Style
- Inventive and ingenious design solutions
- Intricate draping and bodice construction
- Strict adherence to authentic historical silhouettes

Legacy
The Gone with the Wind collection of gowns at the David O. Selznick Archive features real examples and copies of the gowns from the film. Plunkett himself refurbished the originals shortly before his death, but they were never intended to last for decades and so remain fragile.

Academy Awards
Nine nominations. He shared an Academy Award with Orry-Kelly and Irene (who had been an extra with him in *The Merry Widow*) for *An American in Paris*.

MOST FASHIONABLE DESIGNS

THE GAY DIVORCEE (1934)
MARY OF SCOTLAND (1936)
NOTHING SACRED (1937)
GONE WITH THE WIND (1939)
MADAM BOVARY (1949)
SINGIN' IN THE RAIN (1952)

Plunkett has come to life and turned in magnificent Scarlett costumes so we won't need anyone else.
DAVID O. SELZNICK, PRODUCER

THE NINETEEN FIFTIES | HOLLYWOOD FASHION

STYLE MAKER
WALTER PLUNKETT

Even while he was studying law at the University of California, Oakland-born Walter Plunket was more interested in what was going on in the school theater department than in the lecture hall. In 1923 he finally listened to his muse and went to New York to work as an actor, set designer, and costume designer. A move to Hollywood came next, where he could only find work as an extra. When it became clear that acting was not his ticket to fame, he focused on wardrobe and costume design.

Plunkett was hired by RKO in the late 1920s—his first credited film was 1927's *Hard-Boiled Haggerty*—and was asked to develop their costume department. Plunkett not only created a large, well-run wardrobe department that became an asset to RKO, his own designs began to rival those of the best designers at the top studios.

But in 1935, Plunkett abruptly quit and moved to New York. He claimed he had no artistic freedom in films, where his designs were at the mercy of the directors, producers, and actors. He was happily designing afternoon wear for women when he got word that Katharine Hepburn wanted him—and only him—to do the costumes for *Mary of Scotland*. Plunkett took a leave of absence and went west to work on her film.

So Plunkett quit his New York job and entered the Hollywood fray once again. This time, he decided, he would limit himself to historical costumes, where outsiders were less likely to be critical. Plunkett became an authority on period clothing and was soon known for the authenticity of his costumes, like those he designed for both the 1935 and 1948 versions of *The Three Musketeers*.

His most notable achievement was designing the costumes for the Civil War epic, *Gone with the Wind*. Several years before filming was completed, Plunkett traveled the South seeking archival source material—clothing, fabrics, and fashion plates—and met with author Margaret Mitchell. Producer David O. Selznick was not happy with Plunkett's initial sketches for Scarlett's gowns, but the designer soon got up to speed and pleased the finicky studio head. Nearly every outfit worn by Vivien Leigh became iconic—from her green sprigged barbecue dress to her red-velvet dressing gown. But perhaps Plunkett's most famous creation of all was the green-velvet riding ensemble Mammy makes for the impoverished Scarlett from "Miss Ellen's portieres."

Other actresses who enjoyed Plunkett's favor were Ginger Rogers (*Flying Down to Rio* and *The Gay Divorcee*), Carole Lombard (*Nothing Sacred*), Merle Oberon (*Lydia*), Jennifer Jones (*Madame Bovary*), Betty Hutton (*Annie Get Your Gun*), Kathryn Grayson (*Showboat* and *Kiss Me Kate*), Judy Garland (*Summer Stock*), Elizabeth Taylor (*Raintree County*), and Judy Holliday (*Bells Are Ringing*).

The designer also created the costumes for the highly regarded musical *Singin' in the Rain*, fondly parodying his own past with the flapper fashions and lavish film costumes of the late 1920s.

Walter Plunkett retired in 1966, his love-hate relationship with movies finally at an end. Before his death in Santa Monica, he adopted his life-partner Lee so that he could legally inherit Plunkett's estate.

ABOVE

Plunkett used his familiarity with Civil War fashions to design this pink satin hoopskirt gown with waterfall lace sleeves for Elizabeth Taylor in 1957's *Raintree County*.

FULL PAGE

For *Gone with the Wind*, Plunkett created more than 5,000 costumes for over 50 major characters. One notable example was this lush, red-velvet dressing gown with its lace Queen Elizabeth collar, worn by Vivien Leigh during a key confrontation scene with a simmering Clark Gable.

HOLLYWOOD FASHION | THE NINETEEN FIFTIES

FASHION INFLUENCE
TEENAGE TRENDS

> My fans want my shirt. They can have my shirt. They put it on my back.
> ELVIS PRESLEY

During the early 1950s, teens felt marginalized by a society that offered them endless rules, but little in the way of entertainment. Music seemed to be the only thing that felt relevant, especially the rhythmic, beat-driven genre that came to be called rock and roll. But that type of music was controversial and often banned. There wasn't much else for a teenager to do but rebel.

Of course Hollywood was paying attention, and the movie industry responded with a spate of youth-oriented films. Marlon Brando's *The Wild One* from 1953 introduced several teenage style icons: motorcycle jackets, blue jeans, long sideburns, and "greaser" hair. James Dean made only three films, but two of them, *East of Eden* and *Rebel Without a Cause*, also featured teens wearing jeans and T-shirts. (Dean's appearance in a white T-shirt in *Eden* sent undershirt sales skyrocketing.) *Blackboard Jungle* examined school gangs and introduced Bill Haley and the Comets' "Rock Around the Clock"—a song so energizing, it caused teenagers to riot in theaters. Elvis Presley made *Jailhouse Rock*, where his performance of the title song in a stylized cell block is considered by many to be the precursor of music videos. Rock and roll—and its pared-down uniform of denim jeans and T-shirts or "skinny" sharkskin suits—was truly here to stay.

Grease, even though it was filmed in 1978, was a love song to the films of the 1950s, with its pompadours, muscle T-shirts and leather jackets, teased hair, skin-tight capris, and circle skirts. The film even featured a 1950s'-style sleepover, where girls wore baby doll pajamas and dorm shirts while doing each other's hair and listening to the latest tunes.

Surf's Up!
The surfing craze of the late 1950s and early 1960s popularized madras swim trunks, bikinis, huarache sandals, and Hawaiian shirts and led to films like *Gidget*, and later *Ride the Wild Surf*, and a host of "Beach Blanket" films starring 1950s pop singers Annette Funicello and Frankie Avalon.

Teen Trends to Adult Mainstays
Many of the fashions sported by teenagers in the 1950s and early 1960s—and showcased in films of that era—have become enduring staples in adult wardrobes today. These must-have items include denim blue jeans, biker boots, sneakers, muscle T-shirts, black leather jackets, capri and toreador pants, surfer trunks, madras shorts, bikinis, and baby dolls.

ABOVE
The 1959 comedy, *Gidget*, with Sandra Dee—clad in a demure one-piece bathing suit—ushered in the era of surfing and surf music...and sent a beachy, casual-dress wave across America.

TOP RIGHT
Elvis Presley makes prison stripes swing as a singing inmate in *Jailhouse Rock*, his hit film from 1957.

104 1950s

FULL PAGE

James Dean, here wearing the hip "uniform" of a black leather jacket and white T-shirt, became the poster boy for disaffected youth in 1955's *Rebel Without a Cause*.

HOLLYWOOD FASHION | THE NINETEEN FIFTIES

DEBORAH KERR

> *I don't think anyone knew I could act until I put on a bathing suit.*
>
> DEBORAH KERR ON HER ROLE IN *FROM HERE TO ETERNITY*

Forever immortalized by her surf-and-sand love scene with Burt Lancaster, Kerr more typically played proper British ladies.

Deborah Kerr (1921–2007) was known for her sophistication, poise, and dry wit, and for boarding-school posture that could effortlessly carry off both contemporary and period costumes. Born Deborah Jane Trimmer in Glasgow, Scotland, Kerr originally trained as a ballet dancer. After making the switch to acting, her beauty and serene manner led almost at once to lead parts. She was a national hit in *Hatter's Castle*, and her role as a conflicted nun in *Black Narcissus* caught Hollywood's attention.

MGM offered her a contract and, once away from England, the actress seemed game for more adventurous roles. She played opposite dashing Stewart Granger in *King Solomon's Mines*, was persecuted by Nero in *Quo Vadis*, and had a steamy affair with Burt Lancaster in *From Here to Eternity*. She was a less conflicted nun with Robert Mitchum in *Heaven Knows, Mr. Allison*, and a woman of conscience opposite Yul Brynner in *The King and I*. In 1957, she starred in one of Hollywoods most beloved "weepers"—*An Affair to Remember* with exquisite gowns by Charles LeMaire. A key scene from the film at the Empire State Building was fondly reprised in *Sleepless in Seattle*.

In the late 1960s Kerr retired from films, but continued to perform on TV and the stage.

ABOVE
A perennial favorite with women, 1957's *An Affair to Remember*—here in Charles LeMaire's pink satin one-shouldered gown worn with a diamond brooch—and Cary Grant at his most charming.

RIGHT
In this publicity still from 1956's *The King and I*, Kerr models the elaborate—and quite lovely—muslin and lace undergarments necessary to properly carry off a Victorian-era hoopskirt ball gown.

MOST FASHIONABLE FILMS
QUO VADIS (1951)
THE KING AND I (1956)
AN AFFAIR TO REMEMBER (1957)
BELOVED INFIDEL (1959)

Kerr Style
The actress brought a relaxed elegance to everything she wore—from designer gowns to Victorian hoop skirts to a nun's habit. No matter how she dressed, few outfits could outshine Kerr's classic features and red-gold hair.

Signature Look
- Feminine tailored skirts and sweater sets
- Cocktail dresses with sweetheart necklines
- Gloves and pillbox hats

THE NINETEEN FIFTIES | HOLLYWOOD FASHION

DEBBIE REYNOLDS

MOST FASHIONABLE FILMS

SINGIN' IN THE RAIN (1952)
TAMMY AND THE BACHELOR (1957)
THE UNSINKABLE MOLLY BROWN (1964)

Reynolds Style
The exuberant Reynolds kept her style sweet and feminine.

Signature Look
- Short curly bob with bangs
- Tea dresses with illusion necklines
- Beaded gowns

This petite powerhouse has lasted six decades as a singer, dancer and award-winning actress—and a respected collector of film memorabilia.

Debbie Reynolds (1932–2016), a baby-faced, energetic comedian, first made her mark as a dancing ingénue in flapper dresses and tap shoes. She was born in El Paso, Texas, won the Miss Burbank Contest at age 16, and gained a contract with Warner Bros. But it was with MGM that she made her breakout film—1952's Jazz-era musical *Singin' in the Rain* with Gene Kelly and Donald O'Connor (costumes by Walter Plunkett). Reynolds was not a trained dancer and worked tirelessly to keep up with the pros. She later compared the effort to childbirth.

By the mid-1950s, Reynolds was a bona fide star. She scored with teen audiences in 1957 in *Tammy and the Bachelor* (costumes by Bill Thomas), which popularized sundresses, square dance skirts, and pedal pushers—and furnished her with a chart-topping song, "Tammy." Subsequent film hits were 1962's *How the West Was Won* and 1964's *The Unsinkable Molly Brown* (costumes by Morton Hack), which earned her an Oscar nomination.

Reynolds began collecting Hollywood memorabilia in 1972 when MGM auctioned off its props and costumes. Without a home for her vast collection, however, she was forced to start selling it off in 2011. The result was bittersweet—many items sold for much more than estimated… Marilyn Monroe's "subway grate" dress from *The Seven Year Itch* brought $4.6 million.

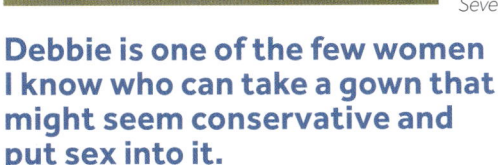

ABOVE

Tammy and the Bachelor, a romantic comedy from 1957, presented Reynolds as an adorable backwoods hick with a "heap" of gumption and a healthy store of common sense.

LEFT

Reynolds, who learned to tap dance for 1952's *Singin' in the Rain*, here wears a fuschia showgirl costume to cavort with more conservatively dressed costar, Gene Kelly.

> Debbie is one of the few women I know who can take a gown that might seem conservative and put sex into it.
> EVA GABOR

HOLLYWOOD FASHION | THE NINETEEN FIFTIES

FASHION INFLUENCE
THE HOLLYWOOD MUSICAL

With the advent of sound technology, Hollywood quickly geared up for the production of musicals, recruiting singing and dancing stars from vaudeville and the stage. These early musicals were immensely popular, yet most lacked a cohesive structure and were little more than filmed revues. As more complex plotlines were added—and more skilled performers were signed—musicals grew more sophisticated.

By the early 1930s, the movie musical reached an apex of sorts, when a thin, balding stage performer and a former chorus girl were paired as a dance team for an RKO musical called *Flying Down to Rio*. They were not the stars, but their sinuous dancing stole the film. They were, of course, Fred Astaire and Ginger Rogers. The popular pair basically saved RKO from bankruptcy and started a national craze for ballroom dancing.

Astaire's tap dance and ballroom style was eventually challenged in the late 1940s by a brash newcomer, an athletic song-and-dance man named Gene Kelly. Kelly incorporated modern dance and jazz moves into his choreography and, working with Stanley Donen, created two musical masterpieces—*Singin' in the Rain*, arguably the best musical ever made, and *An American in Paris*, which won the Oscar for Best Picture.

In the 1950s, the American musical underwent a renaissance, with film versions of Broadway hits *Oklahoma!*, *Carousel*, *The King and I*, and *South Pacific*. Original musicals included *Seven Brides for Seven Brothers*, *Kiss Me Kate*, and *Gigi*. Doris Day came into her own in *On Moonlight Bay*, *Love Me or Leave Me*, and the charming *Pajama Game*. Bing Crosby and Danny Kaye, with Rosemary Clooney and Vera Ellen, longed for a *White Christmas*, while Fred Astaire appeared in *The Band Wagon*

ABOVE
The famous dance team of Fred Astaire and Ginger Rogers first appeared together (as second-billed couple) in 1933's *Flying Down to Rio*, where they performed the carioca—Rogers wearing a flowing black gown trimmed with ostrich feathers.

TOP RIGHT
Audrey Hepburn never looked lovelier than when costumed in gooey Edwardian gowns and lavish picture hats by Cecil Beaton in 1964's *My Fair Lady*.

BOTTOM RIGHT
Singin' in the Rain is frequently voted the best musical of all time. Here its stars, Debbie Reynolds and Gene Kelly, pose in 1950's rain gear—waterproof yellow slickers and rubber gumboots.

108 1950s

THE NINETEEN FIFTIES | HOLLYWOOD FASHION

> **Things danced on the screen do not look the way they do on the stage. On the stage, dancing is three-dimensional, but a motion picture is two-dimensional.**
>
> GENE KELLY

and *Royal Wedding*. Walt Disney produced a number of animated musicals—*Cinderella*, *Lady and the Tramp*, and *Sleeping Beauty*. Finally, Louis Armstrong joined forces with two crooners, Bing Crosby and Frank Sinatra, in Cole Porter's *High Society*.

During the 1960s, Hollywood recreated a number of Broadway hits—the Bernstein/Sondheim collaboration, *West Side Story*, *The Sound of Music*, *My Fair Lady*, *The Music Man*, *Funny Girl*, and *Oliver*—all of them hits. Less successful were versions of *Camelot* and *Hello Dolly*. There was also *Mary Poppins*, which earned Julie Andrews an Oscar.

The 1970s were known more for musical bombs like *Lost Horizon* than hits like *Fiddler on the Roof*, *All That Jazz*, and *Cabaret*. Youthful audiences propped up *Jesus Christ Superstar*, *Tommy*, *The Rocky Horror Picture Show*, *Grease*, *Hair*, and *The Rose*. The 1980s saw failed films like *A Chorus Line*, *Annie*, and *Can't Stop the Music*. *The Muppet Movie* succeeded, however, as did *Victor/Victoria* and Disney's *The Little Mermaid*. Although Disney scored big in the 1990s with *Beauty and the Beast*, *Aladdin*, *The Lion King*, and *Pocahontas*, few live-action musicals were produced. A small light of hope shone for the musical with the new millennium—*Moulin Rouge*, *Chicago*, and *Dreamgirls* were blockbusters.

The Costume Challenge

Creating costumes for dancers posed a new set of challenges for studio designers. Outfits had to flatter the dancers' bodies and complement the choreography. Fabrics had to have enough flex to survive strenuous routines—sleeves had to allow free movement at the armpit and necklines could not be cut so high as to restrict the neck. Men's pants had to be tight enough to allow kicks and lunges, but not so fitted as to inflame the censors.

TOP LEFT

Two musical icons of the 20th century, Bing Crosby and Louis Armstrong, look natty in their tuxedoes as they perform a duet on "That's Jazz" from *High Society* (1956).

BOTTOM LEFT

The *Dreamgirls* in the 2006 musical—Anika Noni Rose, Beyonce Knowles, and Jennifer Hudson—with their coordinated stage costumes and elaborate wigs, were a composite of the great girl groups from the 1950s and 1960s.

109

HOLLYWOOD FASHION | **THE NINETEEN FIFTIES**

JUDY HOLLIDAY

Brash and engaging, the actress-singer won hearts for her portrayal of dizzy blondes.

Judy Holliday (1921–1965) specialized in playing plucky, middle-class heroines who may have dressed for men, but who thought for themselves. Holliday was born in New York City and got an early taste for performing in ballet school. Initially hired as a switchboard operator at the Orson Welles Mercury Theater, Holliday soon took the stage in a cabaret act called *The Revuers* (which included Leonard Bernstein). Minor movie roles followed, including a standout turn in the Tracy-Hepburn comedy *Adam's Rib*.

Holliday originated the endearing character of Billie Dawn, a tycoon's "kept" woman, in the Broadway version of *Born Yesterday*, but Columbia optioned the film for Rita Hayworth. When Hayworth declined, Holliday was in, and the film became a huge success, earning her an Academy Award.

In 1952 Holliday was summoned before the Un-American Activities Committee to answer for suspected Communist affiliations. Although the actress was not blacklisted from films, her career never quite recovered. She made *The Solid Gold Cadillac* in 1956 (with Oscar-winning gowns by Jean Louis), and in 1960 played the switchboard operator in MGM's *Bells Are Ringing* with Dean Martin—a role for which she'd won a Tony on Broadway.

Holliday died after a five-year battle with throat cancer shortly before her 44th birthday.

> **People have a hard time making me dress up to look like a classy gal.**
> JUDY HOLLIDAY

ABOVE
Judy Holliday looks sexy enough, in this black crepe, halter-top cocktail dress, to win Jack Lemmon away from Kim Novak in *Phffft!*

RIGHT
In her Oscar-winning turn as a not-so-dumb blonde in *Born Yesterday*, Holliday—in a black-and-white tuxedo-style lounging pajama—here impresses William Holden.

MOST FASHIONABLE FILMS

BORN YESTERDAY (1950)
PHFFFT! (1954)
THE SOLID GOLD CADILLAC (1956)
BELLS ARE RINGING (1960)

Holliday Style
Holliday was known for playing dumb blondes, but her IQ was above 170. She often said it took a lot of smarts to convince people her characters were stupid. Even in revealing outfits, Holliday never strayed into vulgarity. She was dressed by legends like Jean Louis (*Yesterday, Cadillic*) and Walter Plunkett (*Bells*).

Signature Look
- Off-the-shoulder cocktail dresses
- Swing coats
- Short curly bangs

THE NINETEEN FIFTIES | HOLLYWOOD FASHION

NATALIE WOOD

MOST FASHIONABLE FILMS
MARJORIE MORNINGSTAR (1958)
SPLENDOR IN THE GRASS (1961)
GYPSY (1962)
INSIDE DAISY CLOVER (1966)

Wood Style
The petite Wood, with her early ballet training, had the posture to look good in everything from strapless gowns to men's shirts and jeans. The Creed perfume scent Jasmal was created for her.

Signature Look
- Chin length, bouncy bob
- Stiletto or kitten heels
- Dark, ballerina-style dresses

Wood was that rare child actress who made a graceful transition into adult films after notable performances in several adolescent classics.

Natalie Wood (1938–1981) played both callow ingénues and worldly women, but always with ladylike decorum. Born Natasha Gurdin (of Russian heritage) in San Francisco, Wood was appearing in films by the age of four. After the Orson Welles melodrama *Tomorrow Is Forever*, she entranced audiences as Susan, the little skeptic, in holiday perennial *Miracle on 34th Street*.

As a young adult, Wood was cast opposite two of her generation's most magnetic actors—James Dean in *Rebel Without a Cause* (costumes by Moss Mabry) and Warren Beatty in 1961's *Splendor in the Grass* (Anna Hill Johnstone). That year she also starred in *West Side Story* (costumes by Irene Sharaff), which won the Oscar for Best Picture.

More mature roles include *Gypsy* (Orry-Kelly), *Love with the Proper Stranger*, *Sex and the Single Girl*, *Inside Daisy Clover*, *This Property Is Condemned*—which some critics consider her best film—and *Bob and Carol and Ted and Alice*.

In November of 1981, Wood was on her yacht *Splendor* with husband Robert Wagner and some friends, when she supposedly left for bed. Her body was found floating in the ocean the next morning. Ironically, the actress had always had a deep fear of drowning.

ABOVE
Wood played real-life stripper Gypsy Rose Lee—here making the most of an ecru mesh stage costume encrusted with sequins and jewels—in the musical *Gypsy*, which costarred Rosalind Russell.

LEFT
In 1958's *Marjorie Morningstar*, Wood plays a hopeful young actress who falls under the spell of an older playwright. Here, she wears a satin evening gown with a flowing chiffon drape as she clings to costar Gene Kelly.

111

HOLLYWOOD FASHION | THE NINETEEN FIFTIES

FASHION INFLUENCE
COWBOY COUTURE

Tales of the Old West have always tugged at the American imagination—the notion of vast spaces overrun with hostile forces and patrolled by a few decent men is ingrained in the culture. So it's not surprising that a Western, 1903's *The Great Train Robbery*, was one of the first American movies ever made. Or that early Western film actors like Tom Mix, Ken Maynard, and William S. Hart would become huge stars and sartorial influences.

By the 1930s, Westerns (also called horse operas or oaters) were a fixture of most studios, though often relegated to B-movie status. Eventually, Westerns gained credibility, helped along by critical successes like John Ford's *Stagecoach*, and began attracting major stars such as James Stewart (*Destry Rides Again*) and Gary Cooper (*The Plainsman*). The heroes of some Western serials also became stars; Roy Rogers and Gene Autry were two singing cowboys who parlayed their B-movie fame into record deals, brand merchandising, and television careers. They epitomized the cowboy dandies, with their Nudie shirts, silver-tipped rigs, and fancy, tooled-leather boots.

Most Westerns featured the honor-based "code of the West"—presenting the cowboy as a loner who looks after the weak and the needy, who stands up to evil, and expects nothing in return. These films offered such an appealing blend of action and mythos that many children and adults during the 1940s began to replicate the outfits worn by movie cowboys. Stetson hats, bandanas, yoked shirts with pearl snaps, denim jeans, tooled belts and boots, and fringed buckskin jackets all made their way into retail stores. (Television was not immune to this trend: Disney's Davy Crocket craze during the 1950s had little boys living in coonskin caps.)

Country musicians also adopted Western style, whether their sound crossed over into Western music or not. Nudie suits, shirts with ornate piping, lizard boots, string ties, and the ubiquitous Stetson became the uniform of the aspiring country crooner. Nashville and Memphis began to look more like Nogales and Mesquite.

ABOVE
Jane Fonda plays a female outlaw, complete with western duds—checked ranch shirt, jeans, gunbelt, and flat-crowned hat with stampede strap—in 1965's comic Western, *Cat Ballou*.

TOP RIGHT
Clint Eastwood popularized Italian-made "spaghetti Westerns" like *The Good, The Bad and the Ugly* playing the Man with No Name, seen here in his trademark poncho, scruffy beard, and flat-brimmed hat.

RIGHT
Cowboy actor Roy Rogers, here posing with equine pal, Trigger, and wearing a showy fringe-yoked shirt and tooled cowboy boots, was one of Western clothier Nudie Cohn's best customers.

112 1950s

THE NINETEEN FIFTIES | HOLLYWOOD FASHION

> **I'm an American actor. I work with my clothes on. I have to. Riding a horse can be pretty tough on your legs and elsewheres.**
> JOHN WAYNE

Women were also drawn to "cowgirl" chic, which was exemplified by Dale Evans, the wife of Roy Rogers. Western films with female leads, such as *Calamity Jane*, *Cat Ballou*, *Bad Girls*, *Bandidas*, and *True Grit*, and TV series like *Annie Oakley* helped popularize Western wear for women. As a result, gaucho pants (modeled on the split skirts designed for riding), short bolero jackets, flat-crowned gaucho hats, tooled boots, fringed jackets, ponchos, and even chaps all continue to recur in fashion cycles.

Even though the popularity of Western films has fluctuated over the years, Western wear has become an enduring part of America's fashion landscape.

Nudie Suits
Nudie Cohn and his wife Bobbie began producing embellished, Western-style clothing in California in the 1940s. Their shop, "Nudie's of Hollywood," which incorporated rhinestones and embroidered images on brightly colored suits, soon had a following among actors, country singers, and rock and rollers. Clients over the years included Hank Williams, Porter Wagoner, Gram Parsons, Ronald Reagan, Elton John, ZZ Top, and John Lennon. Nudie designed Elvis Presley's famous gold lamé suit and the rodeo "light" suit worn by Robert Redford in *The Electric Horseman*. Roy Rogers and Dale Evans were often photographed in Nudie outfits and one of Rogers's Nudie shirts recently sold at a Christie's auction for $16,350.

TOP LEFT
In John Ford's psychological 1956 Western, *The Searchers*, John Wayne and Jeffrey Hunter exemplify the simple clothing of the Texas cowboy, while Natalie Wood, as a Comanche hostage, dresses in the traditional velvet tunic and deerskin-wrapped braids of the Southwest tribes.

LEFT
In 1950's *Annie Get Your Gun*, Betty Hutton mugs as Annie Oakley, wearing Hollywood's version of cowgirl garb—white satin shirt, white Stetson, and red silk bandana.

113

HOLLYWOOD FASHION | THE NINETEEN FIFTIES

SANDRA DEE

Dee, who personified the perky, virginal girl next door, had a brief but influential Hollywood career.

Sandra Dee (1942–2005) helped popularize many teen trends, including surfing and beach movies. She was born Alexandra Cymboliak Zuck in Bayonne, NJ, and with encouragement from her mother, began modeling and doing commercials at age 12. She made her screen debut at 14 in *Until They Sail*. In 1959 she made what might be called her signature film, *Gidget*, playing an adorable West-Coast surfer girl. The movie was a hit and set off a craze for surfer gear and two-piece bathing suits (and spawned a TV series starring Sally Field). That year she also starred in two melodramas, *Imitation of Life* with Lana Turner and *A Summer Place*, the latter complete with a pop hit title song and huge teenage audience. Dee now found herself adored by fans across the country.

She married pop singer Bobby Darin in 1960, and they made three films together—*Come September*, *If a Man Answers*, and *That Funny Feeling*. Only the first received decent notices, and Dee's popularity began to decline. She did a few comedies—*Romanoff and Juliet* and *Take Her, She's Mine* and then reprised Debbie Reynolds' role as the shrewd backwoods girl in *Tammy Tell Me True* and *Tammy and the Doctor*. Neither movie was a success; critics complained that Dee did not have Reynolds' homespun charm.

ABOVE
The movie *Gidget* popularized simple, feminine sundresses, like the one Dee is wearing here, as well as youth-oriented beachwear and a flip, breezy way of speaking—"Honest to goodness, it's the absolute ultimate!"

RIGHT
In this scene from *Imitation of Life* Lana Turner, in a satin evening wrap, reassures Dee, who is wearing a popular 1950s' teenage combo—a white open-collared shirt under a pastel pullover sweater.

MOST FASHIONABLE FILMS
UNTIL THEY SAIL (1957)
GIDGET (1959)
IMITATION OF LIFE (1959)
TAKE HER SHE'S MINE (1963)

Dee Style
Softly feminine casual clothing best suited the petite star who was not allowed to wear anything too mature.

Signature Look
- Short sets
- Girlish gowns
- Soft, tousled blonde hair

From the 1970s on, Dee frequently appeared on television, including roles on *Fantasy Island* and *Frasier*. Her screen reputation as a "good girl" was lampooned in the song "Look at Me, I'm Sandra Dee" from the stage play, *Grease*.

THE NINETEEN FIFTIES | HOLLYWOOD FASHION

JANET LEIGH

MOST FASHIONABLE FILMS

SCARAMOUCHE (1952)
MY SISTER EILEEN (1955)
PSYCHO (1960)
BYE BYE BIRDIE (1963)

Leigh Style

With her stunning hourglass figure—she reputedly had a 21-inch waist—Leigh made the most of the form-fitting fashions of the 1950s.

Signature Look

- Tight sweaters
- Black lingerie and bustiers
- Gowns with illusion necklines

Blessed with beauty and an alluring figure, this intense, direct actress was the perfect female foil for the edgy, Method-trained actors of her generation.

Janet Leigh (1927–2004) evolved from playing naïve innocents to savvy women who knew the score. Born Jeanette Helen Morrison, she was the bright child of a couple who kept on the move. When Norma Shearer saw a picture of Leigh as a teen at the ski resort where her parents worked, the girl was offered a screen test.

Her first film, *The Romance of Rosy Ridge*, led to parts in other costume films, including *Little Women* and *Scaramouche* (costumes by Gile Steele); she followed with *Houdini* in 1953, *The Black Shield of Falworth* in 1954, and *The Vikings* in 1958, all costarring husband Tony Curtis. In 1958, she also filmed Orson Welles's *Touch of Evil* while healing from a broken arm, using a coat and other props to hide her cast. Leigh was also noteworthy in the 1962 suspense film *The Manchurian Candidate* and the rollicking musical *Bye-Bye Birdie*.

She is best known to modern audiences for her role as the abruptly terminated embezzler in Alfred Hitchcock's masterful thriller, *Psycho*. Following in her mother's "scream queen" footsteps, Leigh's daughter Jamie Lee Curtis starred in several horror films, and the two appeared together in 1980's *The Fog* and 1998's *Halloween H20*.

ABOVE

Leigh was at the peak of her beauty as a young noblewoman in the 1952 swashbuckler *Scaramouche*; here she models a late 18th-century French gown with a Queen Anne neckline adorned with a velvet bow.

LEFT

Leigh wears a pale belted dress with a subtle stripe while dancing with Dick Van Dyke in 1963's hit musical comedy, *Bye Bye Birdie*.

HOLLYWOOD FASHION | THE NINETEEN FIFTIES

MEN OF THE 1950s
REBELS WITH A CAUSE

The United States entered World War II to battle oppression. But in America during the 1950s—in spite of a national sense of wellbeing—a lot of people were still oppressed. It was no wonder so many of the younger actors of the 1950s had reputations for portraying smoldering rage and alienation, and for seeking roles that reflected an unjust, intolerant, or corrupt society.

The New Method

A new, introspective school of acting, called method acting, helped these young stars get in touch with their own simmering emotions, with sometimes powerful results. The raw, often-stark images they brought to the screen became etched in the minds of teen audiences and influenced them not only in matters of fashion, but also in how they observed the world.

Dramatic actor Marlon Brando was a one-man wrecking crew, stirring events to a fever pitch in *The Wild One*, *On the Waterfront*, and *A Streetcar Named Desire*. He popularized the biker look and what came to be called gang or hoodlum style. James Dean was known for his brooding, angst-ridden roles in *East of Eden* and *Rebel Without a Cause*. His nonconformist stance and shocking death in a car crash at the age of 24 created a lasting cult.

Montgomery Clift was another edgy, modern actor who could play sensitive intellectuals or men of action, while newcomer Paul Newman came into his own with his earthy interpretations of Tennessee Williams and matinee-idol good looks.

From Convicts to Conformists

Tony Curtis and Sidney Poitier in 1958's *The Defiant Ones* demonstrated that racial differences faded when men were faced with basic survival. Curtis was already a budding matinee idol, while Poitier went on to become a polished fashion trendsetter and a role model for black youth. Even Elvis Presley played against type, starring in the prison musical, *Jailhouse Rock*. Yet not every film revolved around the youth culture. Corporate America went under the microscope in 1954's *Executive Suite* with William Holden and in 1956's *The Man in the Gray*

RIGHT
The ever-suave Cary Grant woos Deborah Kerr—here, wearing an ice blue satin robe—in the 1957 "weeper" *An Affair to Remember*.

FAR RIGHT
Escaped convicts Tony Curtis and Sidney Poitier are chained together and must learn tolerance and trust in order to elude the law in 1958's *The Defiant Ones*.

THE NINETEEN FIFTIES | HOLLYWOOD FASHION

> There's a rebel lying deep in my soul. Anytime anybody tells me the trend is such and such, I go the opposite direction. I hate the idea of trends. I hate imitation; I have a reverence for individuality.
> CLINT EASTWOOD

Flannel Suit with Gregory Peck, the title reflected the conformist, conservative clothing and attitudes of the middle class.

Suave or Savage

Elegant, sophisticated gentlemen remained in vogue through much of the decade, with stylish performances by playboy Cary Grant in *An Affair to Remember*, a dapper David Niven in *Around the World in 80 Days*, and sibling rivals William Holden and Humphrey Bogart in *Sabrina*. Military films retained their popularity—*From Here to Eternity*, *The Flying Leathernecks*, *The Enemy Below*—and kept military details in the fashion forefront, while Westerns remained on an upswing with the production of influential classics, such as *High Noon* with Gary Cooper and *The Searchers* with John Wayne.

Signature Menswear Looks of the 1950s
- Less-structured suits without shoulder pads
- Polo shirts
- Hawaiian shirts
- White T-shirts, blue jeans, and sneakers
- Patterned sports jackets
- Penny loafers
- Crew-cut hair or pompadours
- Beat styles: ankle boots, black turtlenecks, berets

ABOVE

Marlon Brando, here sporting a plaid bomber jacket, takes on dockyard corruption in Elia Kazan's hard-hitting *On the Waterfront* (1954).

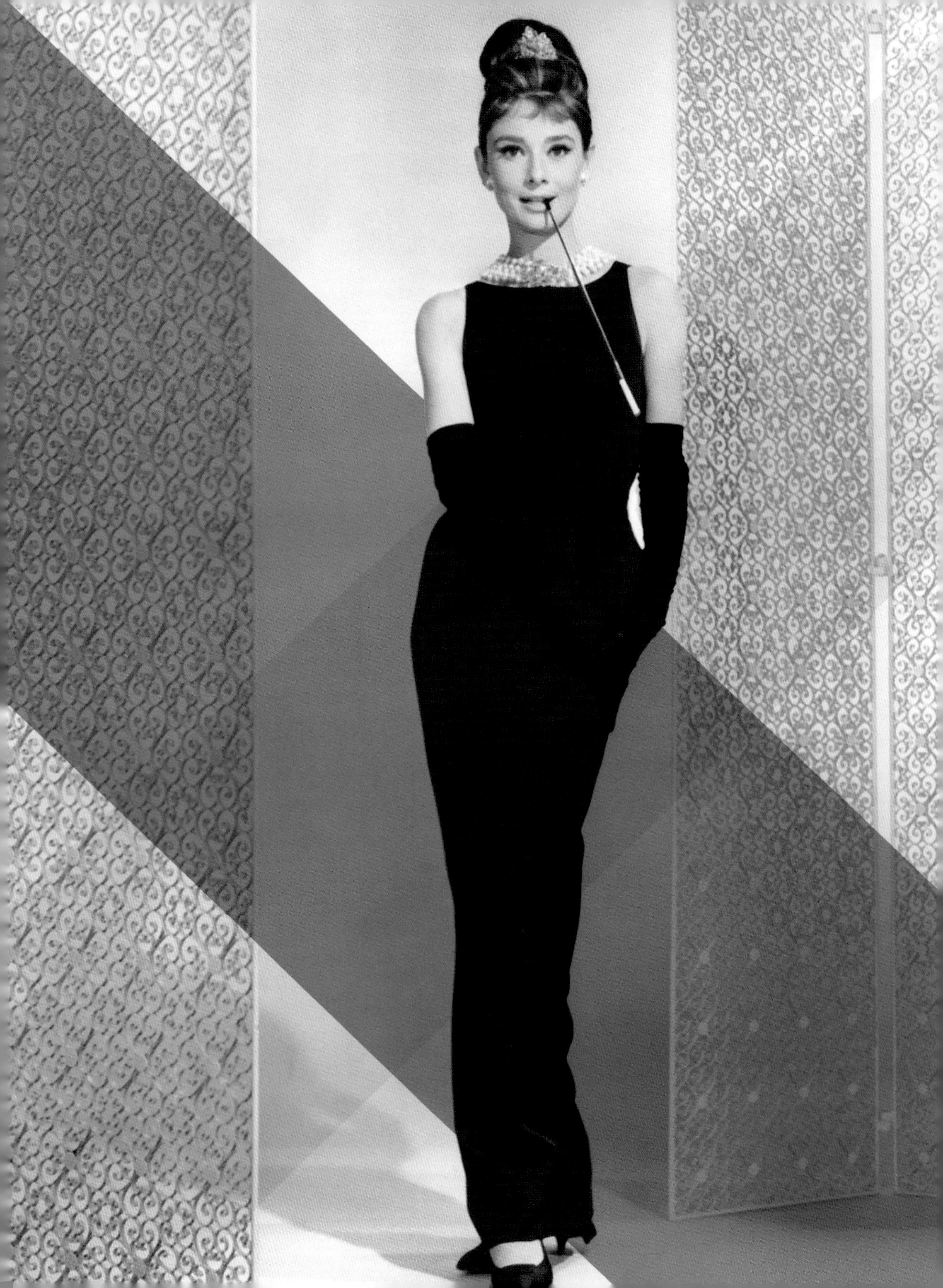

THE NINETEEN SIXTIES

This decade was a time of turmoil and change, encompassing the Vietnam War and its protesters, and the Kennedy and King assassinations. It introduced the hippies and The Beatles (and the whole British Invasion) including their quirky, antiestablishment fashions. Hollywood studios, however, were loathe to acknowledge the controversy over Vietnam—even risk-taker Robert Altman set the antiwar *MASH* in Korea—and the industry was also slow to incorporate the counterculture and its style into movies.

Instead, the focus was on period action films like *Bonnie and Clyde* and *Butch Cassidy and the Sundance Kid* (featuring "likable" outlaws); sweeping period epics like *Lawrence of Arabia* and *Dr. Zhivago*; fluffy period musicals like *Mary Poppins* and *The Sound of Music*; and dark contemporary comedies like *The Graduate* and *Dr. Strangelove*. A few films, however, did address the societal issues of the day—*West Side Story* exposed gang wars and bigotry, *Midnight Cowboy* examined homelessness and male prostitution, and *Guess Who's Coming to Dinner* showcased the changing role of minorities in America.

And while the latest street fashions from England and America's counterculture—bell-bottom trousers, Edwardian suits, Nehru jackets, miniskirts, peasant dresses, knee-high leather boots, go-go boots, and other youthful trends—were huge on the runway, they rarely made it to the cinema screen. The movie industry was not happy to trade the glamorous stars of the 1950s for a group of dressed-down players in granny gowns and tie-dyed shirts.

HOLLYWOOD FASHION | THE NINETEEN SIXTIES

SHIRLEY MACLAINE

This pixie-faced actress began as a Broadway gypsy, graduated to star status, and kept scoring plum roles well into middle age and beyond.

Shirley MacLaine (1934–), known for playing sassy, spirited women, exemplified the Bohemian side of Hollywood, both in fashion and in lifestyle. She was born Shirley MacLean Beaty in Richmond, Virginia, and as a chorus girl in 1954, she lived the Broadway dream. When *The Pajama Game* leading lady Carol Haney broke her ankle, MacLaine filled in for her—and caught the attention of producer Hal Wallis, who signed her with Paramount.

MacLaine played a troubled party girl in *Some Came Running* and an East Indian royal in *Around the World in 80 Days*. She finally found her screen persona with Fran Kubelik, an elevator operator who maintains her sense of humor even while being targeted by a corporate lothario in Billy Wilder's *The Apartment*. Dry humor became MacLaine's signature, whether she was playing a shrewd streetwalker in *Irma La Douce* or watching her adult child die in 1983's *Terms of Endearment*, for which she won an Oscar. MacLaine returned to her singing and dancing Broadway roots in 1964's *What a Way to Go* (gowns by Edith Head) and 1969's *Sweet Charity* (Head). She played lively matrons in *Steel Magnolias* and *Rumor Has It*.

MacLaine, who dabbles in mysticism, wrote a number of books on reincarnation. Her brother, Warren Beatty, is a respected actor-director.

ABOVE
MacLaine puts on a party dress just to play cards with Jack Lemmon in 1960's *The Apartment*.

RIGHT
MacClaine gets dressed in a formal gown with a tiara and jewels to go to the opera in 1967's *Woman Times Seven*.

MOST FASHIONABLE FILMS
ASK ANY GIRL (1959)
THE APARTMENT (1960)
CAN-CAN (1960)
IRMA LA DOUCE (1963)
WOMAN TIMES SEVEN (1967)
SWEET CHARITY (1969)

MacLaine Style
At 5'7" the actress was taller than she appeared on film and had the right figure for the tight skirts and sweaters of the 1950s. Later she would show similar flair as a stylish senior in *The Evening Star* and *In Her Shoes*.

Signature Look
• Short, shaggy hairdo
• Sheath skirts
• Capri pants and novel tops

THE NINETEEN SIXTIES | HOLLYWOOD FASHION

DORIS DAY

MOST FASHIONABLE FILMS
LOVE ME OR LEAVE ME (1955)
PILLOW TALK (1959)
LOVER COME BACK (1962)
THAT TOUCH OF MINK (1962)
THE THRILL OF IT ALL (1963)

Day Style
The actress came to represent the career woman of the 1960s—fashionable, feisty, and indefatigable.

Signature Look
- Pastel business suits with matching pillbox hats
- Gauzy or beaded gowns
- Capes worn with long gloves

This buoyant big-band singer effortlessly made the transition to film, excelling at both drama and light romantic comedy.

Doris Day (1924–2019) is best known for playing perky, ambitious career women in tasteful ensembles who always held out for marriage. She was born Doris Mary Ann Kappelhoff in Cincinnati, Ohio, and planned to become a dancer. A serious auto accident left her bedridden, where she began to sing along with the radio. After her recovery, she worked as a radio singer, and eventually went on to sing with bandleaders Barney Rapp, Jimmy James, Bob Crosby, and Les Brown, with whom she had her first hit song, "Sentimental Journey."

After appearing with Brown's band in a film short, Day was cast in *Romance of the High Seas*, *On Moonlight Bay*, and *Tea for Two*. In 1953's *Calamity Jane* (costumes by Howard Shoup), she sang "Secret Love," which won the Oscar for Best Song. Day turned to drama with the 1955 biography of Ruth Etting, *Love Me or Leave Me* and also starred in Alfred Hitchcock's *The Man Who Knew Too Much*, which introduced her Oscar-winning theme song, "Que Sera, Sera."

Day scored in *The Pajama Game* and *Teacher's Pet*, and followed them with her classic "battle of the sexes" comedies—*Pillow Talk* (gowns by Jean Louis) with rakish Rock Hudson, who also costarred in *Lover Come Back* (Irene) and *Send Me No Flowers*; *The Thrill of It All* (Jean Louis) and *Move Over Darling* with affable James Garner; and *That Touch of Mink* (Rosemary Odell) with a long-suffering Cary Grant.

When her brand of "virginal" film comedy fell out of favor—and her late husband's financial dealings left her deeply in debt—Day took on the challenge of TV, where *The Doris Day Show* had a successful five-year run.

In 1971 Day founded the group "Actors and Others for Animals."

ABOVE
Rock Hudson pursued Doris Day—until she caught him—in *Lover Come Back*. Day played an ambitious ad executive in stylishly tailored, color-blocked suits and perky, matching hats.

LEFT
Pillow Talk created the template for the Doris Day romantic comedies—stubborn career girl butts heads with infuriating playboy type. Here, Day, in a simple and elegant bateau-necked dinner dress, is accosted by frequent-foil Rock Hudson.

121

HOLLYWOOD FASHION | THE NINETEEN SIXTIES

ALBUM OF TRENDSETTERS
OSCAR STYLES 1930s — 1960s

The first presentation of the Academy Awards from the Motion Picture Academy of Arts and Sciences—later called the Oscars—was held at the Hotel Roosevelt in Hollywood and the entire ceremony took 15 minutes.

The first Best Motion Picture winner was the silent film *Wings* (the only silent film so honored until 2011, when the award went to the mostly silent film, *The Artist*). Once the ceremony began to be televised in 1953, studios and press agents realized the awards were a great marketing showcase for their stars. The "red carpet" procession along the cordoned-off entry to the ceremony, where stars were photographed and interviewed about their films and their fashions, became almost as much of an event as the show itself.

An Academy Award for Best Costume Design was not given until 1948, and at that time it was divided into two film categories: black-and-white and color. The former award usually went to a contemporary film, while the latter went to a historical film. After the categories merged in 1967, the Academy has almost always awarded the statuette to a period film; costume designers of modern-era films have won only twice—Albert Wolsky for *All that Jazz* in 1979 and Tim Chappel and Lizzy Gardiner for *The Adventures of Priscilla, Queen of the Desert* in 1994.

Edith Head is the leading lady of the costume design Oscars, having been nominated 35 times and won eight times, while Irene Sharaff was nominated 15 times and won five. It is important to remember, however, that many of Hollywood's legendary designers did their best work before the costume design award even existed.

RIGHT

Judy Garland in an ermine shrug poses with pal Mickey Rooney after winning the Academy's Juvenile Award for 1939's *The Wizard of Oz*.

ABOVE RIGHT

James Stewart received the Best Actor Award for 1940's *The Philadelphia Story* and Ginger Rogers won the Best Actress Award for *Kitty Foyle*. Stewart thought he was better in *Mr. Smith Goes to Washington*, but graciously accepted the award anyway.

BOTTOM RIGHT

Marlon Brando won for *On the Waterfront* and Grace Kelly won for *The Country Girl*. Kelly wore a green silk dress by Edith Head. It was reported to be the most expensive Oscar dress up to that time.

THE NINETEEN SIXTIES | HOLLYWOOD FASHION

If I'd known this was all it would take, I'd have put that eyepatch on 40 years ago.

JOHN WAYNE, UPON WINNING AS ROOSTER COGBURN IN **TRUE GRIT**

ABOVE LEFT

Audrey Hepburn won for 1954's *Roman Holiday*, wearing a flowered evening gown that showed off her shoulders to great effect.

ABOVE RIGHT

Liz Taylor won for 1960's *Butterfield 8*, seen here at an after party wearing a long white dress. Unlike today's food starved stars, Liz had a healthy appetite for both food and drink.

LEFT

John Wayne poses with wife Pilar after winning the Best Actor Oscar for his rollicking performance as Rooster Cogburn in 1969's *True Grit*.

HOLLYWOOD FASHION | THE NINETEEN SIXTIES

JANE FONDA

This two-time Oscar winner, with the leggy appeal of a runway model, evolved from sweet ingénue to sex kitten to complex layered roles.

Jane Fonda (1937–) had a flair for contemporary fashion that made her a trendsetter at an early age. The daughter of screen legend Henry Fonda, the actress began her film career in light comedies—opposite Rod Taylor in *Sunday in New York* and Robert Redford in *Barefoot in the Park*, then made *Barbarella*, a science fiction sex romp with husband French director, Roger Vadim.

Fonda followed up with moving performances in *Klute* with Donald Sutherland, playing a call girl (costumes by Ann Roth), and in *Coming Home* with John Voight, as a straight-laced military wife who falls in love with a paraplegic soldier (women's costumes by Jennifer Parsons). Both films earned her Academy Awards. She was also nominated for Best Actress for 1969's *They Shoot Horses Don't They?*, 1977's *Julia*, 1979's *The China Syndrome*, 1986's *The Morning After*, and as Supporting Actress in *On Golden Pond*, the film for which her father won his only Oscar. She was also in the popular films *The Electric Horseman* and *Nine to Five*.

Fonda was an outspoken critic of the Vietnam War and married activist Tom Hayden. She also married media mogul Ted Turner. Fonda was famous for creating a series of "No pain, no gain" workout videos in the 1980s.

MOST FASHIONABLE FILMS
SUNDAY IN NEW YORK (1963)
BAREFOOT IN THE PARK (1967)
BARBARELLA (1968)
THE ELECTRIC HORSEMAN (1979)

Fonda Style
The actress was known for her cutting-edge fashion sense from the swinging sixties, through the trendy, big-shouldered 1980s into the sophisticated present.

Signature Look
- Sleek, belted trenchcoats with head scarves
- Knee-high boots with concho-belted miniskirts
- Elegant, body-hugging evening gowns

ABOVE
Fonda contemplates a pre-marital fling and dresses for the part in *Sunday in New York* from 1963.

RIGHT
Fonda conquered the galaxy—and invaded many young males' fantasies—wearing this futuristic body suit in Roger Vadim's space romp, *Barbarella*.

THE NINETEEN SIXTIES | HOLLYWOOD FASHION

NANCY KWAN

Kwan not only "enjoyed being a girl," she also enjoyed being an actress, a producer, and a voting activist.

Nancy Kwan (1939–), although typecast as a Chinese sex kitten, was also a role model for aspiring Asian actresses. Born Ka Shen Kwan in Hong Kong, she was the daughter of a Chinese architect father and a British fashion model mother. Kwan was training as a dancer with England's Royal Ballet School when producer Ray Stark discovered her.

He cast her as an Asian prostitute opposite William Holden's artist in the 1960 melodrama, *The World of Suzy Wong* with costumes by Phyllis Dalton. (Ironically, Kwan was made up to appear "more Chinese.") To promote the film, Stark arranged magazine spreads in *Time*, *Look*, *Esquire*, and a cover shoot at *Life*. Kwan became an overnight sensation—some called her the "Chinese Bardot"—and one of the few international stars of Asian heritage.

The following year she won the Golden Globe Award for Most Promising Female Newcomer and starred in the hit musical, *Flower Drum Song* (costumes by Irene Sharaff), where she again played a sexy man-hunter. Kwan grew concerned when Chinese-Americans protested that Hollywood kept portraying their young women as sexually promiscuous.

Unfortunately, after 1962 Kwan's career began to fade. In 1972 she moved to Hong Kong to be with her ailing father, and formed a production company for commercials. Kwan, who now resides in Los Angeles, still does occasional TV and film work and is the spokeswoman for the Asian American Voters Coalition.

MOST FASHIONABLE FILMS

THE WORLD OF SUZY WONG (1960)
FLOWER DRUM SONG (1961)
TAMAHINE (1963)

Kwan Style
The actress made waves in 1963 by having her nearly waist-length hair cut and styled by Vidal Sassoon into a Mary Quant bob. The cut then became known as the "Nancy Kwan."

Signature Look
- Silk cheongsams and high heels
- Sleek hair and smoky eyes
- Short skirts

ABOVE

Kwan impressed audiences with her performance as a free-spirited Chinese singer, and with her cheeky rendition of "I Enjoy Being a Girl," in 1961's *Flower Drum Song*. Here, she models an updated variation of the traditional silk cheongsam.

LEFT

Kwan, here wearing a dusty-pink pleated chiffon dress as she boats with John Fraser, plays a Polynesian girl transported to a British boy's academy in 1963's *Tamahine*.

HOLLYWOOD FASHION | THE NINETEEN SIXTIES

FASHION INFLUENCE
THE COUNTERCULTURE

As with the 1950s, teenagers again drove the fashion trends of this decade. While some extreme clothing options of this era have fallen by the wayside, others are still considered wardrobe staples. And, of course, the denim blue jeans that came to prominence in the 1950s continued their reign as the "signature of youth" garment, mandatory for anyone under 30.

Carnaby Street

Great Britain, for all its grand history, has never been considered a source of cutting-edge fashion, not when compared to Paris, Milan, or New York. And bleak, postwar Britain, with its halting recovery from the bombing and rationing, seemed the least likely place for imaginative new fashions and an upbeat, swinging lifestyle to emerge.

But just as the grim mood in America after World War I gave way to the lively Jazz era, postwar Britain enjoyed a similar resurgence, one that resulted in innovative clothing, flourishing boutiques and dance clubs, and a nation-branded genre of popular music that invaded America...and most of the civilized world. Carnaby Street, a youthful shopper's paradise in London's Soho district, came to emblemize England's new character. The street featured emerging designers, including Mary Quant and Irvine Sellars, and gave rise to trendy shops like Lady Jane, Biba, and Kleptomania.

British moviemakers naturally incorporated the thriving youth scene into their films, as with 1967's good-natured *Smashing Time*, and showcased Carnaby Street-inspired clothing in movies like *Wonderwall*, *Georgy Girl*, and *Blow-Up*.

ABOVE
Mick Jagger, in a stretch top, button-sided bell bottoms and a long red scarf, is caught mid-strut as he performs with the Rolling Stones in the 1969 rockumentary, *Gimme Shelter*.

TOP RIGHT
The Beatles, in lookalike tailored suits, perform during Richard Lester's comic romp, 1964's *A Hard Day's Night*. The Fab Four would later experiment with more individual retro and Bohemian styles.

BOTTOM RIGHT
In 1967's *Smashing Time*, Rita Tushingham seeks fame and fortune in Swinging London and becomes a mod model.

Mods vs. Rockers

During the 1960s, two opposing male styles arose in England—the Brando-esque rockers with their slicked-back hair and tight jeans; and the dandyish mods, with their natty suits and taste for colorful shirts and ties. By the time The Beatles became famous, they had evolved from their Hamburg rocker days into the well-groomed, impeccably tailored mods of *A Hard Day's Night*.

The Counterculture

The American hippie culture, which drew its ideology from youthful war protesters, folk and

THE NINETEEN SIXTIES | HOLLYWOOD FASHION

Hippy is an establishment label for a profound, invisible, underground, evolutionary process. For every visible hippy, barefoot, beflowered, beaded, there are a thousand invisible members of the turned-on underground.
TIMOTHY LEARY

rock musicians, and iconoclastic gurus, influenced young people on the street and college campus much more than was reflected by the few fictional films Hollywood devoted to it at the time. Possibly the best examples of hippie culture were found in documentaries like *Woodstock*, *Gimme Shelter*, and *The Last Waltz*. *Woodstock* could have served as a thesis on the clothing of the love generation: psychedelic, tied-dyed shirts, bell-bottom jeans, headbands, love beads, sandals, peasant dresses, and unisex flower garlands. Naturally, it wasn't long before older fashionistas were demanding hippie clothing. Designers complied with upscale mini-dresses, Nehru jackets, peace medallions, go-go boots, and Afghani sheepskin coats—with often mixed results.

One fiction film that did deal with the counterculture was the 1969 classic, *Easy Rider*, a tale of two alienated motorcyclists. It featured filmmaker Peter Fonda as "Captain America" in a flag-embellished leather jacket, a sleeker version of the 1950s' biker jacket.

A number of later films finally got around to exploring the era—and went on to inspire a revival of hippie fashions. 1979's *Hair* (costumes by Ann Roth) reprised the famous Broadway play of the late 1960s; 1999's bittersweet *A Walk on the Moon*, with Diane Lane and Viggo Mortensen, contrasted the attitudes and clothing of the Woodstock generation with traditional middle-class values (costumes by Jess Goldstein); 2007's *Across the Universe* (Albert Wolsky) paid homage to The Beatles, and *Taking Woodstock* from 2009 followed the evolution of the rock festival (costumes by Joseph G. Aulisi).

TOP LEFT

In 1969's indie classic, *Easy Rider*, bikers Dennis Hopper, in buckskin fringe, and Peter Fonda, in star-spangled helmet (with straitlaced passenger Jack Nicholson) are on a cross-country journey of discovery.

LEFT

Although *Hair: The American Tribal Love Rock Musical*, first appeared on Broadway in 1968, it was not until 1979 that director Miloš Forman produced a film adaptation. With joyful choreography by Twyla Tharp and a puckish performance by Treat Williams, the movie captured the spirit of the Summer of Love.

127

HOLLYWOOD FASHION | THE NINETEEN SIXTIES

AUDREY HEPBURN

This former ballet dancer transformed herself on screen from a gangly girl to the height of sophisticated elegance.

Audrey Hepburn (1929–1993), who played ingénue parts well into her 30s, was known for her wide-eyed air of innocence as well as a drop-dead wardrobe created for her by French couturier Hubert de Givenchy. Hepburn was born in Bussels, Belgium, the daughter of a British banker and a Dutch baroness. After enduring hard times during World War II, Hepburn studied ballet and began modeling in England. Film producers were soon pursuing the gamine beauty with the swanlike neck, and in 1953 she was cast as a runaway princess in *Roman Holiday* (costumes by Edith Head). The film, which costarred Gregory Peck, was a huge hit and earned the actress an Oscar.

Hepburn then found herself paired with the leading actors of the era (often men who were embarrassingly much older)—she was wooed by Humphrey Bogart in *Sabrina* (costumes by Head and Givenchy), danced with Fred Astaire in *Funny Face* (Edith Head), was courted by Gary Cooper in *Love in the Afternoon* (Jay A. Morley, Jr.), sparred with Cary Grant in *Charade* (gowns by Givenchy), and was Peter O'Toole's accomplice in *How to Steal a Million* (her wardrobe by Givenchy).

She created her most memorable character in 1961 with *Breakfast at Tiffany's* Holly Golightly, part pleasure seeker, part wounded bird. One striking ensemble from the film—an elegant black gown worn with pearls, long black gloves, and a cigarette holder—became as iconic as Monroe's white sundress or Garland's *Oz* pinafore.

Hepburn was cast as Eliza Doolittle in place of newcomer Julie Andrews—who originated the role on Broadway—in 1964's *My Fair Lady* (costumes by Cecil Beaton). Andrews bested Hepburn at Oscar time, however, winning Best Actress for *Mary Poppins*. In spite of not doing her own singing, Hepburn was a charming Eliza and helped make the movie a blockbuster.

Other outstanding efforts include *Two for the Road* with Albert Finney, the story of a marriage's ups and downs; *Robin and Marian* with Sean Connery, a tale of renewed love in Sherwood Forest; and *Wait Until Dark*, with Hepburn as a blind woman fending off a killer in her home.

From 1988 to 1993 the actress was a special ambassador to the United Nations' UNICEF fund, helping children in Africa and Latin America. In 1993, Hepburn was posthumously awarded the Gene Hersholt Humanitarian Award by the Motion Picture Academy.

Hepburn Style

Hepburn was the willowy antithesis of the curvy sex goddesses of her era; she popularized the beatnik look—black capri pants, leotard tops, and ballet slippers—that is still a fixture today. Her association with designer Givenchy resulted in a new silhouette for women's evening wear—sleek, minimal, and elegant.

Signature Look

- Little black dresses with clean, straight lines
- Oversized sunglasses
- Pillbox or picture hats

ABOVE
Hepburn was transformed from a shop clerk to a Paris model in 1957's *Funny Face*.

TOP RIGHT
Hepburn's over-the-top beribboned and feathered Ascot Race ensemble from 1964's *My Fair Lady* was designed by Cecil Beaton and is often found on "10 Best" lists. Here, tweedy mentor Rex Harrison peeks around a pole but can barely get close to her.

FULL PAGE
The actress found her perfect role as Holly Golightly, a party girl with a fragile heart, in 1961's *Breakfast at Tiffany's*. Here she poses in a classic LBD—little black dress—and Holly's signature cigarette holder.

MOST FASHIONABLE FILMS

SABRINA (1954)
FUNNY FACE (1957)
BREAKFAST AT TIFFANY'S (1961)
CHARADE (1963)
MY FAIR LADY (1964)

HOLLYWOOD FASHION | THE NINETEEN SIXTIES

FASHION INFLUENCE
GANGSTER CHIC

ABOVE

Uma Thurman, in 1994's *Pulp Fiction*, plays a modern gangster's moll who is not afraid to dance with—or hit on—one of her husband's foot soldiers. Director Quentin Tarantino, with his "skinny" black suits and dark shades, helped reshape the gangster look for the new millennium.

TOP RIGHT

Gangster chic revived in the late 1960s and early 1970s with the advent of several key films, including 1967's *Bonnie and Clyde*, where Faye Dunaway's sporty Depression-era ensembles by Theadora Van Runkle, inspired retail fashion for years.

Films and newsreels of the 1920s first exposed American audiences to gangsters, bootleggers, and racketeers. With their fedoras, silk suits, diamond rings, and spats, these men had a certain cachet for the public, one that outlaws often possessed. They thumbed their noses at the police and flaunted their "fame," their expensive cars, tailored clothing, and beautiful women.

A typical ensemble for racketeer Al Capone was a blue silk suit, white silk hankie, pearl gray spats, and a diamond and platinum watch chain. So it was these sartorial displays that Hollywood copied in its many gangster-based films from the 1930s onward. And it was no wonder gangster styles began to invade the staid showrooms of tailors and the racks of retail stores across the country. Brooks Brothers introduced the "gangster suit" during this decade, as did Gieves and Hawkes in England and Brioni in Italy. And so a men's fashion trend was born.

Gangster movies also often featured the mobster's girlfriend—or moll—who either wore lounging outfits or evening gowns, complete with diamonds, and furs. The moll was typically represented as a powerless plaything— Jean Harlow in *The Public Enemy* and Marilyn Monroe in *The Asphalt Jungle*—or less often as the power behind the boss, as with Ava Gardner's character in *The Killers*. Somewhere in the middle lies Sharon Stone's game-playing moll in *Casino*, whose costumes made her look "packaged for sex" by her criminal lover.

Bonnie's Turn

It wasn't until the 1967 debut of *Bonnie and Clyde* that women were offered a distaff version of gangster chic. When the film's costume designer, newcomer Theadora Van Runkle, dressed Faye Dunaway in a striking homage to classic 1930s'

THE NINETEEN SIXTIES | HOLLYWOOD FASHION

separates, she created a frenzy in women's retail. Everyone and their sister wanted the "Bonnie Parker" look—a long knit skirt, spectator shoes, and ribbed poor-boy sweater worn with a knotted silk scarf and topped off with a jaunty beret. (Van Runkle also designed Dunaway's Oscar gown for 1968 and most of her off-screen wardrobe for that year.)

Modern Trends
In the 1970s, when Francis Ford Coppola's popular *Godfather* saga resulted in a cultural "Godfather effect" across America, gangster chic resurfaced in a big way. Pinstriped, double-breasted suits, pocket squares, and homburg hats worn with expensive Italian dress shoes reappeared on the runways. The first film's trendsetting costumes were by Anna Hill Johnstone, *Godfather II* was styled by Van Runkle, and *Godfather III* was costumed by Milena Canonero, who also worked on Best Picture Oscar winners *Chariots of Fire* and *Out of Africa*.

Director Quentin Tarantino put his own spin on gangster chic in his gritty crime films *Reservoir Dogs* and *Pulp Fiction*, where dapper thieves and stylish hitmen sport fitted black suits, skinny ties, and narrow black shoes.

TOP LEFT

The 1950 cine noir heist film, *The Asphalt Jungle*, provided Monroe with one of her better early roles. Here she models a black, off-the-shoulder cocktail dress.

TOP RIGHT

Sometimes the gangster's moll got in on the action, as with Ava Gardner, here in a seductive, strapless satin gown, in 1946's *The Killers*.

LEFT

James Cagney helped create the iconic look for well-dressed screen gangsters—impeccable tailoring and an ominous scowl—in films like 1931's *The Public Enemy*.

131

HOLLYWOOD FASHION | THE NINETEEN SIXTIES

GOLDIE HAWN

America's favorite flower child played sunny, big-eyed blondes who often got into situations way over their heads.

Goldie Hawn (1945–) with her minidresses, body paint, and shag haircut, became a 1960s' icon and made ditzy behavior both charming and sexy. Born in Washington, DC, to a dancer mother and musician father, Hawn was running a ballet school by the age of 19.

She entered movies with a string of popular comedies, including 1969's *Cactus Flower* (costumes by Moss Mabry) for which she won the Oscar, *There's a Girl in My Soup*, *Shampoo* (costumes by Ossie Clark), and dramas *Butterflies Are Free*, *The Girl from Petrovka*, and *The Sugarland Express*. She followed with two of her biggest comedy hits, 1978's *Foul Play* with Chevy Chase and 1980's *Private Benjamin*, which she also produced. In 1987, she made *Overboard* with life-partner Kurt Russell; initially a box-office failure, it has become a cable TV favorite.

In the 1990s her career speeded up, with *Bird on a Wire*, *Death Becomes Her*, *The First Wives Club* (Theoni V. Aldredge), and Woody Allen's *Everyone Says I Love You*.

Hawn is the mother of actors Oliver Hudson and Kate Hudson.

ABOVE
In *There's A Girl in My Soup*, Hawn epitomizes the iconic look of the late 1960s and early 1970s with her tousled curls, big eyes, and floaty, chiffon minidress in grasshopper green.

RIGHT
Hawn won an Oscar for playing a free-spirited woman-child in *Cactus Flower*, where she got to wear a series of trendy outfits like this hot-pink, pleated minidress.

MOST FASHIONABLE FILMS

CACTUS FLOWER (1969)
THERE'S A GIRL IN MY SOUP (1970)
THE FIRST WIVES CLUB (1996)
THE BANGER SISTERS (2002)

Hawn Style
During her Laugh-In days, the actress was famous for her disheveled blonde hairdo and exaggerated eye makeup. She remains a fashion trendsetter and is often seen on the red carpet.

Signature Look
- Ruffled minidresses
- Mix-and-match Boho separates
- Ethnic-inspired gowns

THE NINETEEN SIXTIES | HOLLYWOOD FASHION

JULIE CHRISTIE

MOST FASHIONABLE FILMS

DARLING (1965)
DOCTOR ZHIVAGO (1965)
FAR FROM THE MADDING CROWD (1967)
PETULIA (1968)
SHAMPOO (1975)

Christie Style

Christie ushered in the age of the natural beauty, but also became a "Swinging Sixties" fashion icon with her minidresses and high boots. The actress was eventually less concerned with her sexy image as she turned her focus to human and animal rights.

Signature Look

- Sun-kissed skin
- Windswept honey-colored hair with lush bangs
- Paisley minidresses and floppy hats

The sun-kissed blonde with the husky voice and sensual mouth was the swinging English girl that every man desired.

Julie Christie (1941–) played sexually adventurous young women in a variety of time periods. Born in Assam, India, she grew up on a tea plantation. After an education in England and Paris, she enrolled in acting school and debuted on the stage in 1957. After appearing in two film comedies, she met director John Schlesinger, who boosted her career with breakout film, *Billy Liar*, and 1965's *Darling*. This tale of an amoral model earned Oscars for Christie, costume designer Julie Harris, and screenwriter Frederic Raphael. Christie was now the face of the Swinging Sixties in England.

The actress then made three classics—the epic *Doctor Zhivago*, which set off a craze for Russian-style clothing and balalaika music; the futuristic cult hit, *Fahrenheit 451*; and the bucolic *Far From the Madding Crowd*, which sparked a trend for country-style Victorian fashions.

The 1970s saw more success, with Robert Altman's Western tragedy *McCabe and Mrs. Miller* and the contemporary comedies *Shampoo* and *Heaven Can Wait*, all costarring her paramour Warren Beatty (for whom, some acting peers claim, she gave up her prime career years). She also starred with Donald Sutherland in 1973's sexually explicit thriller, *Don't Look Now*.

From the 1980s onward, Christie's popularity waned, although she continued to make quality films and was nominated for Academy Awards in 1997's *Afterglow* and 2006's *Away from Her*. The still-striking Christie continues to act in films and also campaigns for animal rights and for environmental issues

ABOVE

Christie looks alluring in 1968's *Petulia*, the tale of a wife determined to cheat on her husband.

LEFT

Christie, here in a matching beach set, plays a model who sleeps her way to the top in *Darling* from 1965.

HOLLYWOOD FASHION | THE NINETEEN SIXTIES

FASHION INFLUENCE
THE BIKINI

In 1957, a French bombshell hit the United States. The sultry blonde's name was Brigitte Bardot…and the film that made her an international sex symbol was Roger Vadim's *And God Created Woman*. In the film, Bardot wears an abbreviated two-piece bathing suit, which came to be known around the world as the "bikini."

Although it had been seen on beaches prior to 1946, that was the year French car engineer Louis Réard and designer Jacques Heim officially unveiled the bikini. Réard declared at the time, "For the record, you do not have a genuine bikini unless you can pull it through your wedding ring!" The term "bikini" was coined by Réard after the Bikini Atoll, where early atomic tests had taken place. (He'd originally christened his creation "the Atome, the world's smallest bathing suit.") When he couldn't find a proper fashion model to wear the scandalous two-piecer, he hired Micheline Bernardini, a nude dancer, to pose in it.

Historically, skimpy two-piece outfits appear on a number of ancient artifacts, including a fourth-century Roman floor mosaic of women exercising and statues of Venus wearing a bikini, several of which were recovered from Pompeii. In the early 20th century, inspired by the inclusion of women in Olympic swimming, designer Carl Jantzen made the first two-piece bathing suit, the great grandmother of the bikini.

As flexible fabrics, such as latex and nylon, were introduced, bathing suits became more clingy and revealing. By the 1940s, the glamour girls of Hollywood like Ava Gardner, Rita Hayworth, and Lana Turner were being photographed in two-piece suits. But it wasn't until the release of Bardot's films, that the bikini caught on in America. By the 1970s, it had decreased in overall size with "barely there" strings, and in the 1990s, with the advent of

ABOVE

Carrie Fisher preens in Princess Leia's metallic bikini from *Star Wars VI: The Return of the Jedi*. The brief bronze costume is an often-copied fan favorite at science-fiction conventions.

RIGHT

A cinema moment that sparked the libido of young men everywhere—Phoebe Cates is about to remove the top of her cherry-red bikini in the pool fantasy scene from 1982's *Fast Times at Ridgemont High*.

FAR RIGHT

French actress Brigitte Bardot became famous for the abbreviated European version.

THE NINETEEN SIXTIES | HOLLYWOOD FASHION

> **This bikini made me into a success.**
> URSULA ANDRESS

the Brazilian bikini, the bottom lost most of its back fabric and became a virtual G-string. More recently hipster bottoms and boy-pant bottoms became the rage.

Although etiquette guru Emily Post insisted that bikinis were only for women "with perfect figures and the very young," there is no doubt that the bikini has continued to attract emancipated women of all ages across the globe. By the mid-2000s, bikinis had become an $881 million-business annually. The revealing suit also is responsible for the introduction of a variety of specialty beauty services, including body waxing and self-tanning.

Bangin' Bikini Bods

Even though various decency leagues begged Hollywood not to succumb to the lure of the bikini, the film capital went its own way…right toward the "two-piece bathing suit that reveals everything about a girl except for her mother's maiden name." In addition to Bardot, a number of actresses got their starts or made their marks by donning bikinis.

LEFT & ABOVE

Ursula Andress, the first Bond Girl, here emerges from the sea clad in iconic white bikini and white, webbed knife belt in 1962's *Dr. No*. Forty years later, Halle Berry, in orange bikini and white belt, pays homage to Andress during this recreation of the scene in 2002's *Die Another Day*.

FAR LEFT & LEFT

Ava Gardner poses in the demure two-piece bathing suit that was the precursor of the bikini; exotic dancer Micheline Bernardini models the first official bikini.

135

HOLLYWOOD FASHION | THE NINETEEN SIXTIES

JULIE ANDREWS

Originally labeled saccharinely sweet—possibly due to early roles as a nanny and a nun—Andrews later graduated to edgier parts.

Dame Julie Andrews (1935–) was known for playing morally upright characters in both comedies and musicals. Born in Walton-on-Thames, England, this gifted singer from a vaudeville family began performing as a child. After playing *Cinderella* at London's Paladium, she did *The Boyfriend* on Broadway in 1954. She next played Eliza Doolittle in *My Fair Lady*, one of Broadway's legendary musicals, and followed with *Camelot* with Richard Burton. Warner Bros. passed over her for the screen role of Eliza, which went to Audrey Hepburn, but Andrews got the last laugh. That same year she won the Best Actress Oscar for her delightful turn in Disney's *Mary Poppins* (costume consultant: Tony Walton).

During the 1960s, she made the non-musicals *The Americanization of Emily*, *Torn Curtain*, and *Hawaii*, and the musicals *Thoroughly Modern Millie*, *Darling Lili*, and *Star!* But the film with which she came to be most identified was 1965's blockbuster, *The Sound of Music* (costumes by Dorothy Jeakins).

She played a long-suffering girlfriend in 1979's sexy comedy *10* (costumes by Patricia Edwards) and hit a career high note in 1982 with the gender-bending musical smash *Victor/Victoria* (costumes by Patricia Norris). She appealed to a whole new generation with *The Princess Diaries* in 2001 and *Shrek 2* in 2004.

The actress was married to director Blake Edwards for 41 years until his death. In 1997 she underwent throat surgery and, sadly, lost her singing voice.

MOST FASHIONABLE FILMS
MARY POPPINS (1964)
THE SOUND OF MUSIC (1965)
DARLING LILI (1970)
VICTOR/VICTORIA (1982)

Andrews Style
The world "ladylike" seems as if it were coined for this star, yet she also famously revealed her bosom in the film *S.O.B.*

Signature Look
- Casual, cropped hair
- White or pastel pant suits
- Fringed gowns and satin stoles

ABOVE
Andrews, in a floral, chiffon frock with butterfly sleeves, shares a tender moment with costar Christopher Plummer in the 1965 blockbuster, *The Sound of Music*.

RIGHT
The actress made a comeback of sorts as a down-on-her-luck soprano who cross-dresses her way to success—as seen here wearing evening tails with Robert Preston—in 1982's smash hit, *Victor/Victoria*.

THE NINETEEN SIXTIES | HOLLYWOOD FASHION

FAYE DUNAWAY

One of Hollywood's most striking faces, the actress typically found roles where her looks were less important than her characters.

Faye Dunaway (1941–) excelled at playing intelligent, deeply flawed women, often in historical settings. Born Dorothy Faye Dunaway in Bascom, Florida, Dunaway was a beauty queen who opted for acting over a teaching career. After two years on Broadway, she transitioned to films and in 1967 found the role of a lifetime—1930s' gangster Bonnie Parker in *Bonnie and Clyde* (after Natalie Wood turned down the part). The rollicking tale of America's favorite desperados, who come to a bad end, made Theadora Van Runkle's bias-cut skirts, knit tops, and tilted berets the new rage in women's wear.

Dunaway followed with some lighter fare—the 1968 heist film, *The Thomas Crown Affair*, costarring Steve McQueen (costumes by Van Runkle) and the 1975 spy caper, *Three Days of the Condor*, with Robert Redford—as well as two intense, critically acclaimed films, Roman Polanski's chilling *Chinatown* with Jack Nicholson and 1976's *Network*, for which she won the Oscar playing an icy TV producer (costumes by Theoni V. Aldredge). Dunaway reached the heights of camp playing a spot-on Joan Crawford in *Mommie Dearest* with evocative mid-century fashions by Irene Sharaff.

MOST FASHIONABLE FILMS

BONNIE AND CLYDE (1967)
THE THOMAS CROWN AFFAIR (1968)
CHINATOWN (1974)
THREE DAYS OF THE CONDOR (1975)

Dunaway Style

The actress is credited with popularizing several fashion trends: the gangster chic of Bonnie and Clyde and the "new" corporate uniform of classic silk separates she wore in Network.

Signature Look

- Pencil skirts with tall boots
- Wind-tossed, sun-streaked hair
- Fitted trousers with feminine blouses

ABOVE

Dunaway's character is at the center of the mystery in Roman Polanski's *Chinatown* from 1974. Here, the actress wears a dove gray suit, matching fedora, and ascot blouse with an Art Deco brooch and carries a large clutch bag.

LEFT

In the 1966 heist film, *The Thomas Crown Affair*, Dunaway showcased a number of stylish outfits, including this piping-trimmed minicoat worn with glossy leather boots, pale tights, and a floppy hat. Costar Steve McQueen wears the decade's ubiquitous khaki topcoat.

HOLLYWOOD FASHION | THE NINETEEN SIXTIES

FASHION INFLUENCE
FOREIGN FILMS

Hollywood has always been a sponge when it comes to foreign influences. Even in its infancy, the industry was importing French designers to improve film wardrobe departments. But by the 1930s, Hollywood had surged ahead of most other countries' cinema in terms of technology, costume design, art direction, and distribution (if not in acting, directing, or screenwriting).

It wasn't until after World War II, that Europe and Asia began to break free of the Hollywood template, creating fresh, compelling cinematic genres, among them the new wave in Europe, neorealism in Italy, the nouvelle vague in France, Japan, and Brazil, Kurasowa's new humanism in Japan, Bergman's quest for a dialog with the profound in Scandinavia. Even America's version of cine noir was drawn from German Expressionism.

These edgy new offerings gained many American fans, and suddenly foreign films were in demand in the U.S. Their popularity increased to such a point, that the Motion Picture Academy inaugurated a Best Foreign Language Film award in 1947. But these films did more than introduce new cinematic forms to America, they introduced a freer, more emancipated lifestyle, including a more sensual—and at the same time, less fussy—manner of dressing. America—and her fashion arbiters—was overdue for a sexual revolution, and the films of the less-puritanical Europeans were ready to light the spark.

ABOVE
The 1960 French melodrama, *Breathless*, starred two sexy newcomers, Jean-Paul Belmondo, here in a casual sports suit and fedora, and Jean Seberg, wearing a très gamine outfit of T-shirt and pencil slacks with flats.

RIGHT
Catherine Deneuve, in a scarlet, double-breasted Eisenhower jacket, seems immune to the charms of husband Jean Sorel in Luis Buñuel's 1967 avant-garde drama, *Belle de Jour*. Roger Vivier designed the costumes, including Deneuve's trendsetting "pilgrim" pumps.

> Being an actress is a very physical thing. If I didn't look the way I looked, I would never have started in films.
> CATHERINE DENEUVE

138 1960s

THE NINETEEN SIXTIES | HOLLYWOOD FASHION

TOP LEFT

Marcello Mastroianni, in a tailored tweed jacket, and Anita Ekberg, in a fitted black dress with draped back panels, costarred in Federico Fellini's 1960 Italian classic, *La Dolce Vita*—and proved why European stars set the standard for style.

TOP RIGHT

Melina Mercouri plays a high-spirited Greek prostitute in 1960's *Never on Sunday*. The title song was the first from a foreign film to win Best Original Song at the Oscars.

LEFT

Penelope Cruz, here in *Volver* first attracted attention in a series of films for Spanish director Pedro Almodovar.

139

HOLLYWOOD FASHION | THE NINETEEN SIXTIES

MIA FARROW

This waiflike actress shocked the world as Rosemary and was Gatsby's undoing as Daisy.

Mia Farrow (1945–), with her boyish figure and cropped hair, exemplified the androgynous look popular during the 1960s. Born Maria de Lourdes Villiers Farrow, she was the daughter of actress Maureen O'Sullivan and director John Farrow. She came to prominence as Allison McKenzie in the hugely popular nighttime soap opera, *Peyton Place*. After a short-lived marriage to Frank Sinatra, Farrow refocused on her film career and in 1968 found a memorable role—the hapless target of Satanists in Roman Polanski's *Rosemary's Baby* (costumes by Anthea Sylbert).

She was deemed the perfect Daisy Buchanan in 1974's *The Great Gatsby* (costumes by Theoni V. Aldredge), ushering in a craze for 1920s' attire, including pleated trousers, gauze gowns, and cloche hats. In the 1980s, Farrow became Woody Allen's romantic partner, beginning a screen collaboration that produced more than nine films, including *A Midsummer Night's Sex Comedy*, *Broadway Danny Rose*, *The Purple Rose of Cairo*, *Radio Days*, and *Alice*. *Hannah and Her Sisters*, with Farrow in the title role (costumes by Jeffrey Kurland), went on to win three Academy Awards.

In 1992 a scandal erupted when Allen admitted to a relationship with Farrow's adopted daughter (with former husband Andre Previn) Soon-Yi Previn. Farrow dealt openly with the event in her autobiography, *What Falls Away*. Farrow has been recognized for her ongoing humanitarian work as a Goodwill Ambassador for UNICEF, especially in Darfur and Chad.

ABOVE
Farrow's outfits, like this Peter Pan-collared dress worn with a schoolgirl hat, were intended to make her look extra innocent and virginal in Roman Polanski's 1968 horror classic, *Rosemary's Baby*.

RIGHT
With her fragile features, whispery voice, and the ideal figure for 1920s' styles, Farrow seemed born to play Daisy in 1974's *The Great Gatsby*, here, wearing a gossamer gown and pearls.

MOST FASHIONABLE FILMS

ROSEMARY'S BABY (1968)
THE GREAT GATSBY (1974)
HANNAH AND HER SISTERS (1986)

Farrow Style
As a young actress, she represented her "flower power" generation while displaying a simple, timeless elegance.

Signature Look
• Dark, scooped-neck tops
• A-line shifts
• Pixie haircut

THE NINETEEN SIXTIES | HOLLYWOOD FASHION

ANN-MARGRET

MOST FASHIONABLE FILMS

BYE BYE BIRDIE (1963)
VIVA LAS VEGAS (1964)
THE SWINGER (1966)

Ann-Margret Style

With her shapely figure and dancer's legs, Ann-Margret looked terrific in the skimpiest outfits—something producers took advantage of throughout her career.

Signature Look
- Short shorts or hot pants
- Colorful, midriff-baring tops
- Tight capri or toreador pants

This electric redhead won hearts as the singing and dancing heroine of Bye Bye Birdie—and became an overnight sensation.

Ann-Margret (1941–), in her ruffled midriff tops and stretch pants, epitomized the dance-crazy teens of the 1960s. Born Ann-Margret Olsson in Sweden, the actress's family moved to America when she was five. After making her live TV debut at 16, she began attending Northwestern University, where comedian George Burns discovered her. She ended up with a record deal from RCA and a movie contract at 20th Century-Fox.

1962's *State Fair* earned her a Golden Globe as Most Promising Newcomer, a prediction she lived up to in her next two films. 1963's *Bye Bye Birdie* (with wardrobe by Marjorie Wahl), featuring Ann-Margret as the fan chosen to kiss an Army-bound pop star farewell, was a smash. *Viva Las Vegas* from 1964 (with costumes by Donfeld)—where she held her own against Elvis Presley—established her as a full-fledged teen icon. A series of sexy parts followed, including *Kitten with a Whip*, *The Pleasure Seekers*, and *The Swinger*.

In the 1970s, she took on more substantive roles in the adult melodrama, *Carnal Knowledge* (costumes by Anthea Sylbert), for which she received an Oscar nod, and the thriller, *Magic* (costumes by Ruth Myers).

In 1967 she married TV actor Roger Smith. In 1972, she survived a 22-foot fall from the stage in Lake Tahoe but suffered facial damage and a concussion. The plucky trouper was back performing ten weeks later. Since the 1980s she has worked in both film and TV.

ABOVE

Ann-Margret, in a pale yellow sheath and matching heels, gets down with Elvis Presley in *Viva Las Vegas*.

LEFT

The actress is a symphony of vivid colors, wearing a yellow ruffled blouse and burnt orange skirt, and holding an aqua "Princess" phone, in this playful scene from 1963's *Bye Bye Birdie*.

141

HOLLYWOOD FASHION | THE NINETEEN SIXTIES

MEN OF THE 1960s
THE CINEMA ANTIHERO

> The noir hero is a knight in blood-caked armor. He's dirty and he does his best to deny the fact that he's a hero the whole time.
>
> FRANK MILLER, ARTIST/WRITER/DIRECTOR

The 1960s was an era of actor-driven films, but many of the parts called for characters to be ambivalent, even conflicted about their lives, such as Peter O'Toole in *Lawrence of Arabia* and Dustin Hoffman in *The Graduate*. Heroes' motivations were no longer clear cut; and some protagonists were literally outside the law—as with Warren Beatty in *Bonnie and Clyde* and Paul Newman and Robert Redford in *Butch Cassidy and the Sundance Kid*.

Contemporary films echoed the decade's unrest—and also provided fashion insights. *West Side Story* exposed gang conflicts and at the same time cemented the popularity of tight jeans, chinos, and flounced mambo dresses.

Though few films of this era addressed the counter-culture, the ones that did made fashion waves. *Easy Rider*'s antihero bikers, Peter Fonda and Dennis Hopper, started the craze for "chopper" motorcycles, fringed leather jackets, and fitted biker "leathers." And even though Jon Voight played a hustler in *Midnight Cowboy*, he also popularized Western outerwear.

The Beatles' neatly tailored appearance in *A Hard Day's Night* set off a trend for pipe-stem trouser suits, while their "Sgt. Pepper" look in *Help!* and *Yellow Submarine* sent American youth into military-band jackets, psychedelic shirts, ornate Victorian coats, and striped bell-bottoms.

TOP RIGHT

Lawrence of Arabia, David Lean's epic film—and Best Picture Winner for 1962—portrays the enigmatic man who united the Arab tribes during World War I. Here, Peter O'Toole, in the snow-white robes of a Harith sharif, allies himself with brigand leader Anthony Quinn.

RIGHT

Richard Beymer and George Chikaris as opposing gang members are ready to rumble in a scene from the revolutionary film musical—and Best Picture winner—*West Side Story*.

142 1960s

THE NINETEEN SIXTIES | HOLLYWOOD FASHION

Signature Menswear Looks of the 1960s
- Longer hair and sideburns, facial hair
- Latin- and Italian-influenced business suits
- Suit vests worn without jackets
- Collarless suit jackets
- Narrow ties
- Flared suit trousers
- Bell-bottom jeans
- Tie-dye shirts
- Mixing and matching colors and patterns
- Peace medallions and chunky chain necklaces
- Desert boots

TOP LEFT

One of the most iconic images from the 1960s—Anne Bancroft's outstretched leg lures the callow Dustin Hoffman into an affair in Mike Nichols' groundbreaking coming-of-age tale, *The Graduate* (1967).

TOP RIGHT

Jon Voight, as a male hustler from Texas, and Dustin Hoffman, as a sickly vagrant, both experience the dark side of New York City in 1969's *Midnight Cowboy*, the first R-rated film to win Best Picture.

BOTTOM RIGHT

Lunacy reigns in the war room in Stanley Kubrick's dark antiwar comedy *Dr. Strangelove or: How I Learned to Stop Worrying and Love the Bomb*.

LEFT

Paul Newman, Katherine Ross, and Robert Redford, clad in their finest turn-of-the-century duds—including three-piece suits and bowler hats for the men and a ribbed-satin two-piece dress and elaborate straw and tulle hat for Ross—strike a pose in 1969's comic western, *Butch Cassidy and the Sundance Kid*.

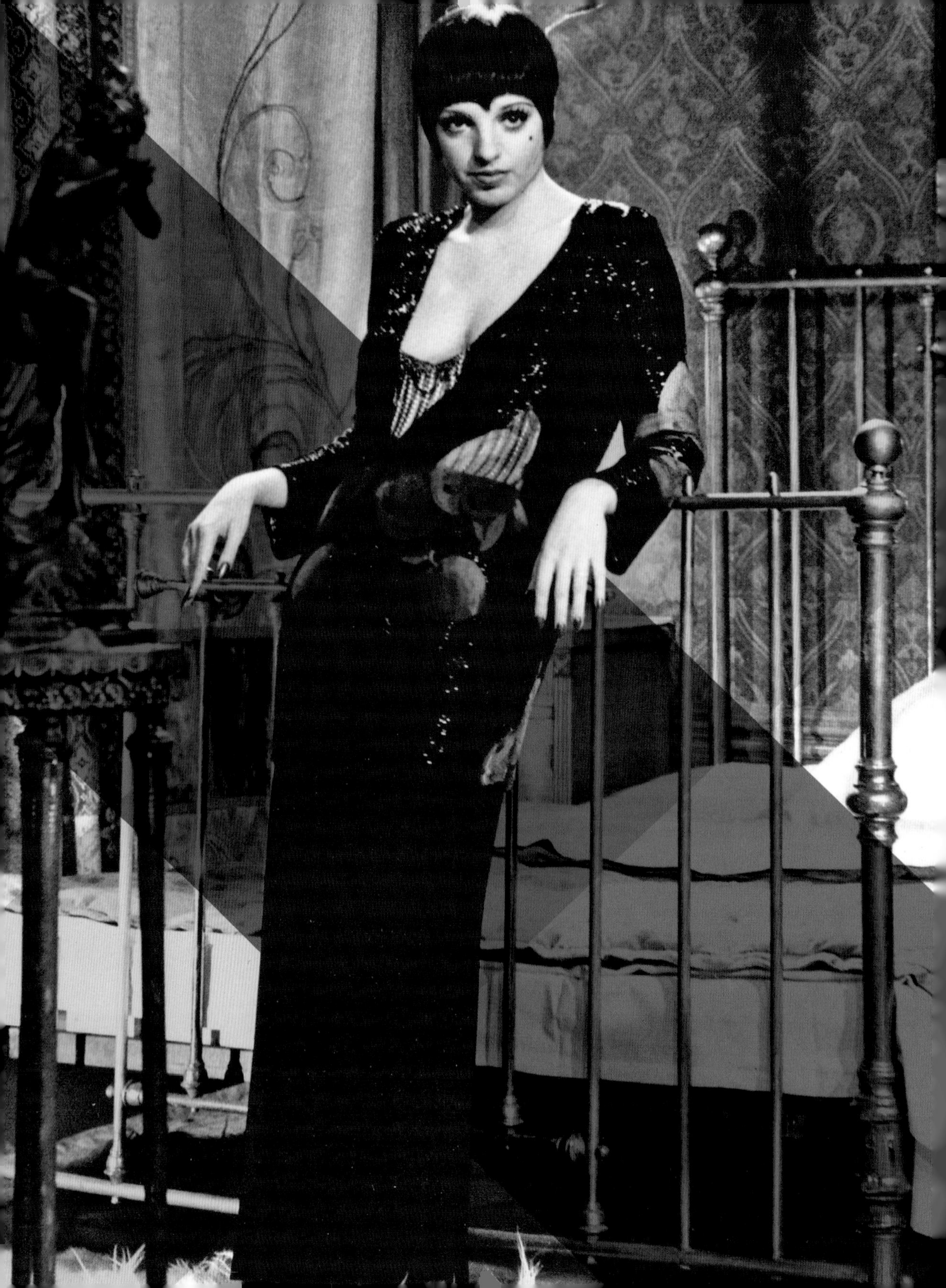

THE NINETEEN SEVENTIES | HOLLYWOOD FASHION

THE NINETEEN SEVENTIES

The decade was a fashion whirlwind, and Hollywood reflected the frenzy. Trendy styles came and went rapidly—as the unisex look of *Annie Hall* vied with a glamorous new romanticism inspired by films like *The Great Gatsby*. Designers Halston and Bob Mackie gained fame through megastar clients like Liz, Liza, and Barbra. And while some fashion holdovers from the 1960s remained popular, the disco dance club style of pastel suits and clingy dresses soon swept the country. Meanwhile, workout gear and leg warmers became street wear, African-American—inspired fashions grew increasingly popular, and torn T-shirts, frayed jeans, and ripped leather jackets reflected the influence of punk music.

Any list of the top films of this "decade of the blockbuster" seems to overflow with male-dominated action or buddy pictures—*Godfathers I* and *II*, ushering in the gangster look, *Chinatown*, *American Graffiti*, *The Deerhunter*, *Serpico*, *Magnum Force*, *The French Connection*, *Jaws*, *Mash*, *One Flew Over the Cuckoo's Nest*, *Rocky*, *Taxi Driver*, and *Saturday Night Fever*, and male-dominated science fiction flicks—*Star Wars*, *A Clockwork Orange*, *The Shining*, *Close Encounters of the Third Kind*, and *Young Frankenstein*.

Memorable films featuring female protagonists (and in some cases, starting fashion trends) include *Klute*, *Annie Hall*, *The Exorcist*, *Shampoo*, *Alice Doesn't Live Here Anymore*, *Cabaret*, *Network*, notable both for Faye Dunaway and Supporting Oscar-winner Beatrice Straight, and finally, *Alien*, with Sigourney Weaver kicking butt and popularizing the industrial jumpsuit and cropped hair.

145

HOLLYWOOD FASHION | **THE NINETEEN SEVENTIES**

BARBRA STREISAND

MOST FASHIONABLE FILMS
FUNNY GIRL (1968)
HELLO DOLLY! (1969)
ON A CLEAR DAY YOU CAN SEE FOREVER (1970)
THE WAY WE WERE (1973)
THE MIRROR HAS TWO FACES (1996)

This actress is living proof that a talented performer can transcend unorthodox looks and become a world-class beauty, a recording superstar, and a screen legend.

Barbra Streisand (1942–), like many Hollywood icons, has frequently played herself on film...or at least a version of herself that her earliest movies introduced: The offbeat young woman with a will of iron.

By the time she was 21, Streisand had performed in summer stock, in nightclubs, and on TV variety shows, and even recorded a Grammy-winning album. After starring as Fanny Brice in the 1964 Broadway hit, *Funny Girl*, Streisand expected Columbia to cast her in the film version. The producers wanted a star, however, and were considering Shirley MacLaine. Ray Stark, Fanny Brice's son-in-law and the producer of the stage play, insisted on Streisand, who more than lived up to his expectations. The 1968 film, with costumes by Irene Sharaff, earned Streisand her first Oscar and made her an overnight sensation. Columbia got its star.

Next, the actress was slightly miscast as a too-youthful Dolly Levi in 1969's *Hello Dolly!* (Sharaff again), but bounced back with a madcap performance in the 1972 screwball comedy, *What's Up, Doc?* (women's costumes by Nancy McArdle). She wrung hearts in the bittersweet 1973 fable, *The Way We Were* (costumes by Dorothy Jeakins and Moss Mabry) and reprised Fanny Brice in *Funny Lady* from 1975 (costumes by Ray Aghayan and Bob Mackie). With the 1976 rock musical, *A Star is Born* (costumes by Seth Banks and Shirlee Strahm), Streisand crossed over to the youth market, gaining new fans and sporting the short, curly perm that became the rage in America, even for men! The film netted her and cocomposer Paul Williams the Oscar for Best Song—"Evergreen."

Streisand's "project of the heart" was the 1983 musical *Yentl*, which she starred in, cowrote, directed, and produced—a Hollywood first for a female. The film, about a Jewish woman who masquerades as a man to attend yeshiva, earned her Golden Globes for Best Director and Best Picture.

The 1990s brought two strong performances, a therapist in *The Prince of Tides*, 1991 (costumes by Ruth Morley); and an ugly duckling in *The Mirror Has Two Faces*, 1996 (costumes by Theoni V. Aldredge).

Notoriously afflicted with stage fright, the actress still performs occasional concerts. Her most recent film appearance has been in Ben Stiller's *Meet the Parents* series. Streisand married actor Elliot Gould in 1963 and they had a son, Jason. She had a long-time relationship with entrepreneur Jon Peters; and has been married to actor James Brolin since 1998.

ABOVE
The Way We Were from 1973 became a sentimental favorite with Streisand's fans. It allowed her to glory in classic late 1940s' costumes and win the heart—for a time—of Robert Redford.

RIGHT
Wearing possibly the most blatant negligee ever designed, Streisand prepares to share George Segal's cramped apartment in comic romp, *The Owl and the Pussycat* (1970).

FULL PAGE
Streisand reflected the style of the time with an open-back dress, platform heels, and permed hair, in 1976's *A Star is Born* with Kris Kristofferson.

146 1970s

> I arrived in Hollywood without having my nose fixed, my teeth capped, or my name changed. That is very gratifying to me.
> BARBRA STREISAND

Streisand Style

Through the many phases of her career, Streisand has always appeared flawlessly turned out from hair, clothing, and makeup to her long, elegant fingernails (often featured in film closeups). She is known for wearing exotic turbans, headdresses, and beaded chokers to accentuate her "Egyptian" profile.

Signature Look
- Empire-waist gowns (which she once bragged about buying wholesale)
- Tea-length dresses or pants with open blazers
- Sporty separates worn with a frosted pageboy

HOLLYWOOD FASHION | THE NINETEEN SEVENTIES

JILL CLAYBURGH

The modern women she portrayed may have been conflicted, but they also managed to be both sleekly urban and sexually earthy.

Jill Clayburgh (1944–2010) became a placeholder for the stylish, intelligent, liberated, slightly self-deprecating women of the 1970s. Born in New York City to a wealthy family, she attended prep schools and Sarah Lawrence College, where she decided on a career in acting. After two Broadway successes, *The Rothschilds* and *Pippin*, she made a move to films and was featured in 1976's comic thriller, *The Silver Streak* and 1977's football comedy, *Semi-Tough*.

Clayburgh's breakout role as a divorcée determined to live life on her own terms in 1978's *An Unmarried Woman* (costumes by Albert Wolsky) won her the Oscar. She was also nominated the following year for *Starting Over* with Burt Reynolds (costumes by John Boxer). In the 1980s she made *It's My Turn* with Michael Douglas (costumes by Ruth Myers), the last film in her "independent woman" trilogy, and then played real life Valium addict Barbara Gordon in *I'm Dancing As Fast As I Can*. She made few notable films after that due to poor script choices.

Clayburgh passed away in 2010 after battling leukemia, leaving behind many saddened fans—including her close friend, Meryl Streep.

ABOVE
Clayburgh relaxes before the mayhem begins in 1976's *Silver Streak*.

RIGHT
Clayburgh plays the bride to Burt Reynolds football star in 1977's *Semi-Tough*.

MOST FASHIONABLE FILMS
GABLE AND LOMBARD (1976)
SILVER STREAK (1976)
SEMI-TOUGH (1977)
AN UNMARRIED WOMAN (1978)
STARTING OVER (1979)
IT'S MY TURN (1980)

Clayburgh Style
The tall, ash-blonde actress, who considered herself a changeable "putty" face, always looked casually pulled together in preppy classics.

Signature Look
- Tailored separates
- Little black dresses
- Tastefully elegant gowns

THE NINETEEN SEVENTIES | HOLLYWOOD FASHION

DIANA ROSS

MOST FASHIONABLE FILMS
LADY SINGS THE BLUES (1972)
MAHOGANY (1975)
THE WIZ (1978)

Ross Style
Ross became a fashion icon early in her career, first for the highly groomed "girl group" look—dressy gowns, long gloves, lots of eyeliner, and stylish wigs—and then for going natural, letting her hair grow out, and wearing ethnic-influenced clothing.

Signature Look
- Exotic wigs and hair extensions
- Ethnic ensembles
- Dramatic gowns

This Motown diva left the world of pop music for a brief film career.

Diana Ross (1944–) played gifted women trying to make their way in a harsh world. Born in Detroit, Michigan, she was of Native-American and African-American descent. Ross started her career as a singer (later lead singer) in the Motown supergroup, The Supremes, and she eventually went solo. Her vivid makeup, designer wigs, and glittery stage costumes soon became the go-to look for black women who wanted to dress up—a retro style that was revived by the 2006 film, *Dreamgirls*.

Her first motion picture, 1972's *Lady Sings the Blues*, a film biography of music legend Billie Holiday (with costumes by Ray Aghayan and Bob Mackie), gained Ross an Oscar nomination for Best Actress, and the film's soundtrack made it to #1 in the U.S. Her second movie, *Mahogany*, in 1975, explored the world of fashion design, with clothing created by Ross herself. Although the film's reception was lukewarm, Ross's title song became a #1 single.

1978 saw her starring in a film version of the Broadway play, *The Wiz*, a remake of *The Wizard of Oz* (costumes by Tony Walton and Miles White). In spite of featuring two major pop stars—Ross as Dorothy and Michael Jackson as the Scarecrow—the film stumbled badly at the box office. Some critics insisted Ross was simply too old for the role. *The Wiz* was her final film.

In 1981, Ross had a hit with the title song from the film *Endless Love*, penned by Lionel Richie. In 1993, *The Guinness Book of World Records* declared her the most successful female singer of all time.

ABOVE

Ross portrayed singer Billie Holiday in 1972's *Lady Sings the Blues*. Here, Ross performs wearing Holiday's trademark gardenia in her hair and a beaded 1930s' dinner dress.

LEFT

In 1975's *Mahogany* Ross played an aspiring designer from the slums of Chicago.

HOLLYWOOD FASHION | **THE NINETEEN SEVENTIES**

ALI MACGRAW

After playing the ultimate coed—leggy, smart-mouthed, and adorable—this actress went on to live her own Love Story...twice.

Ali MacGraw (1939–) was a natural at playing arch, intriguing women of intelligence and humor. Born in Pound Ridge, NY, to commercial artist parents, she was a bright girl who attended Wellesley College and then spent six years at *Harper's Bazaar*. While working as a photographer's stylist, the leggy brunette was recruited as a fill-in model for a photo shoot. After appearing in a number of commercials, MacGraw was cast in the film version of Phillip Roth's *Goodbye, Columbus*.

Emboldened by her positive critical notices, and a Golden Globe for her performance, MacGraw asked Paramount Studios production head Robert Evans to buy a script for her, a story, she said, that had made her weep. Evans, who was smitten with MacGraw—and would subsequently marry her—finally agreed, even though the script's subject was considered "mawkish."

The script was for a movie called *Love Story*. MacGraw and costar Ryan O'Neal had entire audiences weeping by the end of the film. In their classic preppy clothes (designed by Alice Manougian Martin and Pearl Somner), they embodied Ivy League romance and youthful aspiration cut short. Both she and O'Neal were catapulted into mega stardom and were nominated for Academy Awards; McGraw received her second Golden Globe for playing the doomed Jennie. A poignant phrase from the film, "Love means never having to say you're sorry," entered the American mainstream.

MacGraw and Evans had a son, Josh, in 1971. In 1972, McGraw began filming *The Getaway* with Steve McQueen, Hollywood's "King of Cool." MacGraw, who felt neglected by Evans during the filming, began to fall under McQueen's spell. By the end of the shoot, they were lovers. She spent a tempestuous five years with McQueen, ultimately divorcing him. She eagerly sought film projects, but since McQueen had insisted she not work during their marriage, her box-office appeal had faded and she had trouble regaining the momentum of her early career. During the 1980s she made the comedy *Just Tell Me What You Want* with Alan King, and found work on TV, including a stint on *Dynasty* (she was a victim of the infamous "Moldavian wedding massacre"), and a starring role in *The Winds of War* miniseries.

The 1990s saw her interest in Hatha Yoga expand to a video, "Ali MacGraw, Yoga Mind and Body," which according to *Vanity Fair* magazine was greatly responsible for the increased popularity of yoga in America. In 1991 MacGraw was chosen as one of the "50 Most Beautiful People in the World," and in 2008 *GQ* magazine placed her on their list of the "Sexiest 25 Women in Film Ever." A staunch animal rights activist, MacGraw currently lives in Santa Fe, New Mexico. She settled there permanently in 1994 when her rental home in Malibu burned down.

MOST FASHIONABLE FILMS

GOODBYE, COLUMBUS (1969)
THE GETAWAY (1972)
CONVOY (1978)
JUST TELL ME WHAT YOU WANT (1980)

ABOVE
The bittersweet coming-of-age film, *Goodbye, Columbus* from 1969, gave audiences their first taste of MacGraw—seen here in casual mode wearing white duck trousers and a striped tank top.

TOP RIGHT
Cool coed meets hockey jock—MacGraw in a peacoat and costar Ryan O'Neal in a tweed jacket and scarf cross the Harvard Campus in the 1970 blockbuster romance, *Love Story*.

FULL PAGE
It was while filming *The Getaway* in 1972 that MacGraw—here wearing a white wrap dress with woven hip belt—fell in love with costar Steve McQueen.

> **You know, the fashion business is this legendary repository of young girls on their way to getting husbands. I really wanted to work.**
> ALI MACGRAW

MacGraw Style
The actress's distinct flair for fashion was remarked on even when she was a photographer's assistant. Today, she still carries off capes and boots and chunky Southwestern jewelry and makes the look completely her own.

Signature Look
- Tweedy separates worn with dark tights
- Knit hats pulled down low
- Thick eyebrows and slightly crooked front teeth

HOLLYWOOD FASHION | THE NINETEEN SEVENTIES

SUSAN SARANDON

Even as Susan Sarandon evolved from cult-film heroine to respected Oscar winner, she always marched to her own beat.

Susan Sarandon (1946–) often portrays sexually liberated women who feel like outsiders. Born Susan Abigail Tomalin in New York City, she started out as a Ford model. Her first standout performance was as Janet Weiss in 1975's camp film *The Rocky Horror Picture Show* (costumes by Sue Blane). She gained exposure in *Pretty Baby* and *The King of the Gypsies*, and was finally accorded critical approval in 1980 with the Louis Malle crime drama, *Atlantic City*, costarring Burt Lancaster (costumes by François Barbeau).

The 1980s saw *Tempest*, *The Hunger*, *Compromising Positions*, and *The Witches of Eastwick*, but it was in 1988's *Bull Durham* that the actress came into her own, playing baseball guru Annie Savoy in retro 1940s' outfits (by Louise Frogley). She sparred romantically with Kevin Costner, but in real life fell for Tim Robbins… beginning a 21-year relationship.

In 1990's *White Palace*, she was a waitress entangled with a young widower, and in 1991 she became a feminist icon in the morality tale, *Thelma and Louise* (costumes by Elizabeth McBride). The film earned her the first of four Academy Award nominations that decade—1992's *Lorenzo's Oil* earned her another, as did 1994's *The Client*. (That year also saw her as Marmee in the successful *Little Women* remake.) In 1996, she won the Oscar as a compassionate nun in *Dead Man Walking*—and accepted the award in a dramatic copper Dolce and Gabbana gown, which she later donated to the Metropolitan Museum of Art's Costume Institute.

The actress is a long-time supporter of progressive political policies and an activist for human rights.

MOST FASHIONABLE FILMS
THE ROCKY HORROR PICTURE SHOW (1975)
THE WITCHES OF EASTWICK (1987)
BULL DURHAM (1988)
THE BANGER SISTERS (2002)

Sarandon Style
Age has barely diminished her sexual appeal, as her many recent red-carpet appearances can prove.

Signature Look
- Off-the-shoulder tops
- Pencil skirts and stilettos
- Dressy pants suits with classic lines

ABOVE
Sarandon, looking major league in a white off-the-shoulder cowl-neck sweater and matching knit skirt, offers to coach minor league catcher Kevin Costner in 1988's popular baseball comedy, *Bull Durham*.

RIGHT
Sarandon shows she can dress up a little in an embroidered white shirt while enjoying cocktails, during a gritty cross-country journey with Geena Davis in 1991's *Thelma and Louise*.

THE NINETEEN SEVENTIES | HOLLYWOOD FASHION

DIANE KEATON

This quirky actress started a worldwide fashion movement with her eclectic menswear look.

Diane Keaton (1946–) is known for playing slightly offbeat intellectuals with an idiosyncratic fashion sense. Born Diane Hall in Los Angeles, she studied drama first at Santa Ana College and then at the Neighborhood Playhouse in New York. In 1972, she was cast in Woody Allen's stage production of *Play it Again, Sam*, and the two were soon romantically involved. She appeared with him in the film version of the play, as well as in *Manhattan*, *Sleeper*, and *Love and Death*. She won an Oscar for Allen's *Annie Hall*, which also went on to win Best Picture. Meanwhile, she was also getting dramatic roles in *The Godfather* saga and *Looking for Mr. Goodbar*, which earned her a Golden Globe nomination.

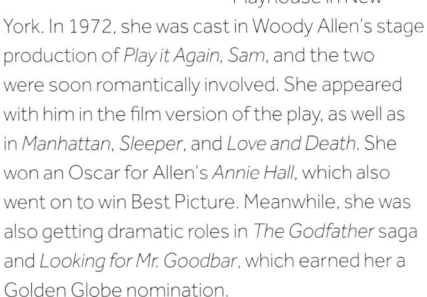

Keaton was later involved with actor-director Warren Beatty and made *Reds* with him, earning both Oscar and Golden Globe nominations for herself. She continued to make quality films like 1987's *Baby Boom* (costumes by Susan Becker), but her career really rebounded in the 1990s with the *Father of the Bride* comedies and the smash hit chick flick, *The First Wives Club*.

MOST FASHIONABLE FILMS
THE GODFATHER (1972)
ANNIE HALL (1977)
REDS (1981)
THE FIRST WIVES CLUB (1996)

Keaton Style
The actress's mother always told her to express herself through clothing and Keaton's peculiar mix-and-match style, so popular in the 1970s, can still be seen today in some versions of Japanese Harajuku fashions.

Signature Look
- Funky thrift-shop ensembles
- Fedora hats
- Sleek, monochromatic pants suits

ABOVE
Keaton, here in a 1950s'-style polka-dot dress and straw hat, gained critical attention as the emotionally torn wife of Mafia scion Al Pacino in *The Godfather*.

LEFT
Keaton, Bette Midler, and Goldie Hawn bonded over having all turned 50 when they costarred in the 1996 revenge comedy, *The First Wives Club*. Here, they celebrate the opening of their women's crisis center in white evening suits.

HOLLYWOOD FASHION | THE NINETEEN SEVENTIES

FASHION INFLUENCE
ANNIE HALL

> Leave her. She's a genius. Let her wear what she wants.
> WOODY ALLEN

ABOVE

In *Annie Hall*, Keaton's idiosyncratic clothing style is clearly in evidence. She combines an Oxford shirt, menswear vest, long tie, and baggy khaki trousers with a felt hat. Woody Allen sticks to his usual understated preppy look.

While shooting his 1977 film, *Annie Hall*, actor-director-screenwriter Woody Allen intended to go "deeper" into the story than he normally did, in part by refining the humor and not just clowning around for laughs.

He hoped that other values would emerge from the film that would be "nourishing and interesting for the audience." The movie succeeded beyond his wildest expectations, becoming a box office hit and winning Academy Awards for Best Picture, Best Director, Best Screenplay, and Best Actress for Diane Keaton. But something else emerged from the film and quickly spread beyond the screen…an eclectic, self-expressive style of dressing that, to some extent, women have never completely relinquished.

THE NINETEEN SEVENTIES | HOLLYWOOD FASHION

Diane Keaton gets to take complete credit for the iconic look. The clothing she wore in the film was from her own closet. Yet when she reported to the set, the wardrobe mistress took one look at her and complained, "She can't wear that." But Allen, who had written the role specifically for Keaton, replied, "Leave her. She's a genius… let her wear what she wants."

Keaton has at times explained the look as the result of her own neurotic desire to cover up as much skin as possible. She credits her mother with encouraging her to express her own personal style with clothing and accessories.

Variations of the *Annie Hall* style have been worn by Marianne Faithfull, Brigitte Bardot, Sienna Miller, Kate Moss, and Rachel Bilson.

ABOVE & BOTTOM LEFT

Kate Moss and Rachel Bilson, both wearing tuxedoes on the red carpet, rock the menswear look popularized by Keaton.

TOP LEFT

Keaton in a double-breasted white pin-stripe suit, pink tie, and a white version of her *Annie Hall* bowler hat arrives at the White House Correspondents Dinner in April 2012.

TOP RIGHT

Keaton sports a formal Ralph Lauren suit, her *Annie Hall* bowler, spectator pumps, and gray gloves at the 76th Academy Awards.

HOLLYWOOD FASHION | THE NINETEEN SEVENTIES

BO DEREK

Bo Derek made only one significant film, but her appearance was so provocative it cemented her status as a love goddess across the globe.

Bo Derek (1956–) played sun-kissed beach blondes like nobody before or since. Born Mary Cathleen Collins in Long Beach, California, her mother worked for Ann-Margret. "Cathy" was discovered backstage at one of the star's Las Vegas concerts at age 16 and wed actor John Derek when she was 20. Her first notable film was in the Jaws clone *Orca*, but even bigger things were in store for her.

In Blake Edwards' comedy, *10*, Dudley Moore's middle-aged movie composer is transfixed by the sight of a young woman on the way to her wedding. For the pivotal bride role, Edwards found a newcomer who was both blushing and nubile—Cathy Collins, now christened Bo Derek. But it was her later appearance on a Mexican beach wearing long, blonde cornrow braids and an eye-popping saffron bathing suit that set audiences aflame. The film, which showcased Ms. Derek's playful persona as well as her physical charms, became a huge hit and made her an international sex symbol.

Unfortunately, most of John Derek's subsequent film choices for his wife, including *Tarzan the Ape Man* and *Bolero*, were panned and damaged her career. Ms. Derek still occasionally makes films and TV movies, but her main focus now is as an activist for horse welfare and as national honorary chairperson for Veterans' Affairs National Rehabilitation Special Events.

MOST FASHIONABLE FILMS
10 (1979)
TARZAN THE APE MAN (1981)
BOLERO (1984)

Derek Style
Even though her film career faded, the actress remained a sex symbol. With her ash-blonde hair and stunning figure, she continues to elicit male admiration at the Kentucky Derby or on the red carpet.

Signature Look
- Long cornrows embellished with beads and shells
- Sheer, flirty dresses
- Ethnic-style skirts and blouses

ABOVE
In the 1979 comedy that made her an international sensation, Bo Derek, here in her iconic ocher bathing suit and cornrow braids, surely deserved a rating of *10*.

RIGHT
In 1981's *Tarzan the Ape Man*, Derek found a jungle love and cavorted in the water in a sheer Victorian-style dress.

THE NINETEEN SEVENTIES | HOLLYWOOD FASHION

LIZA MINNELLI

MOST FASHIONABLE FILMS
CABARET (1972)
LUCKY LADY (1975)
NEW YORK, NEW YORK (1977)

Minnelli Style
The actress has always been more of a chance-taker than her mother when it comes to fashion and is not afraid to be labeled kooky or outrageous.

Signature Look
- Jet-black hair in a shaggy bob
- Hip-length, blousy tops with stretch pants
- Black, knee-high boots

This talented dynamo—the daughter of an entertainment superstar—fought to gain her own brand of fame.

Liza Minnelli (1946–) often plays eccentric or dysfunctional women who manage to maintain a sense of hope. The daughter of Judy Garland and director Vincente Minnelli, the actress, who was born in Los Angeles, debuted on the New York stage when only 16. A year later her mother featured her in a concert at the London Palladium, where Minnelli impressed the audience—and met her first husband Australian singer, Peter Allen. In 1965 she became the youngest actress to win a Tony for her *Flora, the Red Menace*.

Early films like *The Sterile Cuckoo* got her noticed, but it wasn't until her heart-wrenching performance as Sally Bowles in 1972's *Cabaret* (costumes by Charlotte Flemming) that she became an international star—and won the Best Actress Oscar. She appeared in the popular comedy *Arthur* and in Martin Scorsese's retro film, *New York, New York*, but had trouble finding star vehicles. So she switched gears and moved to the concert stage and to TV, where she scored big on variety shows and with her own special "Liza with a Z."

Minnelli is that rare entertainer who has won the Oscar, the Tony, the Emmy and the Grammy. Like her mother, she is prone to addictions and has often been in rehab. With her large gay fan base, she is a favorite subject for impersonation by drag queens.

ABOVE

Minnelli in full stage show gown from 1977's *New York, New York*.

LEFT

The 1972 musical, *Cabaret*, furnished a perfect role for the actress—the conflicted, damaged entertainer, Sally Bowles—seen here on the Kit Kat Club's stage in bowler hat, halter vest, tap pants, and garter belt.

157

HOLLYWOOD FASHION | THE NINETEEN SEVENTIES

FASHION INFLUENCE
DISCO

The image was indelible—John Travolta undulating rhythmically along a Brooklyn street swinging a can of paint to the sound of The Bee Gees in 1977's *Saturday Night Fever*. In this disco-crazy decade, nearly every moment could be an opportunity to "do a little dance." Later, Travolta's Tony Manero dons his white, three-piece suit and platform shoes and struts into the local discotheque, where the hardware clerk now rules the dance floor.

The following year, 1978, Donna Summer, the "Queen of Disco" herself, left the recording studio for the film studio to appear in *Thank God It's Friday*. Produced at the height of the disco craze, the film features Summer performing "Last Dance," which won the Academy Award for Best Song in 1979.

Ballet Staple Hits the Dance Club
The traditional ballerina's leotard became an important female fashion accessory in the mid-1970s, and remained in style throughout the decade. Celebrities—including Joni Mitchell, Cher, and even Rod Stewart—regularly appeared wearing leotards as tops. The trend was abetted by an extensive advertising campaign by Danskin that promoted their leotards and tights as "not just for dancing." But by the late 1970s, the leotard had also become a staple of the disco dance scene, where flexibility and ease of movement were important. The leotard's popularity was still climbing at the end of the decade...and it exploded with the arrival of the aerobics craze in the early 1980s.

Roller Disco
An extension of the disco dance movie, roller disco films briefly appeared in theaters to capitalize on a short-lived roller-skating craze. Roller disco also spawned its own style notes—it featured all kinds of dancewear but added sportier touches, such as tiny satin running shorts (for both sexes), colorful knee and elbow pads, tube socks, and sweatbands.

The Look for Her
Stretch fabrics like spandex and lurex were everywhere, used for tube tops, wrap skirts, hot pants, supershort shorts, or miniskirts. Fabrics like lamé were commonplace. Wide expanses of shoulder and long lines of exposed legs were the preferred silhouette of the disco era. Belts, often metallic or sequined, were important accessories. Hair was big, worn in cascading waves or full Afro style, often with a matching or contrasting scarf tied around the head to complete the look. Of course, platform shoes were de rigueur, though some smart women adopted the "character" shoes worn by stage dancers, while others opted for precarious-but-sexy strappy stilettos.

ABOVE
Roller Boogie, from 1979, featured Linda Blair, whose abbreviated skating costumes attracted a lot of male viewers to the film.

ABOVE RIGHT
Disco fever begat roller dancing, which led to novelty films like 1979's *Skatetown, USA*. Cast members, including Maureen McCormick (center) and Patrick Swayze (left), wore glammed-up sportswear with a disco sheen.

BELOW RIGHT
1998's *The Last Days of Disco*, with Chloë Sevigny and Kate Beckinsale brought back the music and the fashion of disco's heyday.

THE NINETEEN SEVENTIES | HOLLYWOOD FASHION

The Look for Him

Suits, often made of polyester double knit, had wide legs and wide lapels, and while the color choices were wild and varied, white suits were by far the most popular. Shirts were made of stretch materials, such as Qiana, generally in bold prints or vibrant solids, and were worn half unbuttoned so that the chest was visible and the long collars could jut out over the jacket collar. Pants were high-waisted, very tight on top, and then flared from the knee down. Platform shoes and a heavy gold neck chain completed the look.

ABOVE

In *Thank God It's Friday* (1978), Donna Summer plays Nicole, who dreams of becoming a disco star. Summer shows off a lot of leg in her side-split sequin-shot wrap skirt. Her look, copied in discotheques everywhere, featured glitter and shine from the top of her wild waves of hair to the tips of her rhinestone-buckled platforms.

LEFT

John Travolta busts his signature—now iconic—move in his white three-piece suit beside partner Karen Lynn Gorney in 1977's *Saturday Night Fever*. Male disco fans all wanted to look like Travolta and they weren't afraid of wearing body-hugging polyester to get it right.

159

HOLLYWOOD FASHION | THE NINETEEN SEVENTIES

MEN OF THE 1970s
EDGY ACTORS AND MEN OF ACTION

No, Jack Nicholson was NOT in every movie made during the 1970s, though it might have seemed that way to some moviegoers. The laconic, grin-meister starred in at least 15 films, including *Five Easy Pieces*, *Chinatown*, *The Shining*, and *One Flew Over the Cuckoo's Nest*, which earned him the Academy Award for Best Actor. The film, which is set in an antiseptic, neutral-colored mental institution actually inspired a 2007 layout, "Fashion Models Enter Rehab" in Italian *Vogue*.

Gangsters, Grifters, and Graffiti

The cast of *The Godfather*, Marlon Brando, Al Pacino, James Caan, and Robert De Niro, reinvented the gangster look. John Travolta in *Saturday Night Fever* made it acceptable for men to be peacocks again, and then gave new life to the 1950s' "hoodlum" style in *Grease*. The cast of *American Graffiti*, including Ron Howard, Richard Dreyfuss, and Harrison Ford, recreated the iconic styles of the early 1960s, the last years of American innocence, according to director George Lucas, before the Kennedy assassination. Con men Paul Newman and Robert Redford in *The Sting* (and Redford in *The Great Gatsby*) brought back the tailored, pin-stripe suits, suspenders, fat ties, and fedora hats of the 1930s.

ABOVE

In 1974's brilliant *Chinatown*, Jack Nicholson, here wearing a cream-colored suit and graphic tie, emulates the great 1930s' movie detectives when he becomes involved in a murder stemming from water rights outside Los Angeles.

RIGHT

The Rocky franchise—six movies and counting—which got its start in 1976, revived the once-popular boxing film and made Sylvester Stallone, with his pork pie-hat and fingerless gloves, into a style icon.

THE NINETEEN SEVENTIES | HOLLYWOOD FASHION

Signature Menswear Looks of the 1970s
- Three-piece polyester suits
- Wide lapels
- Heavy gold chains
- Bell-bottom trousers
- Wide-leg trousers
- Platform shoes
- T-shirts with iron-on decals
- Painter's pants
- Long fur coats
- Puffy ski jackets
- Frye Western boots
- Cowboy hats

TOP

Best Picture Winner, 1973's *The Sting*, with Paul Newman and Robert Redford, was an example of the quality period films being made during this decade.

BOTTOM LEFT

American Graffiti, from 1973, captured the clothing styles and youth culture of the early 1960s in America, with its souped-up cars, and nights spent cruising down Main Street looking for action. Here, Paul Le Mat shows off his ride to Cindy Williams and Ron Howard.

BOTTOM RIGHT

In 1975's *Jaws*, a trio of men—Roy Scheider, Richard Dreyfuss, and Robert Shaw—bond while doing battle with a mammoth shark. The film popularized nautical New England clothing.

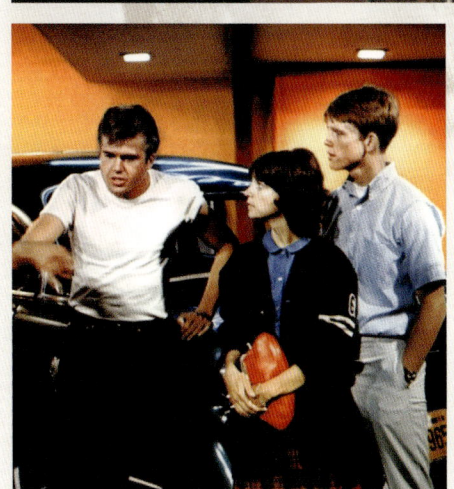

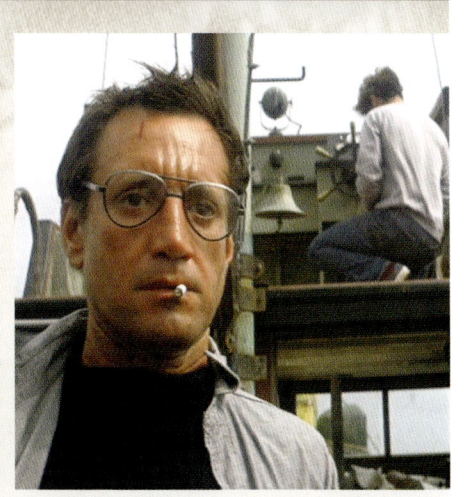

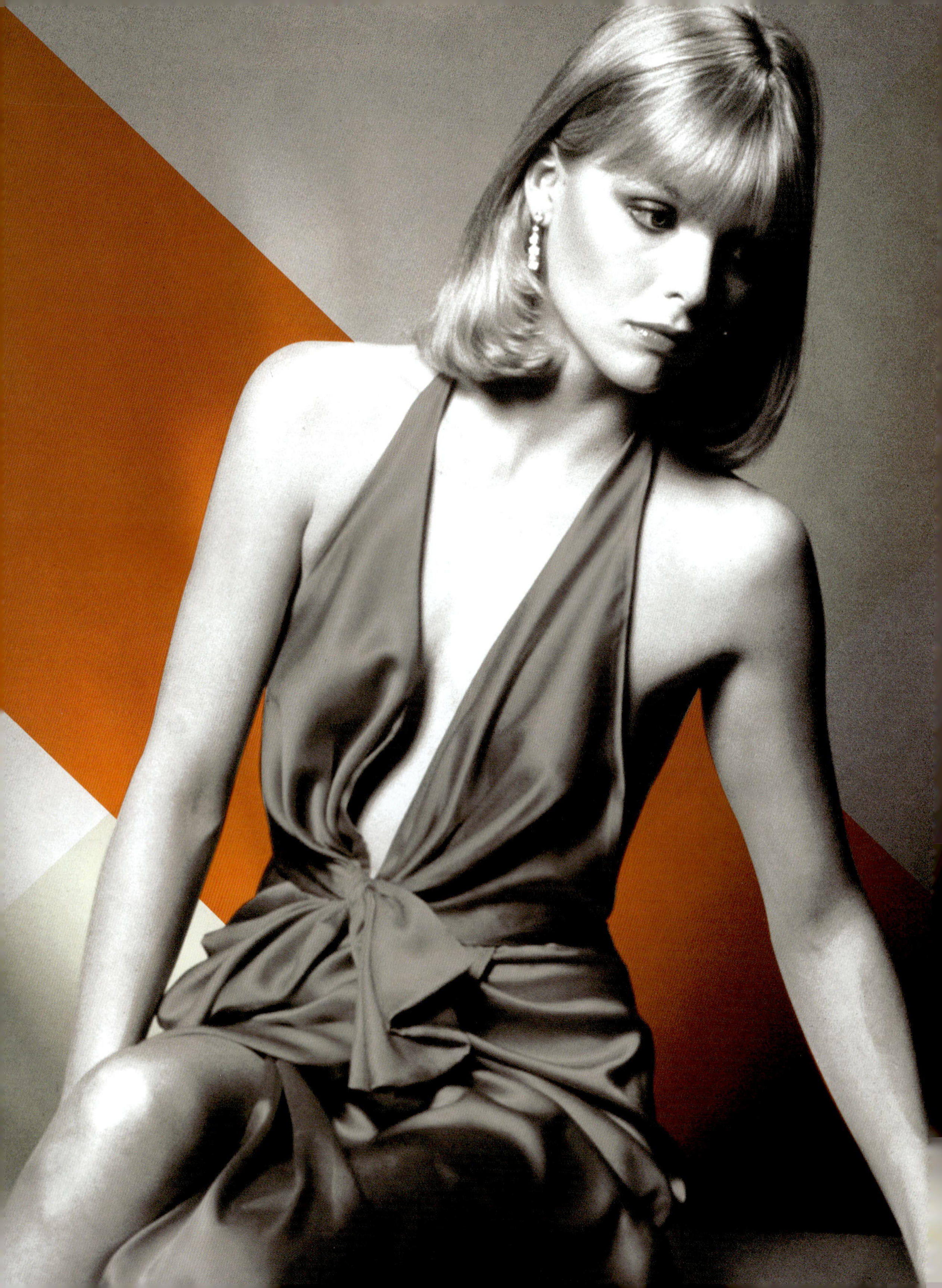

THE NINETEEN EIGHTIES

During the 1980s, Hollywood continued to focus attention on the blockbuster, with offerings like *E.T. the Extra-Terrestrial*, two *Star Wars* sequels, and the manic *Ghostbusters*. With the success of *Back to the Future*, *Animal House*, and *Raiders of the Lost Ark*, retro styles were suddenly all the rage for teens and young adults.

Perhaps the biggest fashion influence of the decade was the advent of MTV on cable television. Music had always had a huge effect on how Americans thought of themselves culturally, but now they were able to watch—and copy the styles of—pop icons in music videos. Hollywood hopped on the youth music bandwagon with *Flashdance*, *Ferris Bueller's Day Off*, and *The Breakfast Club*.

Dance clubs popped up everywhere, and it suddenly felt like everybody could be a star. Hollywood fashionistas geared up with outrageous clothing meant for stealing the spotlight—brightly colored jumpsuits sporting wide shoulder pads, stiletto heels, big fluffy hair, glitter mousse, and banana clips, oversized sweaters, acid-washed jeans with rhinestones, fingerless gloves, neon jewelry, and gaudy clutch handbags. In fact, the only gal in Tinseltown who was still trying to cultivate a classic look was a man—Dustin Hoffman in *Tootsie*.

HOLLYWOOD FASHION | THE NINETEEN EIGHTIES

JESSICA LANGE

After escaping the "bad-career-move" clutches of *King Kong*, this actress came roaring back in complex, demanding roles.

Jessica Lange (1949–) exemplifies the delicate-looking female with a backbone of steel. Born to a middle-class family in Cloquet, Minnesota, she chose studying drama in Paris over an art scholarship. She then went to New York to find modeling work and in 1976 was chosen for the Fay Wray role in Dino De Laurentiis' remake of *King Kong*. The film bombed, and Lange had to wait three years until a decent role opened up, as the Angel of Death in Bob Fosse's *All That Jazz*. Her true comeback occurred in another remake, 1981's scorching *The Postman Always Rings Twice*, with Jack Nicholson. 1982 saw her stellar turn as Frances Farmer in *Frances*, which earned her an Oscar nomination as Best Actress; she did win that year, but it was for Best Supporting Actress in *Tootsie*.

Lange had proved her mettle and was now offered a series of top roles: Patsy Cline in *Sweet Dreams*, the mother in *Cape Fear*, and a frightened wife in *Blue Sky*, which earned her a Best Actress Oscar. She also played an embattled farm wife in *Country*, opposite her life partner at the time, actor/playwright Sam Shepard.

Lange has done well on television, receiving an Emmy for the TV movie *Grey Gardens* and a Golden Globe for the series *American Horror Story*.

ABOVE

In 1981's *The Postman Always Rings Twice*, Lange, seen here dressed in a tweed jacket with a simple top, proved her mettle as an actress in this graphic, gutsy remake

RIGHT

In 1976's *King Kong*, Lange is dressed in a white evening gown for the display of King Kong in New York.

MOST FASHIONABLE FILMS

THE POSTMAN ALWAYS RINGS TWICE (1981)
FRANCES (1982)
TOOTSIE (1982)
SWEET DREAMS (1985)

Lange Style

The actress, who has always combined fragile beauty with earthy sensuality, often chooses unfussy fashions that don't distract from her face, bosom, and wheat-blonde hair.

Signature Look

- Monochromatic dresses and gowns in white, black, and red
- Boat-neck tops and sweetheart necklines
- Simple, classic separates

THE NINETEEN EIGHTIES | HOLLYWOOD FASHION

MERYL STREEP

MOST FASHIONABLE FILMS
THE FRENCH LIEUTENANT'S WOMAN (1981)
SOPHIE'S CHOICE (1982)
OUT OF AFRICA (1985)
THE DEVIL WEARS PRADA (2006)
RICKI AND THE FLASH (2015)

Streep Style
Though not always picture perfect on the red carpet, the tall, striking actress has been a style setter in many of her films, including her iconic sweep of blonde hair in *Manhattan*, her side-knotted shawl in *Out of Africa*, and her chic "mature couture" in *The Devil Wears Prada*.

Signature Look
- Straight blonde hair
- Simple, tailored separates
- Chameleon-like ability to become another person, including accent, posture, and appearance

A cherished Hollywood icon for more than five decades, this actress effortlessly projects poise, pathos, playfulness and a steely resolve.

Meryl Streep (1949–) has convincingly played roles ranging from a tragic Polish immigrant, a distraught Australian mother, a Danish farm owner in Kenya, a tough New York nun, a Midwestern whistleblower, an Italian war bride, an American woman learning to cook in Paris, a British prime minister, and a free-spirited hotelier on a Grecian isle. Born Mary Louise Streep in Summit, New Jersey, she aspired to a career in opera, but turned to acting while at Vassar and ended up doing graduate work at the Yale School of Drama. Streep received an Oscar nomination for her second film, *The Deer Hunter*, and in total was nominated a record 21 times. She won three times—for Best Supporting Actress in 1979's *Kramer vs. Kramer* and for Best Actress for *Sophie's Choice* in 1982 (costumes by Albert Wolsky) and for channeling Margaret Thatcher in *The Iron Lady* in 2011. But Streep is not always about playing it serious— she actually got to sing in *A Prairie Home Companion* and *Mamma Mia!*, and earned laughs in *The Devil Wears Prada* (her wardrobe by Nina Johnston) and *It's Complicated*.

More recently Streep received Oscar nominations for *Into the Woods* and *August: Osage County* in 2014, and played a rocker chick in *Ricki and the Flash* (2015). She continued to gather Best Actress nominations as erstwhile opera singer *Florence Foster Jenkins* in 2016 and portraying publishing legend Kathryn Graham in 2017's *The Post*, adding to her own legendary status.

ABOVE

The tragic World War II melodrama, *Sophie's Choice*, earned Streep her first Best Actress Oscar. Here, she appears pensive in an off-white crepe de chine negligee with a gathered bodice.

LEFT

Streep repeatedly proved herself the mistress of foreign accents—and of stylish period dressing, as seen here in this tweed shooting jacket and wide-brimmed felt hat—in films such as 1985's *Out of Africa*.

165

HOLLYWOOD FASHION | THE NINETEEN EIGHTIES

MELANIE GRIFFITH

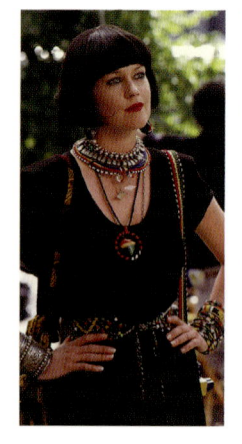

With her little-girl voice and "bod for sin," this second-generation Hollywood actress became both a sex symbol and a respected performer.

Melanie Griffith (1957–) played smart, ambitious women whose sexuality sometimes got them into trouble. Born in New York City, this daughter of Hitchcock star Tippi Hedren had an unorthodox upbringing—raised with the lions and tigers her mother and stepfather trained, while still a minor, she was allowed to move in with actor Don Johnson. They married when she was 18, but separated less than a year later (and were again married from 1989 to 1996). Because Griffith was comfortable working nude, she was cast in a number of nymphet roles before she had turned 20.

Drug and alcohol problems surfaced in the late 1970s, but after Griffith got her act together, she received excellent notices as a porn actress in Brian De Palma's *Body Double* (1984). When Jonathan Demme cast her in *Something Wild* (1986), Hollywood saw that behind her sexual heat was a quirky, original talent. Her true breakthrough came playing an ambitious, resourceful office drone in 1988's *Working Girl* (costumes by Ann Roth). A modern role model for women who aspired to the corner office—she also helped boost the trend for women's suits with linebacker shoulder pads.

Her follow-up films include *Pacific Heights*, *Shining Through*, *Milk Money*, *Nobody's Fool*, and *Crazy in Alabama*.

Griffith's marriage to Spanish actor and American heartthrob Antonio Banderas, whom she wed in 1996, is one of Hollywood's enduring love stories.

MOST FASHIONABLE FILMS

SOMETHING WILD (1986)
WORKING GIRL (1988)
THE BONFIRE OF THE VANITIES (1990)

Griffith Style
The leggy actress has always combined a breezy, relaxed style with smoldering sexuality. Recently she has undergone a number of highly publicized plastic surgery procedures.

Signature Look
- Bee-stung lips and wispy blonde hair
- Power suits and high heels
- Dark evening gowns with illusion necklines

ABOVE
In 1986's road movie, *Something Wild*, Griffith plays a free spirit in early Goth hair, wearing layers of chains and bangles over a belted, slinky black dress.

RIGHT
Check out the killer shoulder pads on this boxy tweed coat! Griffith and her office mates all displayed the wide-shouldered jackets and big hair of the 1980s' secretary pool in *Working Girl*.

KATHLEEN TURNER

No one could make male temperatures rise quicker than this smoky-voiced Midwestern beauty, who was once hailed as the next Lauren Bacall.

Kathleen Turner (1954–) played seductive sirens and adventurous heroines—frequently opposite charismatic leading man, Michael Douglas. She was born in Springfield, Missouri. After appearing in college stage productions, she worked on the soap opera, *The Doctors*, and in 1981 made a sizzling screen debut in *Body Heat* (costumes by Renie Conley).

Her impressive portrayal of homicidal seductress Matty Walker turned costar William Hurt into a whimpering boy toy and nearly ignited the screen. She followed with a comedy, *The Man with Two Brains*, and then played a dowdy author who finds her storybook hero in *Romancing the Stone*—for which she won a Golden Globe—and its sequel, *Jewel of the Nile* (costumes by Marilyn Vance and Emma Porteus, respectively). She won another Globe as an assassin in *Prizzi's Honor* and earned an Oscar nod for *Peggy Sue Got Married*. In 1989 she again costarred with Douglas, this time as his vindictive ex-wife in the comedy, *War of the Roses* (costumes by Gloria Gresham).

Turner has suffered from rheumatoid arthritis since the early 1990s, but the disease is currently in remission. She still occasionally makes movie and TV appearances and is kept busy doing voiceover work.

MOST FASHIONABLE FILMS
BODY HEAT (1981)
ROMANCING THE STONE (1984)
PEGGY SUE GOT MARRIED (1986)

Turner Style
Subscribing to the less-is-more school of fashion, Turner could make a plain white shirtdress or a simple peasant skirt and blouse combo seem as sexy as a negligee.

Signature Look
- Classic, fitted dresses with womanly lines
- Long, tousled, taffy-colored hair
- Tailored sportswear

ABOVE
In 1985's *Prizzi's Honor*, Turner plays a hit man, dressed in a black leather skirt and dark red shirt, who is hired to whack another hit man.

LEFT
In 1981's *Body Heat*, Turner plays a one-woman sexual wrecking crew, with a body and wardrobe to match, including this white dress.

HOLLYWOOD FASHION | THE NINETEEN EIGHTIES

DEMI MOORE

> **I don't like to take my clothes off.**
> DEMI MOORE

With her feline eyes, full-figure, and powerful persona, this actress has kept her sex symbol status for more than two decades.

Demi Moore (1962–) is know for playing sexually liberated, fast-track women who burn the candle at both ends. Born Demetria Gene Guynes in Roswell, New Mexico, her mother and stepfather rarely stopped drinking or fighting. After a short-lived marriage, Moore became a regular on the soap opera, *General Hospital*, and quickly acquired a cocaine habit. It was not until 1985, when she was fired from the set of the Brat Pack film, *St. Elmo's Fire*, that she got clean.

After delivering outstanding performances in *Ghost* (costumes Dawn Jackson); *A Few Good Men*; *Indecent Proposal* (Beatrix Aruna Pasztor, Bernie Pollack, Bobbie Read); and *Disclosure* (Gloria Gresham), Moore entered the rarified ranks of the million-dollar actresses. She made the historical film, *The Scarlet Letter*, in 1995 and then strengthened her standing with her impressive physicality in *G.I. Jane* (1997).

Moore has three daughters with former husband Bruce Willis, and is split from her second husband, Ashton Kutcher.

ABOVE
Moore looked like a milliion bucks in her Thierry Mugler strappy cutaway dress in 1993's *Indecent Proposal*.

RIGHT
This tender interlude from 1990's *Ghost*, shows the increasing popularity of casual clothing in films, even during love scenes.

MOST FASHIONABLE FILMS
ST. ELMO'S FIRE (1985)
GHOST (1990)
INDECENT PROPOSAL (1993)
CHARLIE'S ANGELS: FULL THROTTLE (2003)

Moore Style
The actress's on-screen style has ranged from the Madonna-esque petticoat dresses and scrunchies of *St. Elmo's Fire* to army fatigues in *G.I. Jane*. In spite of some bad fashion choices in the 1980s, Moore remains a red carpet star.

Signature Look
- Gowns in deep jewel tones or metallic shades
- Big sweaters over tank tops
- Short skirts, sexy sandals, and long, tanned legs

THE NINETEEN EIGHTIES | HOLLYWOOD FASHION

MOLLY RINGWALD

> **I do regret...the time that I shaved off half of my eyebrows thinking that I could draw them in better—and they would grow back anyway.**
>
> MOLLY RINGWALD

MOST FASHIONABLE FILMS

SIXTEEN CANDLES (1984)
THE BREAKFAST CLUB (1985)
PRETTY IN PINK (1986)
FRESH HORSES (1988)

Ringwald Style

An impish, red-haired beauty, Ringwald had genuine on-screen presence, plus the courage to make eccentric fashion choices work.

Signature Look

- Preppy separates
- Tousled auburn hair
- Funky retro sweaters

This coltish, auburn-haired Brat Packer became a teen heartthrob in director John Hughes's high-school comedies.

Molly Ringwald (1968–) excelled at playing outsiders, either rich or poor, forced to cope with romantic woes and family troubles. Born in a suburb of Sacramento, California, she was the daughter of a jazz pianist. By the age of ten, she was performing on stage in *Annie* and as a young teen was cast in several TV shows.

Her most notable films were a series of coming-of-age teen comedies written and directed by John Hughes, who utilized a group of young actors who came to be known as the Brat Pack. In *Sixteen Candles*, Ringwald is the birthday girl who gets overlooked by everyone (costumes by Marla Schlom and Mark Peterson); in *Pretty in Pink* she is a Gen X Annie Hall, with her eclectic, retro outfits and repurposed prom gown (costumes by Donna Roberts-Orme and Michael W. Hoffman); and in *The Breakfast Club* she plays the rich girl in designer clothes who yearns for the bad boy (costumes by Marilyn Vance).

A more mature Ringwald starred with Robert Downey Jr. in *The Pickup Artist* and with fellow Bratpacker Andrew McCarthy in the melodrama, *Fresh Horses*.

As an adult, Ringwald made some unfortunate career choices, turning down the Julia Roberts role in *Pretty Woman*, the Demi Moore role in *Ghost* and the Laura Dern part in *Blue Velvet*. In 1994, Ringwald played Franny in the TV miniseries of Stephen King's *The Stand*.

ABOVE

In 1986's *Pretty in Pink*, Ringwald displays her knack for off-beat fashion choices.

LEFT

In 1984's *Sixteen Candles*, Ringwald, still clad in her pink chiffon bridesmaid's dress, finally gets to celebrate her overlooked birthday with crush Michael Schoeffling.

HOLLYWOOD FASHION | THE NINETEEN EIGHTIES

FASHION INFLUENCE
DUDES AND VALLEY GIRLS

During the final decades of the 20th century, high schools became a rich source for a variety of fashion trends as students segregated themselves into groups or cliques based on social hierarchy or shared interests. As Grace, the principal's secretary in *Ferris Bueller's Day Off*, says to her boss, "Oh, he's very popular, Ed. The sportos, the motorheads, geeks, sluts, bloods, waistoids, dweebies, dickheads—they all adore him. They think he's a righteous dude."

Even if the average 1980s' American high school lacked so many influential subsets, it could still offer the standard groups—the elite in-crowd, the jocks, the brainiacs, the artists/actors, and the misfits—each with their own distinct "uniform."

The Brat Pack

The loose-knit group of young actors that came to be known collectively as the "Brat Pack" included Molly Ringwald, Judd Nelson, Anthony Michael Hall, Demi Moore, Rob Lowe, Ally Sheedy, Jon Cryer, Emilio Estevez, and Andrew McCarthy. Their métier was the coming-of-age film and their impresario was director John Hughes, who was responsible for sweet-natured gems like *Sixteen Candles*, *The Breakfast Club*, *St. Elmo's Fire*, and *Pretty in Pink*. As a group, they popularized hair crimping, banana clips, rooster bangs, skinny ties, cardigan sweaters, rolled cuff jeans, and argyle vests. Films like *Ferris Bueller's Day Off* and *Pretty in Pink* also showcased a funky, retro style of teen dressing that quickly caught on.

Valley Girls

During the 1980s and 1990s an affluent female teen protagonist arose, one with Daddy's credit cards and a killer wardrobe. Examples include Molly Ringwald in *The Breakfast Club*, with her designer separates and riding boots; Alicia Silverstone's Cher in *Clueless*, who never met a minidress she didn't like; and the vicious in-crowd clique in

ABOVE
Matthew Broderick may have been a slacker when it came to school, but he proved a most motivated truant in 1986's *Ferris Bueller's Day Off*. He poses here in a two-tone bomber jacket, with Mia Sara in a white, fringed, leather jacket and Alan Ruck in a football jersey.

RIGHT
Valley girls just wanted to have fun in 1995's *Clueless*. Here, Stacey Dash in a plaid suit and lampshade hat, Alicia Silverstone in a red spandex dress and white boa, and Brittany Murphy in a fitted minidress

> I think that *Clueless* was very deep. I think it was deep in the way that it was very light.
> —ALICIA SILVERSTONE

THE NINETEEN EIGHTIES | HOLLYWOOD FASHION

Heathers with their trendy, eclectic, rich-girl outfits.

Surfer Dudes

The 1980s also saw the return of the hip, laid-back surfer dude from the early 1970s, as personified by Sean Penn's irritatingly detached Jeff Spicoli in 1982's *Fast Times at Ridgemont High*. Surfers also had their own slang—"tubular," "radical," "stoked," and "gnarly"—their own fashion style consisting of Hawaiian shirts, board shorts, and cargo pants, and they were often portrayed as stoned on marijuana and living in anticipation of the next big wave.

Slackers

Surfers evolved into another cultural prototype, the Gen-X slacker ...a lazy or unmotivated young man with no discernable goals in life except hanging out. Slackers often wore a grunge version of preppy clothing—baggy cardigans and vests, ratty concert T-shirts, khakis or dockers, and painter's hats. Cinematically, they were represented by Crispin Glover's George McFly in *Back to the Future*, Jeff Bridges's Dude in the Coen Brothers' *The Big Lebowski*, Jay and Silent Bob in *Clerks*, the unmotivated drones of *Office Space*, Mike Myers and Dana Carvey in *Wayne's World*, and the metal-heads played by Keanu Reeves and Alex Winter of *Bill and Ted's Excellent Adventure*.

TOP LEFT

It wasn't only teens who became slackers. In the 1998 cult favorite, *The Big Lebowski*, Jeff Bridges's character, The Dude, spends his time in a bowling alley. Bridges's lack of sartorial style—faded plaid shorts and a Peruvian cardigan, courtesy of Mary Zophres—in itself became a recognized "look."

TOP RIGHT

Valley Girl, from 1983, displayed valley speak and showed valley girls' preoccupation with shopping and fashion.

LEFT

The Breakfast Club from 1985, with Judd Nelson, Emilio Estevez, Ally Sheedy, Molly Ringwald and Anthony Michael Hall—are all charter members of what came to be called the Brat Pack. The film covered the spectrum of high-school archetypes—the greaser, the jock, the weirdo, the rich girl, and the geek.

HOLLYWOOD FASHION | THE NINETEEN EIGHTIES

WHOOPI GOLDBERG

Arguably Hollywood's most original star, this standup comic has played everything from an unwitting spy to a skeptical psychic to a singing nun.

Whoopi Goldberg (1955–) incorporates many odd characters into her standup routines, which has doubtless helped her many screen portrayals ring true. Born Caryn Elaine Johnson in New York City, she started in show business doing comedy improv and standup. Her breakout film, however, was the bittersweet 1985 drama, *The Color Purple*, which earned her an Oscar nomination. She played a banker caught up in spy games in 1986's *Jumpin' Jack Flash*, then made a few formulaic films, but hit her stride again with 1990's *Ghost* (costumes by Ruth Morley). As a fake psychic who taps into her real power, Goldberg took home Oscar gold for Supporting Actress—only the second African-American woman to win after Hattie McDaniel. 1992 brought another smash comedy, *Sister Act* (costumes by Molly Maginnis), where Goldberg plays a Las Vegas lounge singer hiding out in a convent.

Goldberg (who took her first name from "whoopee cushion" and her surname because she needed to "sound more Jewish") is an outspoken liberal who has worked for HBO's Comic Relief since its start in 1986. In addition to an Oscar, she has also won a Tony, two Daytime Emmys and a Grammy. In 1994, she became the first solo woman to host the Academy Awards. She is also a TV mainstay, with appearances on *Hollywood Squares* (which she coproduced) and *Saturday Night Live*; since 2007, she has been a moderator on *The View*.

ABOVE
In 1990's *Ghost*, Goldberg, in a vivid cherry red dress suit with feathered toque, played a fake medium who discovers she really does have psychic powers.

RIGHT
Goldberg has remained a proponent of ethnic patterns and fashions throughout her career; here, from 1992's *Sarafina!*, she wears a traditional South African-style dress, bangle bracelets, and dreadlocks.

MOST FASHIONABLE FILMS
GHOST (1990)
SARAFINA! (1992)
MADE IN AMERICA (1993)

Goldberg Style
Whoopi is a fashion original and proud of her heritage, incorporating several different ethnic styles of dressing with unusual jewelry. She can also carry off sophisticated evening looks on occasion.

Signature Look
- Long dreadlocks
- Mix-and-match African or Island-inspired outfits
- Sweeping gowns in rich fabrics

THE NINETEEN EIGHTIES | HOLLYWOOD FASHION

JAMIE LEE CURTIS

Curtis Style
While getting in shape for *Perfect*, Curtis claimed she reduced her level of body fat to that of an Olympic gymnast. When at normal weight, she is known for her curvy figure and shapely legs.

Signature Look
- Short, angular haircut
- Straight skirts with cinched waists
- Stiletto heels with ankle straps

MOST FASHIONABLE FILMS

PERFECT (1985)
A FISH CALLED WANDA (1988)
TRUE LIES (1994)

After graduating from "scream queen" roles, this daughter of Hollywood royalty carved out a career niche playing funny, savvy women.

Jamie Lee Curtis (1958–) can always be counted on for a breezy, affable performance in comedies and thrillers. The daughter of Janet Leigh and Tony Curtis, she was born in Santa Monica, California, and first made her mark as an actress in 1978 in John Carpenter's hit thriller, *Halloween*. She followed with a series of horror films, including *The Fog*, *Prom Night*, *Terror Train*, *Road Games*, and *Halloween II*.

In the early 1980s, Curtis crossed over into comedy, playing a kind-hearted hooker in 1983's *Trading Places* (costumes by Deborah Nadoolman), a driven aerobics instructor in 1985's *Perfect* (costumes by Michael Kaplan), and an adorable con artist in *A Fish Called Wanda* (costumes by Hazel Pethig) in 1988. She shared action sequences with Arnold Schwarzenegger in 1994's *True Lies* (costume supervisor Lisa Lovaas)—and won a Golden Globe.

In 1984, Curtis married British actor/director Christopher Guest. The son of a nobleman, Guest inherited the Barony of Haden-Guest in 1996. Curtis supports a number of charities including Women in Recovery and has been writing children's books since 1993.

ABOVE

Curtis, here with costar Kevin Kline, modeled a parade of sexy outfits in the 1988 cult comedy, *A Fish Called Wanda*, including this red-sprigged, cotton minidress.

LEFT

Curtis discovers that every woman needs her little black dress, especially when trying to outwit the bad guys in 1994's *True Lies*.

HOLLYWOOD FASHION | THE NINETEEN EIGHTIES

FASHION INFLUENCE
WORKOUT CLOTHES

Americans have always sought a combination of fashion and comfort, and the 1980s gave it to them in the form of soft, stretchy workout clothing. It wasn't long, however, before the leotards, bike shorts, gym shorts, tights, legwarmers, and sleeveless T-shirts that had been reserved solely for the gym or dance class were being sported on the street. Until the sleep pants and pajama jeans phenomena of the late 2000s, this was by far the biggest trend to condone the wearing of indoor clothing outdoors.

A lot of the "blame" goes to films like *Flashdance*, *Fame*, *Perfect*, *Stayin' Alive*, and *The Turning Point*, which put attractive stars into workout or dance-rehearsal gear and furthermore made these outfits appear both sexy and comfortable.

Flashdance from 1983, with its unrestricted, physical style of dancing, filled in some of the musical vacuum left after the demise of disco, though few dancers had Jennifer Beals' athleticism (including Beals herself, who was dance doubled by Marine Jahan.) The film, which showed Beals performing in slouchy, off-the-shoulder tops, leotards, and granny boots, started the workout clothing craze; reported sales of legwarmers alone increased 340 percent after the film debuted.

Perfect, the 1985 film about a magazine reporter investigating upscale urban gyms who forms a relationship with an aerobics instructor, was based on a series of articles in *Rolling Stone* chronicling how L.A. health clubs had become the new singles bars. Jamie Lee Curtis, who already had a sleek, sexy figure, toned and sculpted it even more for the film. Her colorful, high-cut bodysuits and matching leg warmers were soon being copied in gyms across America.

ABOVE
In 1977's *The Turning Point*, real-life ballerina Leslie Browne looks right at home in a rehearsal leotard with a knit shrug tied at her waist.

TOP RIGHT
John Travolta brings the heat wearing a micro-mini toga during *Stayin' Alive*, the sequel to *Saturday Night Fever* that also featured the music of The Bee Gees.

BOTTOM RIGHT
Jamie Lee Curtis, here in a high-cut bodysuit, was aiming for the same body fat percentage as an Olympic gymnast while she trained for 1985's *Perfect*.

THE NINETEEN EIGHTIES | HOLLYWOOD FASHION

> **I wanted to dance on tabletops during math class with leg warmers.**
> —NAOMI WATTS

Singer-actress Olivia Newton-John helped popularize the trend even more in her music video for "Let's Get Physical."

Not for Dancers Only
The Turning Point in 1977, *Fame* in 1980, *Stayin' Alive* in 1983, *A Chorus Line* in 1985, *Dancers* in 1987, and *All That Jazz* in 1989 featured key scenes set during dance tryouts, rehearsals, or actual performances. It wasn't long before dance clothing— jazz shoes, ballet flats, warm-up pants, jersey wrap skirts, leotard tops, knit boleros, tutu-style gauze skirts, and those ubiquitous leg warmers—had crept into America's everyday wardrobe. The 2010 ballet film, *Black Swan*, with its lavish dance costumes by Rodarte, again revived this look when ballet-inspired designs— lace dresses, crystal-encrusted fabrics, and Nutcracker-style military jackets—hit the runways that year.

TOP LEFT
Jennifer Beals rehearses in a basic black leotard during the filming of 1983's *Flashdance*, one of the first films to reflect the influence of music videos in certain sequences.

BOTTOM LEFT
The cast of 1985's *A Chorus Line* wear a variety of rehearsal clothing—from warm-up pants with leg warmers to midriff tops with tights—as they run through their grand finale.

175

HOLLYWOOD FASHION | **THE NINETEEN EIGHTIES**

WINONA RYDER

This delicate, pale-skinned actress has seamlessly moved back and forth between period films and cutting-edge modern dramas.

Winona Ryder (1971–) often portrays women who are driven, neurotic, and high-strung—clearly some of the same qualities she herself possesses. Born Winona Horowitz in Winona, Minnesota, she grew up on a commune in California. After playing an alienated Goth teen in *Beetlejuice*, she followed with her breakthrough film, the cult favorite, *Heathers*, the story of a free-spirited high-school girl who gets to be part of the "in crowd." The film, in addition to showcasing a young Christian Slater, was notable for its dark humor and on-trend fashions by Rudy Dillon, including patchwork blazers with padded shoulders, lacy socks, tiered skirts, and menswear jackets.

In 1990 Ryder starred in Tim Burton's tragic-comic *Edward Scissorhands*, then made three period films—*Dracula* in 1992, Martin Scorsese's *The Age of Innocence* (costumes by Gabriella Pescucci), which earned her an Oscar nod, and *The House of the Spirits* in 1993. 1994 brought the Gen X anthem, *Reality Bites*, about conflicted college grads (costumes by Eugenie Bafaloukos). Another career high was playing Jo March in Gillian Armstrong's 1994 remake of *Little Women*, which brought her a second Oscar nomination.

MOST FASHIONABLE FILMS
HEATHERS (1988)
EDWARD SCISSORHANDS (1990)
THE AGE OF INNOCENCE (1993)

Ryder Style
The actress has appeared in at least three films—*Beetlejuice*, *Heathers*, and *Reality Bites*—where the styles of a particular segment of the youth culture—goths, high school queen bees, and Gen-Xers—were reflected.

Signature Look
- Dark, shaggy cropped hair
- Black or dark separates
- Dresses with clean, spare lines worn with few accessories

ABOVE
Ryder is striking with her shaggy hair and simple separates in 1994s' *Reality Bites*.

RIGHT
Winona Ryder cozies up to the backstabbing high school clique known as the three *Heathers*. The film featured a host of popular 1980s' looks—big-shouldered plaid blazers, pleated skirts, colored tights, Mary Janes with frilled socks, big hair, and scrunchies.

THE NINETEEN EIGHTIES | HOLLYWOOD FASHION

SIGOURNEY WEAVER

Although well equipped for leading lady roles, the lanky brunette came into her own as the indomitable heroine of the futuristic *Alien* franchise.

Sigourney Weaver (1949–) is best known for portraying capable, intelligent women who can cope during a crisis. Born in New York City, her father was TV producer Sylvester L. Weaver Jr. She made her mark as tough ship's officer Ellen Ripley in Ridley Scott's 1979 space thriller *Alien*, then reprised the role in *Aliens* and two more sequels. (In the 1999 space comedy *Galaxy Quest*, Weaver played against the Ripley model as a sex-kitten communications officer.)

In other early roles she was cast as career women—a TV news reporter in *Eyewitness* (costumes by Hilary Rosenfeld), a diplomatic attaché in *The Year of Living Dangerously* (costumes by Terry Ryan), and an art restorer in *Ghostbusters*. As she matured, she sought serious roles in dramatic films such as *Gorillas in the Mist*, *The Ice Storm*, and *A Map of the World*. She also scored as an unscrupulous lady boss in *Working Girl* (costumes by Ann Roth).

MOST FASHIONABLE FILMS

ALIEN (1979)
THE YEAR OF LIVING DANGEROUSLY (1982)
GHOSTBUSTERS (1984)
DAVE (1993)

Weaver Style
The actress's dark beauty, statuesque height, and willowy figure make her as sensational in military jumpsuits as in couture gowns.

Signature Look
- Curly dark hair
- Smart business suits
- Classic dresses and gowns

ABOVE
Weaver, primed for action in a blue jumpsuit and holding some serious firepower, proves a formidable opponent to the Geiger-faced monsters in 1979's blockbuster, *Alien*.

LEFT
In spite of her role as a suspicious First Lady, Weaver shines in an alluring evening gown with jeweled straps and white opera gloves in the 1993 political comedy, *Dave*.

177

HOLLYWOOD FASHION | THE NINETEEN EIGHTIES

MICHELLE PFEIFFER

In spite of her angelic face, this actress has played gangsters' molls, seductive singers, and other good girls gone bad.

Michelle Pfeiffer (1958–) is known for adding a heart-breaking vulnerability to tough-cookie roles. Born in Santa Ana, California, Pfeiffer pursued an acting career after becoming Miss Orange County in 1978. Although she starred in the 1982 sequel, *Grease 2*, she didn't gain real acclaim until the following year's cult hit, *Scarface*, with Al Pacino (costumes by Patricia Norris).

Her ethereal blonde beauty was captured in 1985's fantasy *Ladyhawke* (costumes by Nana Cecchi), 1987's *The Witches of Eastwick* with Jack Nicholson (costumes by Aggie Guerard Rodgers) and the period melodrama, *Dangerous Liaisons*. Yet she was just as lovely as a brunette in 1988's dark comedy, *Married to the Mob* (costumes by Colleen Atwood). 1989 offered a career-defining, Golden Globe-winning role, where she turned a baby grand piano into a sex toy in *The Fabulous Baker Boys* (costumes by Lisa Jensen).

Pfeiffer's career continued to flourish—she was nominated for an Oscar and a Golden Globe for 1992's *Love Field* and a Golden Globe for 1993's *The Age of Innocence* (costumes by Gabriella Pescucci). In the mid-to-late 1990s, she made *Wolf*, again with Nicholson, *Dangerous Minds*, *Up Close and Personal* with Robert Redford, and the cute comedy *One Fine Day* with George Clooney.

Pfeiffer has been married to TV auteur David E. Kelley since 1993 and is frequently seen on both movie and TV red carpets.

ABOVE
Pfeiffer, wearing a white wrap dress with a peplum waist and the typical wide-shouldered silhouette of the 1980s, becomes a drug lord's plaything in *Scarface*.

RIGHT
In 1989's *The Fabulous Baker Boys*, the actress nearly sets the piano on fire when she croons "Makin' Whoopee" in a killer red-velvet gown with a slit up to there.

MOST FASHIONABLE FILMS

SCARFACE (1983)
THE FABULOUS BAKER BOYS (1989)
BATMAN RETURNS (1992)
THE AGE OF INNOCENCE (1993)

Pfeiffer Style
Whether she's sprawled on a piano or teaching in an inner-city classroom, this actress understands that clothes make the woman—or the character.

Signature Look
- Black, neutral, or metallic tone red carpet gowns
- Classic, feminine separates—pencil skirts and stiletto heels
- Long, blonde, loosely waving hair

THE NINETEEN EIGHTIES | HOLLYWOOD FASHION

BETTE MIDLER

MOST FASHIONABLE FILMS

THE ROSE (1979)
JINXED (1982)
FOR THE BOYS (1991)
THE FIRST WIVES CLUB (1996)

Midler Style
The Divine Miss M has always been a fashion innovator, from reviving 1940s' styles to her tacky mermaid lounge act costume to her couture concert ensembles.

Signature Look
- Brassy red hair in wild curls
- Cinch-waisted dresses with wide skirts
- Platform shoes

This outrageous red-haired lounge singer showed her acting range in *The Rose* and has continued to be a force of nature on both stage and screen.

Bette Midler (1945–) is known for her portrayals of brash, determined women bent on making their mark. Born in Honolulu, she studied theater at the University of Hawaii and began performing in gay bathhouses along with pianist, Barry Manilow. Her first two albums from the early 1970s went platinum and quickly made her a pop star.

After a few small film parts, she found her breakout role as a troubled rock star in 1979's *The Rose* (costumes by Theoni V. Aldredge). The film earned her a Best Actress Oscar nomination and Golden Globes as Best Actress and New Star. Her next movie, *Jinxed*, fared badly but she redeemed herself with 1986's comedy hit *Down and Out in Beverly Hills* (Pamela Wise). That same year she played a furious hostage in *Other People's Money* (costumes by Rosanna Norton). She shone in 1988's buddy film *Beaches* (costumes by Robert Da Mora) and was part of a vengeful trio in *The First Wives Club* (costumes by Theoni V. Aldredge). Her performance as Mama Rose in 1993's TV adaptation of *Gypsy* (Bob Mackie) won her another Golden Globe.

Midler, who has won four Grammy's, still sells out her concert/comedy shows. She continues to be a major contributor to the urban gardening movement in New York City. In 2017 she won a Tony for the smash revival of *Hello Dolly!*

ABOVE

In 1991's *Scenes From a Mall* (1991), Midler is at her brassiest with her red hair and red dress, along with Woody Allen's red hair.

LEFT

Midler brings back the 1940's in *For the Boys*, with this square neck print dress, as she sings and dances to entertain the troops.

HOLLYWOOD FASHION | **THE NINETEEN EIGHTIES**

FASHION INFLUENCE
ROCK AND ROLL

Since its inception, rock and roll music has increasingly dictated the clothing choices of its fans.

Yet before the advent of live Internet feeds, a concert could only reach a limited audience—a stadium show might be seen by 100,000 fans at most. A movie featuring rock and roll, on the other hand, could reach—and influence—millions. Hollywood had got on the rock and roll bandwagon back in the 1950s with *The Blackboard Jungle* and its throbbing rendition of "Rock Around the Clock" by Bill Haley and the Comets, and then with Elvis Presley's *Jailhouse Rock*. Both films added to the popularity of loose, wide-shouldered jackets, blue-suede shoes, and straight-leg jeans.

And as rock and roll became more pervasive, more mainstream, Hollywood increased the number of films that revolved around it. Meanwhile, moviegoers were soon parading hip, new fashion trends that had traveled from the concert stage to the film screen and right onto Main Street. Over time, the Hollywood film industry became a critical factor in spreading rock-and-roll style—including heavy metal, glam rock, punk, grunge, New Wave and Goth—to the world at large.

RIGHT
Based on the smash Broadway show, 1978's *Grease* introduced 1950s' high-school fashions—black leather jackets, motorcycle boots, bouffant hairdos, mambo dresses, and skintight jeans—to a whole new generation.

TOP RIGHT
Glam rock, as personified by David Bowie, The New York Dolls, and Marc Bolan, was the source for the gender-bending rock melodrama, *Velvet Goldmine* (1996).

BOTTOM RIGHT
In 1984's *Purple Rain*, Prince takes his music—and his funky, androgynous, dandy style—to new heights.

180 1980s

> **I don't go to the sale rack. But I wouldn't say I am decadent in my spending. I am careful.**
> MADONNA

FULL PAGE

In *Madonna: Truth or Dare* from 1991, the Material Girl shows her knack for mixing high fashion in low-brow ways to create a look that is distinctly hers.

HOLLYWOOD FASHION | THE NINETEEN EIGHTIES

CHER

After successful careers in music and TV, the legendary pop singer reinvented herself as an actress...and found cinematic gold!

Cher (1946–) is best known for earthy, appealing roles where character and humor outweigh glamour. She was born Cherilyn Sarkisian LaPiere in El Centro, California, and by age 19 was half of the hippie singing duo Sonny and Cher with husband Sonny Bono. The couple went on to host a hit variety show, where Cher became a fashion trendsetter in her glittering Bob Mackie gowns.

After two forgettable "pop" films with Sonny, Cher entered serious films cautiously, taking supporting roles. Her second film, as the lesbian friend of whistleblower Meryl Streep in *Silkwood* (1983), earned her an Oscar nomination and a win at the Golden Globes.

Her bravura performance as the mother of a disfigured teen in *Mask* (Cher's costumes by April Ferry), earned her leads in *The Witches of Eastwick* (costumes by Aggie Guerard Rodgers) and *Suspect*. But it was as a dowdy bookkeeper caught between two brothers in *Moonstruck* (costumes by Theoni V. Aldredge) that she found the role of a lifetime—and won the Oscar for Best Actress.

She continues to perform on the stage and in film— recently playing a theater owner in *Burlesque* (costumes by Michael Kaplan) opposite Christina Aguilera. She holds the distinction of being the only American female singer to have produced #1 singles in four decades.

MOST FASHIONABLE FILMS

MOONSTRUCK (1987)
THE WITCHES OF EASTWICK (1987)
TEA WITH MUSSOLINI (1999)

Cher Style

Cher was a fashion icon long before she ever appeared on a movie screen. The bell bottoms and fur vests from her Sonny and Cher years eventually gave way to the sleek, revealing gowns designed by Bob Mackie for the duo's hit variety show.

Signature Look

- Long, glistening black hair or extreme wigs
- Form-fitting, transparent gowns
- Off-the-shoulder sweaters and tops

ABOVE
Cher, with her 1940s' marcelled hair and elegant tea dresses, plays a wealthy, cultured American who secretly sponsors a motherless Italian boy in *Tea with Mussolini* (1999).

RIGHT
In 1987's romantic comedy, *Moonstruck*, Cher undergoes a radical makeover from dowdy Brooklyn accountant to "uptown" girl in a black strapless cocktail dress with a red flounce and red stiletto heels.

182 1980s

THE NINETEEN EIGHTIES | HOLLYWOOD FASHION

KIM BASINGER

After appearing as a sultry Bond girl, this actress struggled to get meatier roles and eventually earned herself an Oscar.

Kim Basinger (1953–) is known for playing beautiful, fragile women who are rarely in control of their own destinies. Born in Athens, Georgia, she studied ballet as a child, became a teen beauty queen, and was a top Ford model by age 20. After appearing in several hit TV shows, she was cast opposite Sean Connery in *Never Say Never Again*. That led to 1984's baseball classic, *The Natural* (Gloria Gresham, Bernie Pollack), which earned her a Golden Globe nomination. Basinger was now truly big box office. She shared notoriously steamy scenes with Mickey Rourke in *9 ½ Weeks*, costarred with Richard Gere in *No Mercy*, and with Bruce Willis in *Blind Date*. In 1989, she played *Vicky Vale* in Tim Burton's *Batman* (costumes by Linda Henrikson).

After a career hiatus, she came back strong, winning an Oscar in 1997 for playing a hired escort in *L.A. Confidential* (costumes by Ruth Myers) and then giving a heartfelt performance in *I Dreamed of Africa* (2000).

Basinger was married to actor Alec Baldwin from 1993 to 2000, and has a daughter, Ireland, with him. In 1989 she formed an investment group that purchased the small Georgia town of Braselton in an effort to revive it and make it a tourist attraction. A hefty lawsuit filed by her studio forced Basinger to sell off her interest; today, it is one of the fastest growing cities in America.

MOST FASHIONABLE FILMS

THE NATURAL (1984)
THE MARRYING MAN (1991)
L.A. CONFIDENTIAL (1997)

Basinger Style
The white-blonde actress has been a fashion icon since her days as a "Breck Shampoo Girl."

Signature Look
- Monochromatic black or white evening gowns
- Off-the-shoulder sweaters
- Sophisticated separates

ABOVE

In 1984's *The Natural*, Basinger is a temptress paid to lure 1930s' baseball phenomenon Robert Redford from the straight and narrow. Here, she poses in a viscose scarf and sequined gown.

LEFT

Basinger, striking in a black skirt, white sleeveless blouse, and wide black belt, in 1994's *The Getaway*.

183

HOLLYWOOD FASHION | THE NINETEEN EIGHTIES

MEN OF THE 1980s
DECADE OF DECADENCE

ABOVE

Harrison Ford played adventuring 1940s' archeologist Indiana Jones in *Raiders of the Lost Ark*—and single-handedly brought the leather bomber jacket and fedora hat back into style.

TOP RIGHT

Don Johnson as Detective Sonny Crockett and Philip Michael Thomas as Detective Rico Stubbs added a major fashion vibe to TV's *Miami Vice*—T-shirts worn under pastel suits, no socks, rolled-up sleeves, Ray-Ban sunglasses—and influenced both screen characters and the man on the street.

BOTTOM RIGHT

No one wore the power suit better than Michael Douglas's Gordon Gecko in 1987's *Wall Street*. Here, he instructs a most willing pupil, Charlie Sheen.

The 1980s—the decade of decadence—brought a revolution to men's fashion. Designers strayed from previous norms and broke the barriers that limited the fashion of earlier generations. Bright colors, long hair, and even makeup were all popular trends for males in the 1980s.

An American Original

Richard Gere's performance as an *American Gigolo* started the 1980s with an explosion of testosterone—and a closet full of Georgio Armani suits. (The pulsing sound of Blondie's "Call Me" didn't hurt, either.) The provocative film put Gere on the Hollywood map.

Miami Vice

The 1980s were full of bright colors, even in men's fashion. Men began to emulate the look from the hit television series, *Miami Vice*, which paired casual T-shirts with suit jackets, typically worn open. T-shirt colors ran from pastel to tropical and the suit was either a pale hue or Florida-sunshine white.

Power Dressing Is Good

When Gordon Gekko proclaimed that "greed is good" in *Wall Street* (1987), he did so wearing a classic power suit with all the key accessories: suspenders, cuff links, gold watch, striped shirt with contrasting white collar. Men's retailers quickly took note.

Musically Inspired

Michael Jackson's "Thriller" video, released in 1982, inspired a whole new fashion craze, including lighter-weight leather jackets. In films like *The Lost Boys* (1987), the jackets were often studded and left undone to create a tougher look.

A Preppy Comeback

Michael J. Fox in 1985's *Back to the Future* (as well as in his TV show, *Family Ties*, as conservative Alex P. Keaton) helped return the preppy look to the mainstream. Preppy style for men encompassed plaids, checks and tweeds, iconic golf and polo shirts—Izod, Brooks Brothers, Ralph Lauren—as well as khakis, suspenders, nautical vests, argyle sweaters, and loafers. Plain pullover sweaters might be monogrammed and would be worn tossed over the shoulders with the sleeves knotted in front.

THE NINETEEN EIGHTIES | HOLLYWOOD FASHION

Signature Menswear Looks of the 1980s
- T-shirts worn under Armani jackets
- Ray-Ban Wayfarer sunglasses
- Aviator shades worn by Tom Cruise in *Top Gun*
- High-rise, acid-washed jeans and denim jackets
- Aviator bomber jackets à la Indiana Jones
- Clunky hiking boots worn with flannel shirts
- Five o'clock shadow all day long

> The secret of my success is my hairspray.
> —RICHARD GERE

TOP LEFT

Richard Gere displays the new attitude in men's suits—relaxed lines, muted colors, and sleek, elegant fabrics—in *American Gigolo* (1980).

BOTTOM LEFT

The Lost Boys (1987), led by Kiefer Sutherland (center back), evoked the rising Goth and New Romantic fashions inspired by Michael Jackson and Prince; hair was either a punk-style mullet or the flowing locks of MTV's heavy-metal bands.

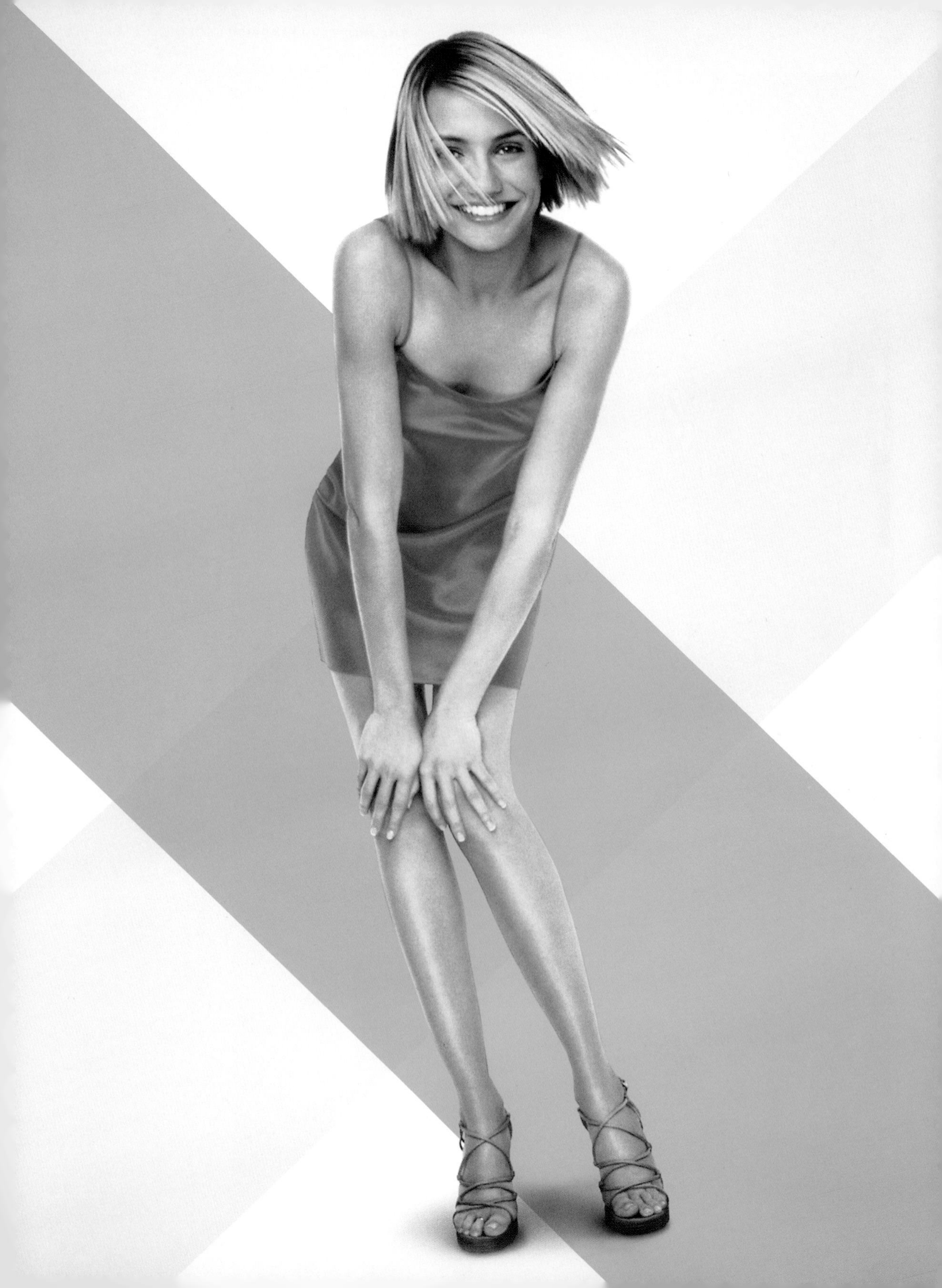

THE NINETEEN NINETIES

This decade simultaneously saw the debut of the biggest blockbuster of its time—*Titanic*—and the rise of independent filmmakers who offered critical favorites like *Pulp Fiction*, with its sly homage to 1960s' fashions, *The Big Lebowski*, with its laid-back slacker look, and *American Beauty*, with its fashion-plate mom and misfit, grunge-favoring son. Men's films dominated the box office—*Goodfellas, Saving Private Ryan, Braveheart, The Usual Suspects, Reservoir Dogs, Unforgiven, The Shawshank Redemption, The Green Mile, Fight Club, Glengarry Glen Ross,* and *Heat.*

Films with female appeal included *The Piano, Thelma and Louise,* and *Howard's End*, as well as two law-enforcement thrillers, *The Silence of the Lambs* and *Fargo*, which both featured determined female heroines who put more emphasis on crime solving than clothing choices. Moviegoers of both sexes were compelled by *Schindler's List, Philadelphia, Dances with Wolves, The Sixth Sense, Shakespeare in Love, Jurassic Park,* and, of course, *Titanic*.

This last film, with costumes by Deborah L. Scott, made fashion waves by reinjecting glamour into American cinema and reintroducing the high-waisted gown to the couture runway. Globally, young men copied Leonardo DiCaprio's haircut and jewelers reproduced Kate Winslet's fabulous blue diamond, "The Heart of the Ocean."

HOLLYWOOD FASHION | THE NINETEEN NINETIES

JULIA ROBERTS

With a smile the size of the Hollywood sign, this hugely popular actress has been charming film fans since her *Mystic Pizza* **days.**

Julia Roberts (1967–) often plays hip, earnest seekers of truth in contemporary films. Born in Smyrna, Georgia, to a theatrical family (her parents founded the Atlanta Actors and Writers Workshop, and brother Eric is a respected actor), Roberts endeared herself to audiences in *Mystic Pizza* and *Steel Magnolias*—the latter earning her an Oscar nomination and Golden Globe win for Supporting Actress. She made a rapid climb to the A-list with 1990's smash hit, *Pretty Woman*, costarring Richard Gere (costumes by Marilyn Vance). The film earned her an Oscar nomination and won her a Golden Globe as Best Actress.

Roberts then appeared in two thrillers—*Flatliners* and *Sleeping with the Enemy*, a melodrama, *Dying Young*, and 1993's *The Pelican Brief* with Denzel Washington (costumes by Albert Wolsky). She was warmly appealing in the romantic comedies *Notting Hill* (costumes by Shuna Harwood) and *Runaway Bride*, which reunited her with Gere. But it was her performance in 2000's *Erin Brockovich* (costumes by Jeffrey Kurland)—as a working-class mom fighting corporate corruption in a push-up bra—that finally earned her the Best Actress Academy Award. More recently she's starred in *Ocean's Eleven*, *Charlie Wilson's War*, *Eat Pray Love*, *August: Osage County*, and *Wonder*.

Now firmly devoted to family life with her husband and children, the actress spends time in both Taos, New Mexico, and New York City.

MOST FASHIONABLE FILMS
PRETTY WOMAN (1990)
NOTTING HILL (1999)
CHARLIE WILSON'S WAR (2007)
EAT PRAY LOVE (2010)

Roberts Style
This "*Pretty Woman*" conveys a relaxed style that incorporates touches of preppy classics mixed with slightly boho touches.

Signature Look
- Feminine Indo-Asian separates with ethnic jewelry
- Pastel twin sets
- Form-fitting gowns in rich fabrics

ABOVE
The off-the-shoulder red dress, with its plunging décolletage, that Roberts wears to the opera in *Pretty Woman* often appears on Best Gowns lists.

RIGHT
The redhead, here in a striking black one-shoulder dress—went blond for the political docudrama *Charlie Wilson's War*.

188 1990s

THE NINETEEN NINETIES | HOLLYWOOD FASHION

KATE WINSLET

This rosy-cheeked British import made a splash in that "ship" movie and went on to succeed in both period and contemporary roles.

Kate Winslet (1975–) seems destined to play headstrong women in dark, complex melodramas. Born in Berkshire, England, to a family of stage performers, her work as an obsessive teen in 1994's *Heavenly Creatures* won her critical approval—and paved the way for a starring role in *Sense and Sensibility* (costumes by Jenny Beavan and John Bright). The film earned her a British Academy Award, and she followed with two more period pieces, *Jude* and Kenneth Branagh's *Hamlet*.

After being cast as the female lead in James Cameron's 1997 epic, *Titanic*, Winslet was on the fast track to international stardom. With her pre-Raphaelite hair and sumptuous gowns by Deborah L. Scott, she brought old-time glamour back to American movies. Winslet then scaled back with a pair of independent films—*Holy Smoke!* and *Hideous Kinky*—and then made the period movie *Quills* in 2000, the biography *Iris* in 2001, and the quirky comedy *Eternal Sunshine of the Spotless Mind* in 2004.

The 2000s saw her gaining stature with powerful and poignant performances in *Finding Neverland*, *Little Children*, and *Revolutionary Road*. After six nominations, she finally won the Best Actress Oscar in 2009 as a Nazi guard in *The Reader*. She was also honored with an Emmy and a Golden Globe for her 2011 TV portrayal of *Mildred Pierce*.

MOST FASHIONABLE FILMS

SENSE AND SENSIBILITY (1995)
TITANIC (1997)
ETERNAL SUNSHINE OF THE SPOTLESS MIND (2004)
REVOLUTIONARY ROAD (2008)

Winslet Style

After her success in *Titanic*, the softly rounded actress became a fashion inspiration for women with "average" figures. She continues to be a red carpet favorite.

Signature Look

- Lace or draped fitted evening gowns
- Crop pants and flats worn with an oversized sweater
- Jeans tucked into suede boots

ABOVE

The actress made a memorable entrance in 1997's megahit *Titanic*, wearing a white with black pinstripe walking dress and peering out from under the brim of an oversized hat with an enormous striped bow.

LEFT

Winslet was reunited with her *Titanic* costar, Leonardo DiCaprio in the 1950s'-based melodrama *Revolutionary Road*. Here, she cuddles with Leo in an ice-blue sheath with an openwork neckline.

HOLLYWOOD FASHION | THE NINETEEN NINETIES

FASHION INFLUENCE
SCIENCE FICTION/ FANTASY

Science fiction and fantasy films stimulate our imaginations with visions of dreamscapes, fanciful alternative worlds, and far-fetched inventions that just might come to pass. These films also serve as a major influence on fashion design, and have done so since the earliest cinematic ventures into the realm of make-believe.

Americans have always been intrigued by the future and are quick to adopt any look from science-fiction films that smacks of the uber-modern, no matter how ridiculous. They have embraced window-blind sunglasses, vinyl moon boots—as worn by Napoleon Dynamite, metallic vests, and paper or Mylar clothing.

While movie fans might be more hesitant to incorporate fantasy fashions into their daily wear—which explains why the Luke Skywalker leg-wrap look never caught on—fashion designers love the playfulness and expansiveness of fantasy costumes and borrow freely from the genre.

While science-fiction fashions tend to be pared down, minimalist, and sleek—incorporating either drab, *1984*-type fabrics or glossy metallic vinyl—fantasy fashions are apt to be over-the-top and include feathers, fur, leather, suede, melted plastic, steel studs, gauze, ripped fabric, and prosthetic ears, horns, and antennae.

Fashion designers or design houses that incorporate fantasy or science-fiction looks into their lines include Rick Owens, Manish Arora, Alexander McQueen, Charlie Le Mindu, Rodarte, Gareth Pugh, John Galliano, and Topshop Unique.

Steampunk

Steampunk—a subgenre of science fiction—has also become a fashion and design esthetic whose followers appreciate both steam-powered technology and ornate adornment. Steampunk

ABOVE

Robby the Robot supposedly fabricated Anne Francis's seductive gowns in *Forbidden Planet* (1956) but they were actually designed by human Helen Rose.

TOP RIGHT

Buster Crabbe, circa 1938, poses in his abbreviated *Flash Gordon* costume.

BOTTOM RIGHT

In 1997's *The Fifth Element*, Milla Jovovich plays the "perfect being" sent to save humanity, and here models a futuristic "wrap" costume by Jean-Paul Gaultier.

THE NINETEEN NINETIES | HOLLYWOOD FASHION

> If you can tune into the fantasy life of an 11-year-old girl, you can make a fortune in this business.
>
> GEORGE LUCAS

TOP LEFT

The Matrix from 1999 (costumes by Kym Barrett) was all about cinematic style; it ramped up the appeal of sweeping black leather trench coats and skintight cat suits and continued to influence fashion designers years after it debuted.

BELOW LEFT

George Lucas's *Star Wars* franchise, here with Mark Hamill, updated the sci-fi serials from the 1930s and they are still going strong.

BELOW RIGHT

1982's *Blade Runner* (costumes by Michael Kaplan) combined dystopian futuristic styles with those of the 1940s for a look sometimes called "tech noir" or "neo-noir." The film, voted the second most visually influential by the Visual Effects Society, left its mark on movies, TV shows such as *Battlestar Galactica*, animé series like *Ghost in the Shell*, and many video games.

fans, with their Edwardian outfits, clockwork or nautical jewelry, and scientific instruments, are not only drawn to the "science battling the undead" aspect of the *Dracula* mythos, but also to Victor Frankenstein's world of technology and reanimation, and to Jules Verne's and H.G. Wells's visions of "the future that may be." Films in the steampunk genre include *Metropolis*; *20,000 Leagues Under the Sea*; *The Time Machine*; *Time After Time*; *Wild, Wild West*; *Brazil*; *The League of Extraordinary Gentlemen*; 2009's *Sherlock Holmes*; and *Hugo*.

Cyberpunk

This subgenre of science fiction combines the hardboiled detective mystery with a futuristic setting—often described as "high tech and low life." Film examples include *Blade Runner*, *The Matrix*, *12 Monkeys*, *Strange Days*, and *The Fifth Element*.

191

HOLLYWOOD FASHION | THE NINETEEN NINETIES

JENNIFER LOPEZ

After a breakout role as a Latina singing star, this multitalented actress founded herself headed for major stardom.

Jennifer Lopez (1969–) is known for playing fiery women who know how to go after what they want. Born in the Bronx to Puerto Rican parents, young Jennifer began taking singing and dancing lessons at age five. In 1991 she became a Fly Girl dancer on the TV series *In Living Color* and in 1997 found a breakout film role as a tragic Tejano singer in the biopic *Selena*. She then sparked with George Clooney in the 1998 comic heist film, *Out of Sight*, playing a federal marshal with a taste for Chanel suits and SIG Sauer pistols.

Over the next few years, while maintaining a successful recording career, she made a science-fiction thriller, *The Cell* (costumes by Eiko Ishioka and April Napier), a pair of melodramas, *Angel Eyes* and *Enough*, and two romantic comedies—*The Wedding Planner* (Pamela Withers) and *Maid in Manhattan* (Albert Wolsky). She had a much-publicized romance with Ben Affleck, playing a lesbian opposite him in the box office disaster, *Gigli*. She taught Richard Gere about life and love in *Shall We Dance?* and then fell victim to Jane Fonda's wrath in *Monster-in-Law*. 2010's *The Back-up Plan* put her back in familiar rom-com territory (costumes by Karen Patch). Lopez wed singer Marc Anthony in 2004 and is the mother of twins, Maximilian and Emme. In 2011 she became a judge on American Idol; she and Anthony split in 2014. Lopez remains a fixture of the red carpet.

ABOVE
Lopez, playing an expectant single mother in 2010's *The Back-up Plan*, models a frothy, one-shouldered, off-white maternity dress from Karen Patch.

RIGHT
The Cell, a futuristic thriller from 2000, featured some of the most original, if not outrageous, clothing designs courtesy of Eiko Ishioka and April Napier. Here, Lopez wears a feathery white gown with an Elizabethan collar and complex, structured bodice.

MOST FASHIONABLE FILMS
OUT OF SIGHT (1998)
THE CELL (2000)
THE WEDDING PLANNER (2001)
MAID IN MANHATTAN (2002)
SHALL WE DANCE (2004)
THE BACK-UP PLAN (2010)

Lopez Style
This Latina icon is proud of her womanly curves and likes showing them off in eye-popping outfits. Lopez has her own clothing, accessory, and perfume line and has inspired the look of other performers for years.

Signature Look
- Plunging necklines
- Form-fitting workout suits with couture labels
- Sexy, sky-high heels

THE NINETEEN NINETIES | HOLLYWOOD FASHION

SHARON STONE

MOST FASHIONABLE FILMS
BASIC INSTINCT (1992)
CASINO (1995)
THE MUSE (1999)

Stone Style
The actress still turns heads on the red carpet and can mix couture with menswear in a pinch.

Signature Look
- Monochromatic black or white ensembles that showcase her ash-blonde hair
- Combining menswear white shirts with couture evening skirts
- Lately seen in 1920s' style vintage dresses, coats, and cloche hats

This sleek, leggy blonde has had an uneven career, but at her best, she possesses the cool sting of a stiletto blade.

Sharon Stone (1958–) is known for playing icy, predatory women. Born in Meadville, Pennsylvania, Stone was a bright child who loved Astaire and Rogers movie musicals. She entered and won the Miss Pennsylvania contest, and then her work as a Ford Agency model led to small parts in forgettable movies. She finally gained media attention playing Arnold Schwarzenegger's wife in *Total Recall* (1990)—and by posing nude for *Playboy*—which paved the way for her breakthrough role, the detached, lipstick lesbian murder suspect in 1992's *Basic Instinct* (costumes by Nino Cerruti and Ellen Mirojnick). The interrogation scene, where Stone crosses her legs and purposely flashes the policemen, became a cinematic sensation, replayed and parodied even today.

Stone went on to play a stalker victim in *Sliver*, a vengeful woman luring Sylvester Stallone in *The Specialist*, and a female gunfighter in *The Quick and the Dead*, all box-office disappointments. She came roaring back in 1996's *Casino* with Robert De Niro and Joe Pesci, as a trophy mob wife (costumes by John A. Dunn and Rita Ryack). The role earned her an Oscar nomination and won her a Golden Globe.

Stone is a dedicated AIDS activist who currently splits her time between film and TV work.

ABOVE
Stone, as the amoral mob wife in 1995's *Casino*, aims for elegance in this Mackie-esque, bead-spangled golden gown from designers John A. Dunn and Rita Ryack.

LEFT
Stone—and this provocative scene from 1992's *Basic Instinct*—became a Hollywood icon when her character, wearing a tight, white dress hiked up to her thighs, crosses her legs during a police interrogation and shockingly reveals her lack of underwear.

193

HOLLYWOOD FASHION | THE NINETEEN NINETIES

SANDRA BULLOCK

With her doe eyes, vulnerable air, and impish humor, she might be the most endearing actress to grace the screen since Audrey Hepburn.

Sandra Bullock (1964–) excels at playing the capable-but-sensitive woman who cannot always speak her heart. Born in Arlington, Virginia, to a voice coach father and German opera singer mother, Bullock decided to go into acting shortly before her college graduation. After appearing on TV and in a few indie films, she played a supporting character in *Demolition Man*, which led to her showcase role in the 1994 mega-hit, *Speed*.

By the late 1990s she was a box-office titan, guaranteeing high revenue for films like *While You Were Sleeping* and *Miss Congeniality* (costumes by Susie DeSanto). Although the sequels to *Speed* and *Miss Congeniality* were not well received, Bullock bounced back in 2002 with *Two Weeks Notice* costarring Hugh Grant, and a critically acclaimed turn in the 2005 drama, *Crash*. Other films from that period include *The Lake House*, *Infamous*, and *Premonition*.

2009 was a banner year for Bullock; she made a blockbuster comedy, *The Proposal*, with Ryan Reynolds (costumes by Catherine Marie Thomas), and a heart-warming drama, *The Blind Side* (costumes by Daniel Orlandi), the latter earning her the Oscar, the Golden Globe, and the Screen Actors Guild Award for Best Actress. In 2013 she was again nominated for an Oscar for her bravura performance in *Gravity*, where she portrays a female astronaut set adrift in space...outside her craft. Bullock is known for her philanthropic gestures—like making million dollar donations to selected charities.

MOST FASHIONABLE FILMS

MISS CONGENIALITY (2000)
TWO WEEKS NOTICE (2002)
THE PROPOSAL (2009)
THE BLIND SIDE (2009)

Bullock Style
The actress has always preferred flattering, feminine separates and classic, unfussy evening gowns.

Signature Look
- Voile or chiffon tops
- Pastel or neutral-colored gowns with natural lines
- Tailored suits with feminine blouses

ABOVE
Nobody looked more adorable driving a runaway bus than Bullock in 1994's *Speed*. Her slightly Boho college student look was created by Ellen Mirojnick, who also styled *Fatal Attraction* and *Basic Instinct*.

RIGHT
In 2002's *Two Weeks Notice*, the actress attempts to charm costar Hugh Grant by appearing in this strapless black gown worn with black lace gloves and topped with a voluminous tulle shawl.

THE NINETEEN NINETIES | HOLLYWOOD FASHION

MEG RYAN

This wide-eyed blonde became America's comedy sweetheart gasping over a plate of salad, but also sought and mastered more challenging roles.

Meg Ryan (1961–) is best known for playing adorable, if somewhat idiosyncratic, free spirits. Born Margaret Hyra in Fairfield, Connecticut, she initially began acting to help pay for her college degree. Her first significant roles were in *Innerspace* and *D.O.A.* with future husband, Dennis Quaid. In 1989, she costarred with Billy Crystal in *When Harry Met Sally* (costumes by Gloria Gresham) and found her career-making role. She was equally memorable in *Sleepless in Seattle* with Tom Hanks (costumes by Judy Ruskin), went darker with Andy Garcia in *When A Man Loves a Woman*, then returned to her cute persona with Kevin Kline in *French Kiss* (costumes by Joanna Johnston).

Ryan took on a taxing dramatic role as a chopper pilot in 1996's *Courage Under Fire*, and then charmed Tom Hanks in *You've Got Mail* (1998). In 2000, she played the wife of a kidnap victim in *Proof of Life*, and in 2001 met time-traveling English nobleman Hugh Jackman in *Kate and Leopold*.

MOST FASHIONABLE FILMS

WHEN HARRY MET SALLY (1989)
SLEEPLESS IN SEATTLE (1993)
FRENCH KISS (1995)
THE WOMEN (2008)

Ryan Style
Her loosely preppy style layers classic pieces—cardigans or wool blazers—over more casual separates like jeans, ethnic skirts, and T-shirts.

Signature Look
- Short, scrunched blonde hair
- Tailored khakis with sweaters
- Severely plain, form-fitting evening gowns

ABOVE

In this scene from the 1998 romance, *You've Got Mail*, Ryan models a taupe sweater set—typically a sleeved cardigan over a sleeveless shell—a favorite style from the 1950s' that underwent a renaissance in the 1990s.

LEFT

In 1989's *When Harry Met Sally*, friends Meg Ryan and Billy Crystal reconnect. Here, Ryan riffs on Annie Hall, with a tweed blazer, felt hat, polka-dot blouse, sling bag, and menswear-style trousers.

> I do every fitting, and I choose every fabric. I like to create the character, or if it's a lot of background people, I like to create the look of it—the spectacle, the atmosphere.
>
> ANN ROTH

FULL PAGE
The 1976 remake of *A Star Is Born* provided an interesting mix of styles—Kris Kristofferson's "hard rocker" leather and jeans and Barbra Streisand's glittering disco dresses and tailored suits. Here, Babs opts for a silver lamé gown with a waterfall bustle worn with chunky-heeled silver platform shoes.

TOP RIGHT INSERT
In 1996's epic melodrama, *The English Patient*, Kristen Scott Thomas—shown here with Colin Firth—wore a variety of simple-yet-provocative outfits, including this white satin gown with flat straps and a sweetheart neckline.

BOTTOM RIGHT INSERT
In 1996's *The Birdcage*, Ann Roth was not only faced with dressing Nathan Lane and Robin Williams—a gay couple trying to pass for straight when meeting their future in-laws—she also had to create extravagant stage costumes for drag-club revues. Here, the actors, in their island-hued sportswear, still look like the pride of Miami's South Beach.

Academy Awards
Roth won the Oscar for *The English Patient*, and was nominated for *Places in the Heart*, *The Talented Mr. Ripley*, and *The Hours*.

Fashion Legacy
- Costumes for prostitutes, con artists, and drifters
- Rigorous attention to detail
- Forensic approach to researching period clothing

THE NINETEEN NINETIES | HOLLYWOOD FASHION

STYLE MAKER
ANN ROTH

Ann Roth had every intention of becoming a production designer for the stage—until she met costume designer Irene Sharaff, who convinced the fledgling artist to become her assistant on both film and stage productions.

Ann Roth was born in 1931 in Hanover, Pennsylvania, and graduated from Pittsburgh's Carnegie Mellon Institute. She began as a production designer for the Pennsylvania Opera and was painting scenery in Bucks County Playhouse when Sharaff recruited her, convincing the talented young woman she would be happier designing costumes. After a five-year apprenticeship, Roth was ready to embark on her own career. She points out that Sharaff had been an excellent mentor and that, unlike the queen of Hollywood costumers, Edith Head, she designed everything for her films, including the costumes for bit players.

Roth went on to design costumes for more than a hundred films, including *Midnight Cowboy*, *Klute*, *The Goodbye Girl*, *Hair*, *Nine to Five*, *Working Girl*, *Silkwood*, *The Birdcage*, *Primary Colors*, *Cold Mountain*, *Closer*, *Evening*, and *Julie and Julia*. Her numerous stage credits include *The Odd Couple*, *Purlie*, *Seesaw*, *They're Playing Our Song*, *Best Little Whorehouse in Texas*, *Biloxi Blues*, and *The Book of Mormon*. She was fortunate to have formed a close working relationship with both playwright Neil Simon and director Mike Nichols.

One thing Roth always insisted on was authenticity in her period costumes, especially when compared to many West Coast designers. "I am the first girl in this business to use real period clothes," she declares. "I work out of museums; they go into stockrooms and pull stuff that was used in another movie."

Among her many honors, Roth won the 2000 Irene Sharaff Lifetime Achievement Award from the Theater Development Fund, the 2003 Outstanding Achievement in Costume Design Award from the Hollywood Film Festival, and the 2012 Golden Starfish Award for Lifetime Achievement in Costume Design from the Hamptons International Film Festival.

In a recent interview, Roth admitted, "I'm simply not a fashion person. I've never been near a runway." Yet that hasn't stopped her film creations, such as those from *Klute*, *Nine to Five*, and *Working Girl* from influencing fashion designers.

MOST FASHIONABLE DESIGNS

MIDNIGHT COWBOY (1969)
KLUTE (1971)
THE BIRDCAGE (1996)
THE ENGLISH PATIENT (1996)
THE TALENTED MR. RIPLEY (1999)
THE HOURS (2002)

ABOVE LEFT

Roth went for a real contrast of styles when outfitting the two down-and-out protagonists of 1969's *Midnight Cowboy*. It was hard to tell which made the worse fashion statement: Jon Voight's garish Western wear or Dustin Hoffman's dull, seedy suits and dark, oily hair.

ABOVE RIGHT

For Jane Fonda, as a call girl attempting to break into acting in 1971's *Klute*, Roth created a streamlined look—layered, cap haircut; long, belted, A-line skirts worn with boots; and knit tops—that was copied by women across America.

HOLLYWOOD FASHION | THE NINETEEN NINETIES

CATE BLANCHETT

This porcelain-skinned actress manages to be utterly convincing whether she's portraying a pampered Tudor queen, a dogged Russian agent, or a work-roughened American rancher.

Cate Blanchett (1969–), who describes herself as "part extrovert, part wallflower," is known for playing vulnerable women in great peril. Born in Australia to an American father and an Australian mother, she studied for a career as a stage actress. After a series of Australian TV roles and movies—including the lyrical *Oscar and Lucinda*—she gained international notice in 1998's *Elizabeth*, playing the resolute daughter of Henry VIII (costumes by Alexandra Byrne).

She was a troubled psychic in 2000's *The Gift*, a kidnapped housewife in 2001's *Bandits*, and a World War II spy in *Charlotte Gray*. During the 2000s, she also appeared as elf queen Galadriel in Peter Jackson's *The Lord of the Rings* trilogy (costumes by Ngila Dickson and Richard Taylor). In 2003, she played a rancher hot on the trail of the Apache renegade who abducted her daughter in *The Missing*.

Blanchett won the 2004 Best Supporting Actress Oscar for her wry portrayal of Kate Hepburn in *The Aviator* (costumes by Sandy Powell). She was a sniper victim in 2006's *Babel* (Michael Wilkinson), and then reprised her role in 2007's *Elizabeth: The Golden Age* (with Oscar-winning costumes by Alexandra Byrne). She was also notable as a lethal Russian agent in 2008's *Indiana Jones and the Kingdom of the Crystal Skull*, and as a ballet dancer in *The Curious Case of Benjamin Button*. Blanchett won the Best Actress Oscar for Woody Allen's 2013 dramedy, *Blue Jasmine*. In 2015's *Carol*, she added a 1950's sensibility to a lesbian love story, and in 2017's *Thor: Ragnarok* brought down Asgard as villainess Hela.

The actress again plays Galadriel in Peter Jackson's three *Hobbit* films, the first of which debuted in 2012.

ABOVE
In 1999's *The Talented Mr. Ripley*, Blanchett looks relaxed but well dressed in her sweater set and knit hat.

RIGHT
Blanchett plays legendary actress Katharine Hepburn in suitable 1940's evening wear in 2004's *The Aviator*.

MOST FASHIONABLE FILMS

OSCAR AND LUCINDA (1997)
ELIZABETH (1998)
THE AVIATOR (2004)
THE CURIOUS CASE OF BENJAMIN BUTTON (2008)
CAROL (2015)

Blanchett Style
A red-carpet favorite, Blanchett likes gowns with a little oomph—ruffles, embroidery, trains, or unusual necklines. Out of the public eye, she prefers a more relaxed look for her frequent travels with her playwright husband, Andrew Upton, and their four children.

Signature Look
- Gowns with lavish skirts or eye-catching embroidery
- Suede or leather jackets
- High boots and jeans

THE NINETEEN NINETIES | HOLLYWOOD FASHION

NICOLE KIDMAN

MOST FASHIONABLE FILMS

BATMAN FOREVER (1995)
THE PORTRAIT OF A LADY (1996)
MOULIN ROUGE! (2001)
AUSTRALIA (2008)
QUEEN OF THE DESERT (2015)

Kidman Style

The camellia-skinned redhead varies her look between masses of natural curls and sleek upsweeps.

Signature Look

- Sheath gowns, often with an ethnic twist
- Lacy, feminine dresses
- Tailored jackets with boyish trousers

Classy and beautiful, this "sparkling diamond" personifies the barely obtainable object of desire.

Nicole Kidman (1967–) is known for playing ambitious, emotionally distant women in both period and contemporary films. Born to Australian parents in Honolulu, Hawaii, Kidman grew up in Sydney. She left school to pursue an acting career at age 16, and made her U.S. film debut in the 1989 thriller, *Dead Calm*. She next filmed *Days of Thunder* with future-husband, Tom Cruise, with whom she also costarred in *Far and Away*.

Kidman received critical raves—and a Golden Globe—as a ruthlessly ambitious weather girl in *To Die For* (wearing pastel power suits by Beatrix Aruna Pasztor). She and Cruise shot Stanley Kubrick's erotic *Eyes Wide Shut* in 1999, but their marriage ended in 2001. That year she triumphed, earning an Oscar nomination as a singing courtesan in Baz Luhrmann's *Moulin Rouge!*—while the opulent costumes by Catherine Martin and Angus Strathie went on to win.

In 2002, Kidman received the Academy Award for Best Actress as Virginia Woolf in *The Hours* (costumes by Ann Roth). She followed with several independent films, the historical romance *Cold Mountain*, comedies *Bewitched* and *The Stepford Wives*, and two thrillers, *The Interpreter* and *The Invasion*. She reunited with Luhrmann for the 2008 epic, *Australia*, and received positive reviews playing mothers under duress in 2010's *Rabbit Hole* and 2015's *Lion*.

Kidman married country singer (and New Zealander) Keith Urban in 2006 and they have two children. Kidman is frequently seen on movie red carpets and at country music award shows.

> **You don't have to be naked to be sexy.**
> NICOLE KIDMAN

ABOVE

In one of her first big-budget films, 1995's *Batman Forever*, Kidman wears a bronze satin boat-necked gown that accentuates her mane of red-blonde hair.

LEFT

As a tragic courtesan in love with an idealistic young writer, Kidman broke hearts in *Moulin Rouge!*, here, in a stunning red dress offset against her milky-white skin.

HOLLYWOOD FASHION | THE NINETEEN NINETIES

CAMERON DIAZ

With her sun-kissed hair, wide smile, and breezy attitude, this actress brings an easy, West Coast vibe to most of her films.

Cameron Diaz (1972–) has enough sex appeal to heat up the screen, but she is also known for her comic timing (and for charming little dances in her underwear). She was born in San Diego and began modeling for the Elite agency when she was 16. At 19, she auditioned for the role of a sexy lounge singer in the Jim Carrey comedy, *The Mask*—and virtually never looked back. Two mainstream roles, *My Best Friend's Wedding* and *A Life Less Ordinary* led to her breakout film, 1998's irreverent *There's Something About Mary*, which earned her a Golden Globe nomination.

Diaz earned more critical praise in 1999 for playing against type as a dowdy brunette in *Being John Malkovich*, made the first of the *Charlie's Angels* films in 2000 (costumes by Joseph G. Aulisi), and played the other woman in the 2001 science fiction flick, *Vanilla Sky*.

The actress turned to period films—playing an 1860s' pickpocket—in *Gangs of New York*, gave a sensitive performance as a self-destructive club girl in *In Her Shoes* (costumes by Sophie de Rakoff), and found true love with Jude Law in *The Holiday*.

> I'm like every other woman: a closet full of clothes, but nothing to wear. So I wear jeans.
> CAMERON DIAZ

MOST FASHIONABLE FILMS
THE MASK (1994)
MY BEST FRIEND'S WEDDING (1997)
CHARLIE'S ANGELS (2000)
IN HER SHOES (2005)

Diaz Style
Whether she is glamming it up in couture gowns and designer shoes in a Vogue feature, or clomping around Hollywood in her Ugg boots, sweater, and jeans, Diaz seems to have discovered the fountain of youth.

Signature Look
- Solid-color gowns, especially black, red, dove gray, and nude
- Ankle boots or high leather boots.
- Statement earrings and long scarves

ABOVE
Diaz proved herself a good sport as the butt of the Farrelly Brothers' "hair mousse" sight gag in 1998's *There's Something About Mary*.

RIGHT
IIn *Bad Teacher* Diaz plays dumb but looks smart in an outfit not often found in school, a tight beige skirt with a red short sleeve turtleneck and heels higher than she can count.

200 1990s

THE NINETEEN NINETIES | HOLLYWOOD FASHION

HALLE BERRY

She may have been a Bond Girl, Catwoman, and an X-Men mutant but this actress can also portray achingly real heroines.

Halle Berry (1966–) is known for playing strong, resilient women in both slick action movies and earthy dramas. Born in Cleveland, Ohio, her first screen role, as a crack addict in *Jungle Fever*, lead to a part in Eddie Murphy's *Boomerang* (costumes by Francine Jamison-Tanchuck). She paired with Warren Beatty in *Bulworth* in 1998 and won a Golden Globe for the TV biography *Introducing Dorothy Dandridge* in 1999. The following year she appeared as the weather-controlling mutant, Storm, in the first *X-Men* movie.

In 2001 she played a sexy mercenary in *Swordfish* and then a grieving mother in *Monster's Ball* (costumes by Frank Fleming). The latter film netted her the Oscar for Best Actress, and her tearful acceptance speech reminded her peers that few black women had been so recognized.

She went on to play a Bond Girl in *Die Another Day*, a "crazy" therapist in *Gothika*, and another mutant superhero in *Catwoman*. In 2012, she appeared as multiple characters in the fantasy film, *Cloud Atlas*. Berry has yet to match the intensity of her *Monster's Ball* performance, but she still has many challenging roles ahead of her.

MOST FASHIONABLE FILMS

SWORDFISH (2001)
DIE ANOTHER DAY (2002)
CATWOMAN (2004)
CLOUD ATLAS (2012)

Berry Style

The face of Revlon Cosmetics for many years, Berry possesses a natural beauty that seems to owe little to cosmetics or trendy clothes. Yet even when dressed down, she remains a favorite with the paparazzi.

Signature Look

- Short, wispy, razor-cut hair
- Loose-fitting tops with tight jeans
- Big sunglasses, ethnic scarves, and couture handbags

> I'm not the girl for superhigh fashion because I don't have the right body.
>
> HALLE BERRY

ABOVE

Berry as Bond girl, in 2002's *Die Another Day*, shows off her trim midriff in a raspberry-and-white polka-dot top and slinky hip skirt.

LEFT

Berry looks gorgeous in a skin tight black gown in 2004's *Catwoman*.

HOLLYWOOD FASHION | THE NINETEEN NINETIES

ALBUM OF TRENDSETTERS
OUR FAVORITE BRUNETTES

They play the spies, the seducers, and the exotic sirens, the divas and the hellions, the girl Fridays and, often, the trusted wives. Always exciting, sometimes sultry and frequently spicy, Hollywood's most cherished brunettes included a number of foreign-born beauties.

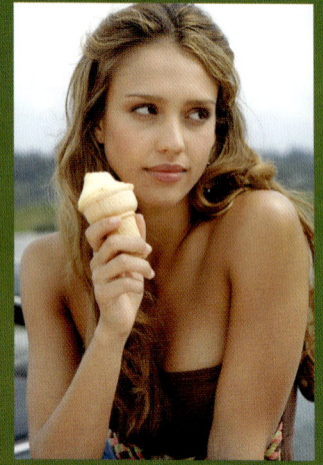

TOP LEFT
Winsome Jessica Alba knows just how to work the strapless dress and the ice-cream cone in 2007's comedy *Good Luck Chuck*.

TOP RIGHT
The appealing Rachel Weisz, here in a classic black-and-white color-blocked top, is one of a young boy's potential mothers in 2008's *Definitely, Maybe*.

BOTTOM LEFT
Green-eyed Jennifer Connelly plays a 1950s' murder victim in the 1996 military thriller, *Mulholland Falls*. Here, she models a v-neck halter top in an era-specific jungle print in shades of turquoise and black.

BOTTOM RIGHT
Salma Hayak, in a doeskin midriff top and buckskin wrap skirt, shows she's armed and dangerous in 2003's *Once Upon a Time in Mexico*.

THE NINETEEN NINETIES | HOLLYWOOD FASHION

> Yes, Howard Hughes invented a bra for me. Or, he tried to. And one of the seamless ones like they have now. He was way ahead of his time. But I never wore it in *'The Outlaw'*. I just told him I did
>
> JANE RUSSELL

TOP LEFT

Dorothy Dandridge, wearing a belted rayon summer dress and free-form necklace, costarred with John Justin in 1957's controversial tale of mixed-race couples, *Island in the Sun*.

TOP RIGHT

Although she was born in rural North Carolina, sloe-eyed Ava Gardner possessed an earthy, Old World appeal that was perfect for period films like 1958's *The Naked Maja*, where she played an 18th-century Spanish noblewoman, the Duchess of Alba.

LEFT

Jane Russell's killer smile, glorious hair, and voluptuous curves made her a standout in films and even allowed her to steal a scene or two from Marilyn Monroe. Here, she poses in a halter-neck turquoise sheath for 1956's *The Revolt of Mamie Stover*.

203

HOLLYWOOD FASHION | THE NINETEEN NINETIES

DREW BARRYMORE

The world fell in love with her in *E.T.* and never lost their admiration for this sometimes-troubled actress from a legendary film family.

Drew Barrymore (1975–) remains appealingly childlike and winsome, even when playing more mature characters. Born in Culver City, California, Barrymore is the granddaughter of screen legends John Barrymore and Dolores Costello. After winning hearts as a child actress in 1982's *E.T. the Extra-Terrestrial*, she embarked on a wild adolescence—including rehab at age 13—and eventually starred in *Poison Ivy*, *Bad Girls*, *Boys on the Side*, *Batman Forever*, *Everyone Says I Love You*, and *Scream*.

Fortunately, by the late 1990s, Barrymore left the drugs and drinking behind and turned her talent to romantic comedies such as *The Wedding Singer*, *Ever After*, and *Fever Pitch* (costumes by Sophie de Rakoff). In 1996 she formed Flower Films with associate Nancy Juvonen and produced *Never Been Kissed* (costumes by Mona May), *Charlie's Angels*, *50 First Dates*, and *Music and Lyrics* (costumes by Tom Soluri), and the indie cult classic, *Donnie Darko*. In 2009 Barrymore was lauded for playing Little Edie in the TV miniseries *Grey Gardens*, receiving both the Screen Actors Guild Award and the Golden Globe.

Barrymore was named Ambassador Against Hunger for the UN World Food Programme (WFP) and in 2007 donated more than one million dollars to the project.

ABOVE

In *Music and Lyrics*, Barrymore looks funky but put together in a Bohemian way.

RIGHT

In *Lucky You*, Barrymore looks graceful and tastefully madeup in a red evening dress as she sings her heart out.

MOST FASHIONABLE FILMS

CHARLIE'S ANGELS (2000)
50 FIRST DATES (2004)
FEVER PITCH (2005)
MUSIC AND LYRICS (2007)

Barrymore Style

Since 2009, she has been modeling for Cover Girl cosmetics and remains a much sought-after celebrity spokeswoman.

Signature Look

- Long, tousled, ombre-effect hair
- Boho separates in bold patterns
- Draped, feminine gowns

THE NINETEEN NINETIES | HOLLYWOOD FASHION

GWYNETH PALTROW

Paltrow Style
The actress enjoys showing off her shapely legs, and frequently wears micro-minidresses with stiletto heels.

Signature Look
- Simple, unadorned dresses and trouser suits
- Classic high heels
- Long, straight, ash-blonde hair

The thinking man's playmate, Paltrow has moved from charming corset roles to modern melodramas.

Gwyneth Paltrow (1972–) typifies the beautiful, self-assured ice queen who rarely steps down from her pedestal. Born in Los Angeles to a show-business family—her mother is actress Blythe Danner and her father was producer Bruce Paltrow—she began acting in 1990 and gained early notice in *Flesh and Bone* and *Seven*.

For an actress with such a modern sensibility, Paltrow managed to be convincing in period films like *Jefferson in Paris*, *Emma*, and *Great Expectations* before landing a career-making starring role in *Shakespeare in Love* (costumes by Sandy Powell), which earned her the Best Actress Oscar. She followed with the romantic mystery *Possession* in 2002 and the grim film biography, *Sylvia*, in 2003.

Paltrow proved she was a good sport, sparring with Robert Downey Jr. in 2008's blockbuster, *Iron Man* (costumes by Rebecca Bentjen and Laura Jean Shannon) and again in the two sequels. She received critical accolades for *Two Lovers* with Joaquin Phoenix and showcased her singing voice as a troubled bluegrass star in *Country Strong* (costumes by Stacey Battat). Once romantically linked with Brad Pitt and Ben Affleck, Paltrow has two children—daughter, Apple, and son, Moses, from her 13-year marriage to Chris Martin of Coldplay; in 2018 she wed writer/producer Brad Falchuk.

MOST FASHIONABLE FILMS

EMMA (1996)
SHAKESPEARE IN LOVE (1998)
THE TALENTED MR. RIPLEY (1999)
THE ROYAL TENENBAUMS (2001)
POSSESSION (2002)
IRON MAN (2008)

ABOVE
Paltrow looks relaxed with a print skirt and white blouse tied at the waist in *The Talented Mr. Ripley*.

LEFT
In *Country Strong*, Paltrow rocks her legs and boots with a hot red dress and showed everyone her fine singing voice.

205

HOLLYWOOD FASHION | THE NINETEEN NINETIES

MEN OF THE 1990s
TENDER-HEARTED TOUGH GUYS

ABOVE

Mel Gibson, clad in leather armor and wearing blue woad face paint, rouses his men as Scots leader William Wallace in the 1995 epic, *Braveheart*. The film went on to win the Academy Award for Best Picture and also earned Gibson a Best Director Oscar.

TOP RIGHT

As the world's swinging-est spy, Mike Myers—in blue-velvet Edwardian suit and white-lace jabot—raises a glass to these bouffant-haired baby-dolled beauties in *Austin Powers: The Spy Who Shagged Me* (1999).

BOTTOM RIGHT

Doomed lovers Kate Winslet, in a bronze, tiered Edwardian dinner gown with crystal beading, and Leonardo DiCaprio, wearing a collarless shirt and broadcloth trousers, share what will become their last dance in 1997's chart-topper, *Titanic*.

Director Quentin Tarantino's early 1990s' crime duo, *Reservoir Dogs* and *Pulp Fiction*, introduced the modern hoodlum uniform of narrow ties and fitted black suits, co-opting the staid corporate look and transforming it into outlaw hip. He did something similar to spice up Uma Thurman in *Pulp Fiction*, adding a naughty black bra beneath her demure white shirt.

Heavy Metal and Hip Hop

This was also the decade when Arnold Schwarzenegger introduced us to the heavy metal and leather look of the *Terminator*, hip-hop street style ruled the *Boyz n the Hood*, stoner/grunge styles identified characters in *Slackers* and *Clerks*, and preppy duds got a new lease on life in films such as *Rushmore*, *Good Will Hunting*, and *Scent of a Woman*.

Other Favorites

Science-fiction films grew increasingly popular, especially entries like 1993's *Jurassic Park* from director Steven Spielberg, 1996's *Independence Day* with Jeff Goldblum, 1997's *Men in Black* with Will Smith and Tommy Lee Jones, and 1998's *Armageddon* with Bruce Willis and Ben Affleck. Willis also appeared in 1999's unsettling thriller, *The Sixth Sense*, playing a soulful shrink in a rumpled raincoat.

Comedy got a Bond-size boost with Mike Myers' 1999 send-up of the British spy franchise, *Austin Powers: The Spy Who Shagged Me*, which simultaneously lampooned and popularized many 1960s' fashion trends, including velvet suits and puffy shirts for men, and mini-dresses and hip-huggers for women. And 1998's *Rush Hour* paired dapper comedian Chris Tucker with martial arts legend Jackie Chan.

Romance fans, of course, reveled in the tragic glory—and lush costumes—of *Titanic* and saw the reunion of *Pretty Woman* costars Richard Gere and Julia Roberts in 1999's *Runaway Bride*. (Note to Roberts: You tried, but those cuffed jeans don't cut it!) For adventure aficionados, Brendan Fraser proved to be a scoundrel with a heart of gold—and an Indiana Jones wardrobe—in 1999's *The Mummy*.

THE NINETEEN NINETIES | HOLLYWOOD FASHION

In a period movie, everybody pretty much accepts that you got it right...But when you do contemporary every single person has an opinion, and believes that their vision of the 1970s or last year is the vision.

KYM BARRETT, COSTUME DESIGNER

Signature Menswear Looks of the 1990s
- Grunge-style oversize flannel shirts
- Hip-hop styles
- Slogan T-shirts
- Track suits
- Preppy khaki slacks
- Bomber jackets

TOP LEFT

Dancing to Chuck Berry's "You Never Can Tell" in 1994's *Pulp Fiction*, John Travolta and Uma Thurman have all the right moves. This dark, campy groundbreaker by Quentin Tarantino created a whole new gangster ethos—"skinny" black suits, foolish, impromptu dialogue laced with foul language, and a nonstop send-up of the conventions of earlier crime films.

BOTTOM LEFT

Arnold Schwarzenegger, as a time-traveling cyborg in 1991's *Terminator 2: Judgment Day*, brings back black...black leather jackets and biker pants, tight black T-shirts, and black-and-chrome motorcycles.

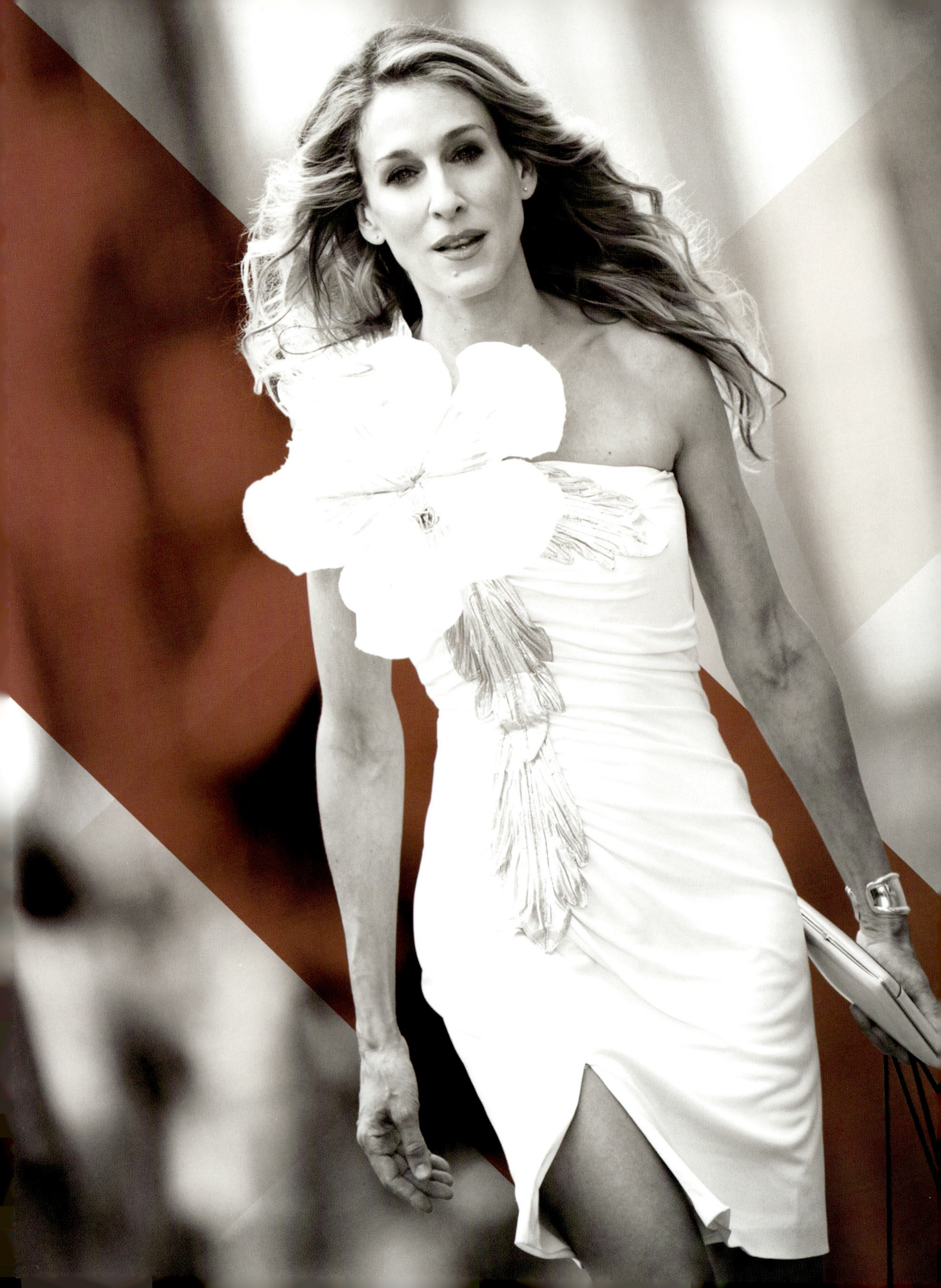

THE NEW MILLENNIUM

As the old century gave way to the new, the 2000s clearly became the decade of big-budget adventures— *Harry Potter*, *Lord of the Rings*, *Spider-Man*, and *Pirates of the Caribbean*—and their numerous sequels. Fashion in the 2000s was also about recycling ideas, perhaps because in sober post-9/11 America, it seemed disrespectful to pursue edgy, new trends. In this fashion mash-up, vintage styles from the 1940s to the 1980s blended with African, Bollywood, and other global themes as well as pop music staples— hoodies, high-top sneakers, military jackets, Western shirts and Lolita/Harajuku fashions.

Yet couture was by no means dead in Hollywood. Anne Hathaway in *The Devil Wears Prada* went from drab to fab... and sent sales of knee-high boots and designer handbags soaring. The *Sex and the City* movie had women craving those Blahniks, Louboutins, and Jimmy Choos. And fashionable coeds and working girls got wardrobe inspirations from stylish young blondes like Reese Witherspoon.

By the 2010s, some trendspotters claimed Hollywood was no longer inspiring fashion choices, but then came the mighty Marvel incursion. Tony Stark's preppy CEO in *Iron Man*, both *Thor*'s long golden locks and his retro mullet, Peter Quill's steampunk space pirate in *Guardians of the Galaxy*, and *Black Panther*'s sleek futuristic uniform all borrowed from past films but offered something new as well—superhero pizzazz. Not be outdone, DC Comics gave us a *Wonder Woman* for the ages...with beautiful period costumes.

Only time will tell what future fashion trends will be inspired by movies yet to be made... or what hip street wear will wind up being glorified in film.

HOLLYWOOD FASHION | THE NEW MILLENNIUM AND BEYOND

ANNE HATHAWAY

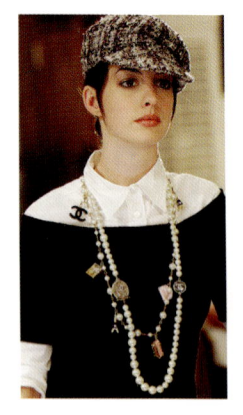

Whether playing a klutzy princess, a fashion disaster, or a lovelorn British author, this actress ultimately ends up cool and collected.

It could be said of Anne Hathaway (1982–) that her progression has matched that of Mia in *The Princess Diaries*—gawky, free-spirited teenager gives way to polished and poised aristocrat. Born in Brooklyn, she grew up in New Jersey and by high school was starring in dramatic and musical plays.

Hathaway's 2001 debut film, Disney's *The Princess Diaries* (costumes by Gary Jones) was an instant hit. She followed up with convincing costume roles—a cursed damsel in *Ella Enchanted* and Jane Austen in *Becoming Jane*—and poignantly portrayed a neglected wife in *Brokeback Mountain*. In Hathaway's signature film, 2006's *The Devil Wears Prada*, she held her own against the awesomeness of Meryl Streep—and got to wear designer duds assembled by Patricia Field.

Hathaway received critical acclaim for the 2008 indie film, *Rachel Getting Married*, which costarred Debra Winger, and returned to mainstream comedy to spar with Kate Hudson in 2009's *Bride Wars*. In 2010 she played the White Queen in *Alice in Wonderland*, and in 2011 she morphed into a lithe Catwoman in *The Dark Knight Rises*. 2012 finally brought her a bona fide singing role—the tragic Fantine in the long-awaited film of the stage hit *Les Misérables*, for which she won the Best Supporting Actress Oscar.

MOST FASHIONABLE FILMS

THE PRINCESS DIARIES (2001)
ELLA ENCHANTED (2004)
THE DEVIL WEARS PRADA (2006)
ALICE IN WONDERLAND (2010)

Hathaway Style
The actress laments that she has a small face with large features, but no one else is complaining. Her aura of great robustness and charming playfulness is reflected in her sporty-yet-feminine fashion choices. In January 2008 Hathaway became the face of the Lancôme fragrance, Magnifique.

Signature Look
- Romantic, retro gowns
- Feminine blouses with tweed skirts and jackets
- Simple, monochromatic separates

ABOVE

Hathaway's character, post screen makeover, now sports a Chanel tweed newsboy cap and necklaces over a white Oxford shirt and black, drop-shouldered sweater in *The Devil Wear Prada*.

RIGHT

For her role as a secret agent in *Get Smart*, Hathaway goes undercover in a mini-skirt with long sleeve shirt and wide black belt.

CATHERINE ZETA-JONES

This luminous Welsh actress proved that a beautiful woman with a quirky smile and a sense of humor could take Hollywood—and America—by storm.

Catherine Zeta-Jones (1969–) portrays sexually confident women who often keep their true agendas a secret. A native of Swansea, Wales, Zeta-Jones was a born entertainer who took to the stage at 11 and was starring in the British revival of *42nd Street* by 15. She then became a sensation on British television with the hit series *The Darling Buds of May*.

After her smoldering Hollywood breakthrough in 1998's *The Mask of Zorro* with Antonio Banderas (costumes by Graciela Mazón), the actress seemed destined to play opposite Hollywood's sexiest men. She starred with Sean Connery in *Entrapment* (costumes by Penny Rose), Liam Neeson in *The Haunting*, George Clooney and Brad Pitt in *Ocean's Twelve*, and, more recently, Tom Cruise in *Rock of Ages*.

Critics began taking her seriously in 2000 after her turn as a pregnant, hard-nosed drug kingpin in best picture nominee, *Traffic*, which also starred Michael Douglas and Benicio del Toro. In 2002, she costarred (and sang and danced in the early stages of pregnancy) with Renée Zellweger and Richard Gere in the Oscar-winning musical *Chicago*. Zellweger was nominated for Best Actress, while Zeta-Jones took home the statuette for Best Supporting Actress. (Colleen Atwood also won for costume design.)

In a very public courtship, the Welsh beauty was wooed and won by Hollywood auteur actor/producer Michael Douglas. They have two children, Dylan and Carys.

MOST FASHIONABLE FILMS

THE MARK OF ZORRO (1998)
ENTRAPMENT (1999)
CHICAGO (2002)

Zeta-Jones Style
Like most Hollywood royalty, Zeta-Jones prefers richly embellished fabrics for evening and classy separates for daytime.

Signature Look
- Strapless gowns in jewel tones
- Knee-length dress and coat ensembles
- Tailored, feminine skirt suits

ABOVE

Zeta-Jones made an indelible impression as a fiery senorita from Old California in 1998's *The Mask of Zorro*. Here, she looks muy caliente in a white ruffled gown worn with a burgundy velvet vest and red sash.

LEFT

In 2002's *Chicago*, Zeta-Jones relied on her stage experience as a dancer to perform her own strenuous routines while wearing Jazz Age outfits, including this midnight-blue velvet and ecru lace costume.

HOLLYWOOD FASHION | THE NEW MILLENNIUM AND BEYOND

CHARLIZE THERON

This South African beauty is not afraid to downplay her looks when a gritty role requires it.

Charlize Theron (1975–) is known for portraying determined women who don't always play by the rules. Born in the Johannesburg area, at 15 she experienced personal trauma when her mother was forced to shoot her drunken father in self-defense. She flew to Hollywood in 1994—the ticket a gift from her mother—to pursue an acting career. After she made a scene in a bank over a misunderstanding, an agent gave her his card.

Early films like *That Thing You Do!* led to lead roles in *The Devil's Advocate*, *Mighty Joe Young*, *The Astronaut's Wife* (costumes by Isis Mussenden), *The Cider House Rules* (Renee Ehrlich Kalfus) and *The Italian Job* (Mark Bridges).

After establishing herself as a glamorous presence in Hollywood, Theron stunned audiences with her 2003 turn as blowsy serial killer Aileen Wuornos in *Monster*—a grueling performance that landed her an Oscar for Best Actress.

She again hid her looks behind miner's gear as an employee fighting for women's rights in *North Country*, and then played a futuristic assassin in *Æon Flux* (Beatrix Aruna Pasztor), a determined cop in *In the Valley of Elah*, a closeted alien in *Hancock*, a scheming, immature writer in *Young Adult*, and an icy space explorer in Ridley Scott's *Prometheus*.

The actress has a son, Jackson, who was born in 2011 and whom she adopted in 2012.

> **Hey, I'm a girl, and we like to play dress-up.**
> CHARLIZE THERON

ABOVE
Theron models a classic menswear-look jacket and white Oxford blouse with one of her "Mini" costars in the 2003 heist thriller, *The Italian Job*.

RIGHT
Theron's fierce warrior Imperator Furiosa helped make *Mad Max: Fury Road* a box office hit. The stark post-apocalyptic costumes by Jenny Beavens earned the designer an Academy Award and a BAFTA.

MOST FASHIONABLE FILMS
THE CIDER HOUSE RULES (1999)
THE ITALIAN JOB (2003)
ÆON FLUX (2005)
SNOW WHITE AND THE HUNTSMAN (2012)

Theron Style
The face of Dior's J'Adore fragrance, the actress is also a red-carpet darling. Off screen, she prefers trendy separates.

Signature Look
- Sexy black or white evening gowns
- Pencil jeans with masculine jackets and fedoras
- Leather pants with oversize tops

THE NEW MILLENNIUM AND BEYOND | HOLLYWOOD FASHION

UMA THURMAN

MOST FASHIONABLE FILMS
DANGEROUS LIAISONS (1988)
KILL BILL VOL. I (2003)
THE PRODUCERS (2005)

Thurman Style
When out with her kids, Thurman favors casual jeans and cotton separates, but this spokeswoman for Lancome Cosmetics is also a perennial red-carpet favorite, often showcasing designer Christian Dior.

Signature Look
- Feminine, flowing evening gowns in white or neutral colors
- Dark suits with bold accents
- Asian-influenced tops and jewelry

This leggy, gilded cinema goddess was an ungainly, insecure child who used her imagination to escape taunting classmates.

Uma Thurman (1970–) is known for playing smart, sexy women who can take care of themselves. Born in Boston, this child of a European socialite and a Buddhist scholar grew up in an eccentric but spiritual household. This unorthodox upbringing has often informed her choice of film roles. Thurman first gained notice in 1988, with the historical melodrama, *Dangerous Liaisons* (costumes by James Acheson), and followed with the Henry Miller biography, *Henry & June*. She got her big break—and a Supporting Actress Oscar nomination—in Quentin Tarantino's *Pulp Fiction* playing a gangster's reckless wife (costumes by Betsy Heimann), who shares an inspired dance with John Travolta.

After starring in two notorious flops—*Batman & Robin* and *The Avengers*, she quickly redeemed herself—and won a Golden Globe—with the TV drama, *Hysterical Blindness*. Thurman was a lethal bride in Tarantino's *Kill Bill, Vol. I and II* (costumes, including that standout yellow tracksuit, by Kumiko Ogawa and Catherine Thomas), and sang and danced in "gooey gowns" in the musical version of *The Producers*.

ABOVE
Thurman made the most of her leggy appeal while singing and dancing as a Broadway musical wannabe in a white V-neck dress with a slit skirt and playful panel scarf in 2005's *The Producers*.

LEFT
Thurman, as The Bride, looks sharp with her trademark yellow tracksuit and Samurai sword in Quentin Tarantino's violent duo, *Kill Bill Vol. I & II*.

HOLLYWOOD FASHION | THE NEW MILLENNIUM AND BEYOND

ALBUM OF TRENDSETTERS
OSCAR STYLES 1970s — 2000s

The first color telecast of the Academy Awards was in 1966, and from then on Hollywood provided enough glitz and glamour to bring viewers back year after year. Since 1969 the show has been broadcast internationally. At present, the Oscars are telecast in at least 200 countries and the Academy claims as many as one billion viewers worldwide.

As for the Best Costume Design Award, sadly, the Oscar telecast has gone from featuring actual examples of a costume designer's work in past years to barely mentioning the nominees' names. Now the real fashion show is on the red carpet rather than on the stage. Attendees of both sexes are regularly asked by the TV media to name their designer and jeweler.

TOP RIGHT

Cher has never shied away from dressing dramatically. Love it or hate it, her 1988 Bob Mackie gown for when she won for *Moonstruck* is still on *Vogue*'s list of best Oscar dresses.

RIGHT

In 1989, Jodi Foster won for *The Accused* and Dustin Hoffman won for *Rain Man*. Foster's dress was not as much of a success and Giorgio Armani offered to style her for the following year's show.

BOTTOM RIGHT

At the 1970 awards, Elizabeth Taylor, with Richard Burton, wore a plunging violet dress from Edith Head that matched her eyes along with a 69-carat, pear-shaped Cartier diamond necklace.

214 2000s & BEYOND

THE NEW MILLENNIUM AND BEYOND | HOLLYWOOD FASHION

You can never be overdressed or overeducated.
OSCAR WILDE

TOP LEFT

Cosmopolitan magazine called Cate Blanchett's 2007 Giorgio Armani Prive sheath one of the best Oscar gowns of all time.

TOP RIGHT

In 1998, Sharon Stone, with Phil Bronstein, went for hi-low chic in a Vera Wang skirt with a white Gap shirt.

LEFT

The 2019 Academy Awards telecast was Lady Gaga's night to dazzle—and win a Best Song Oscar—in a sweeping black ball gown by Brandon Maxwell, her former stylist.

HOLLYWOOD FASHION | THE NEW MILLENNIUM AND BEYOND

ANGELINA JOLIE

Some says its her voluptuous mouth, others claim its her catlike walk, but whichever of her physical attributes strike a chord, there is no doubting this actress's sensual appeal.

Angelina Jolie (1975–) is known for playing sexy women of intelligence and immeasurable cool. Born in Los Angeles, she is the daughter of actor Jon Voight and French actress Marcheline Bertrand. Jolie began studying with Lee Strasberg at age 11 and by her late teens was modeling and appearing in indie films. After receiving Golden Globes for the TV movies *George Wallace* and *Gia*, she was cast in the 1999 big budget thriller *The Bone Collector* with Denzel Washington. Next came *Girl, Interrupted*, the true story of young women coping with mental illness and Jolie's powerful performance opposite Winona Ryder earned her a Best Supporting Oscar and another Golden Globe.

Jolie, who suffered from depression, became notorious for her bizarre behavior. wearing second husband Billy Bob Thornton's blood in a vial. With the release of the hit *Lara Croft: Tomb Raider*, the public grew more tolerant of the young actress. In 2006, she starred with Brad Pitt in *Mr. and Mrs. Smith* (costumes by Michael Kaplan) and the two were soon a major tabloid "item." After living together—and creating a family that included six children—they married in 2014...and officially split in 2016.

In 2007, Jolie starred in a pair of melodramas—*A Mighty Heart* and *Changeling*, then in three thrillers—*Wanted*, *Salt*, and *The Tourist* with Johnny Depp. 2014 saw her portray *Maleficent*, a powerful misunderstood fairy, in the Disney hit film. A sequel is in progress.

Jolie is known for her tireless humanitarian work for refugees and is a former UN Goodwill Ambassador.

MOST FASHIONABLE FILMS
ORIGINAL SIN (2001)
MR. AND MRS. SMITH (2005)
THE TOURIST (2010)

Jolie Style
Considered by many to be the most beautiful woman in Hollywood, Jolie's fashion choices are often obscured by her overall aura of glamour.

Signature Look
- Dramatic couture gowns
- Sleek, dark upswept hair with striking earrings
- Sexy, yet understated daywear

ABOVE
In 2008's *Changeling*, Jolie plays a Jazz-era mother who searches for her missing son after being presented with an imposter. Here, she models a peach-colored cloche hat and boxy brown wool coat with mink collar and cuffs.

RIGHT
In 2005's *Mr. and Mrs. Smith*, both Jolie and future husband, Brad Pitt, prove that even hired assassins can find time to dance—and look fashionably swanky.

216 2000s & BEYOND

THE NEW MILLENNIUM AND BEYOND | HOLLYWOOD FASHION

SARA JESSICA PARKER

America's favorite fashionista, this leggy actress has conquered stage, screen, and television.

Sarah Jessica Parker (1965–) plays sassy, confident New York women who are not afraid to buck the trends. Born in Ohio, Parker's early training in singing and ballet led to a year as *Annie* on Broadway. She soon added TV roles like *Square Pegs* to her resume and found work in films such as *Footloose*.

Her first movie lead was 1985's *Girls Just Wanna Have Fun*, followed by a notable turn as Steve Martin's lover in 1991's *L.A. Story*. She kept up her momentum with *Honeymoon in Vegas* (costumes by Julie Weiss), *Hocus Pocus*, *Ed Wood*, and *Miami Rhapsody*. 1996 found her on screen in *The First Wives Club*, *If Lucy Fell*, and *Mars Attacks!*. She also took to the stage in *Sylvia*, playing a dog, *How to Succeed in Business Without Really Trying* with husband Matthew Broderick, and the Tony-nominated *Once Upon a Mattress*.

TV called again in 1998, offering Parker a series about female friendships, sexual relationships, and designer shoes. *Sex and the City* lasted six years and spun off not one but two movie sequels. As Carrie Bradshaw, sage sex columnist, Parker became a fashion guru (abetted by designer Patricia Field), sparking a return to retro styles and encouraging women to dress up.

Recent films include *The Family Stone* (Shay Cunliffe), *Failure to Launch* (Ellen Mirojnick), and the ensemble comedy *New Year's Eve*.

MOST FASHIONABLE FILMS

MIAMI RHAPSODY (1995)
THE FAMILY STONE (2005)
SEX AND THE CITY (2008)

Parker Style

While TV's Carrie managed to combine ballet tutus, Hawaiian shirts, tube tops, and 3D purses, the real SJP opts for a more glamorous tone. In 2007, Parker launched her own line of clothing, Bitten. Her three signature fragrances are Covet, Lovely, and SJP NYC.

Signature Look
- Cinch-waisted short dresses
- Strapless evening gowns with pouf skirts
- Endless supply of high-heeled designer shoes

> **But there are no rules with Pat when it comes to fashion. It's liberating.**
> SARAH JESSICA PARKER ON WORKING WITH *SEX AND THE CITY* DESIGNER PATRICIA FIELD

ABOVE

In 1992's *Honeymoon in Vegas*, Parker is dressed for a wedding she hopes won't happen.

LEFT

Parker again reprised her TV character, Carrie Bradshaw, in the 2010 film *Sex and the City 2*. Here, she keeps her cool in a short white dress while walking down the street in New York.

HOLLYWOOD FASHION | THE NEW MILLENNIUM AND BEYOND

FASHION INFLUENCE
HORROR FILMS

From *Dracula* and *The Wolf Man* to *Rosemary's Baby* and *Twilight*, horror movies have always had a powerful effect on American culture and subsequently on American fashion. And it wasn't only Halloween or masquerade costumes that were being influenced; fashion designers have been borrowing from the horror genre for decades.

In recent years, Alexander McQueen's designs were influenced by Jack the Ripper and Dante's *Inferno*; Dame Vivienne Westwood, Karl Lagerfeld, Chanel, and Dior all sent models to the catwalk in zombie makeup and goth clothing; and in 2012 Christian Siriano created a line of gowns based on the film, *The Vampire Bat*.

Dracula's Children

Early vampire films such as 1922's *Nosferatu* and 1931's *Dracula* with Bela Lugosi established the persona of the now-familiar count, with his formal Victorian clothing, sinister expression, mesmerizing glance, oddly elongated fingers, and ability to transform into a bat.

Vampire films remained popular and influenced several cultural movements during the latter part of the 20th century, including Goth fashions and Japanese animé. Goths, with their pale skin, black fingernails, tattoos, biker boots, and leather clothing embellished with chains and spikes were influenced by early punk rockers, who clearly took their sartorial cues from the vampire genre. Films with a Goth sensibility include *Beetlejuice*; *The Hunger*; *The Addams Family*; Tim Burton's *Edward Scissorhands* and *Batman*; *The Crow*, and *The Girl with the Dragon Tattoo*.

The *Twilight* film franchise of the 2000s, based on the books by Stephenie Meyer, also harks directly back to the *Dracula* canon. Meyer's pale-skinned vampires "sparkle" when exposed to sunlight and have superhuman strength. Though the good vampires dress in modern clothing, their amoral leaders, the Volturi, are attired, as one would expect, in dark velvet and hooded capes. The popularity of these and other recent vampire films and TV series has given rise to a thriving vampire culture, where some fans have taken their obsession to an

ABOVE
In 2011's *The Girl with the Dragon Tattoo*, Rooney Mara's Goth style was influenced by earlier vampire films.

RIGHT
Angelica Huston and Raul Julia get into the mood for amore as Morticia and Gomez Addams in the film version of the popular TV series, *The Addams Family*. Both Goth and steampunk styles were influenced by the film's eclectic, Bohemian costumes.

THE NEW MILLENNIUM AND BEYOND | HOLLYWOOD FASHION

> **I never play without my cape.**
> BELA LUGOSI

TOP LEFT

Even though Hungarian Bela Lugosi was the "Drac Daddy" of screen vampires, officially he only appeared twice as the bloodthirsty Count—in Tod Browning's *Dracula* in 1931 and in *Abbott and Costello Meet Frankenstein* in 1948.

TOP RIGHT

The Wolf Man from 1941, which starred Lon Chaney Jr., followed an earlier template and told the story of a nice guy who transforms into a monster after being bitten by a werewolf. Variations on the theme include *I Was a Teenage Werewolf*, *The Howling*, *An American Werewolf in London*, *Teen Wolf*, and *Wolf* with Jack Nicholson.

CENTER LEFT

Imperiled mother Mia Farrow arms herself against devil-worshippers—yet manages to look crisp and fresh in her lace-trimmed summer robe—in *Rosemary's Baby*.

BOTTOM LEFT

The angst-ridden, romantic *Twilight* films—which debuted in 2008—were based on the novels of Stephenie Meyer and featured Kristen Stewart as a mortal girl torn between brooding teen vampire, Robert Pattinson, and moody, Native American werewolf, Taylor Lautner.

extreme, displaying extensive tattoos, surgical body sculpting, and fang implants.

Dying to Look Good

Of the many horror films offering fashion-conscious protagonists along with the screams and scares, at least three were directed by Alfred Hitchcock: In *The Birds*, Tippi Hedren spends the film in a pale-green Chanel-style suit; in *Rear Window*, Grace Kelly is a fashion editor in designer dresses and a killer charm bracelet; and in *Psycho*, motel owner Anthony Perkins wears classic preppy shirts and chinos—and carries a very large knife.

Other fashion-forward horror films include *Rosemary's Baby*, with Mia Farrow in her schoolgirl collars and tasteful cotton maternity frocks; *The Mummy*, with Rachel Weisz's multiethnic riding outfits; *Alien* with Sigourney Weaver kicking butt in iconic Rambo-esque fatigues; and *Halloween*, with Jamie Lee Curtis and friends embodying the late 1970s in wide-leg bell-bottoms, sweater vests, and big hair.

HOLLYWOOD FASHION | THE NEW MILLENNIUM AND BEYOND

KEIRA KNIGHTLEY

Her continued success in costume dramas makes this British actress with the angular cheekbones the natural successor to Norma Shearer and Deborah Kerr.

In spite of her delicate appearance, Keira Knightley (1985–) often plays tomboys or feisty, independent young women in period films. Born in London, England, to a theatrical family, Knightley first gained international attention in the popular 2002 film *Bend It Like Beckham*. She then played a fur-enrobed Lara—the role made famous by Julie Christie—in the TV miniseries *Doctor Zhivago*.

After appearing in 2003's ensemble film *Love Actually*, Knightley was cast in the Disney romp, *Pirates of the Caribbean: The Curse of the Black Pearl*. The resulting blockbuster franchise (costumed by Penny Rose) would properly launch her career and make her winsome face one of the most recognized on the planet.

After costarring with Clive Owen in *King Arthur* ("swords and sandals" costumes by Penny Rose), she was offered the part of Elizabeth Bennett in a 2005 remake of *Pride and Prejudice*. The subsequent hit film (with costumes by Jacqueline Durran) earned her an Oscar nomination and confirmed her true star power.

She gave a poignant performance in the 2007 tragedy, *Atonement*, (and wore an iconic green dinner dress from Jacqueline Durran that landed on many "favorite" lists). In 2008's *The Duchess*, she did credit to the lavish Academy Award–winning Georgian costumes of Michael O'Connor. By the end of that year, she was the second-highest-paid actress in Hollywood. In 2012 she earned critical raves for her performance as the tragic *Anna Karenina* (costumes again by Jacqueline Durran).

ABOVE
In 2007's *Atonement*, Knightley, in a sumptuous green backless dress, has her ife thrown off course by misunderstandings and the coming war.

RIGHT
In 2004's *Love Actually*, Knightley wears a modern white gown at her wedding.

MOST FASHIONABLE FILMS
PIRATES OF THE CARIBBEAN: THE CURSE OF THE BLACK PEARL (2003)
ATONEMENT (2007)
THE DUCHESS (2008)
ANNA KARENINA (2012)

Knightley Style
Even when she is not wearing period gowns and beribboned bonnets, this actress frequently gets dolled up for red-carpet and charity events.

Signature Look
- "Barely there" gowns
- Designer daywear dresses
- Hip-hugger, skintight jeans with trendy tops

THE NEW MILLENNIUM AND BEYOND | HOLLYWOOD FASHION

NATALIE PORTMAN

MOST FASHIONABLE FILMS

CLOSER (2004)
MY BLUEBERRY NIGHTS (2007)
THE OTHER WOMAN (2009)
BLACK SWAN (2010)

Portman Style
This young actress is not above experimenting with her clothing choices. She sometimes opts for trendy or modern on the red carpet, but usually relies on timeless glamour.

Signature Look
- Ruffled or draped gowns
- Balloon skirts
- Man-tailored daywear worn with girly shoes

The ultimate professional, this brilliant young actress nearly disappears into her many varied roles.

Wise beyond her years, Natalie Portman (1981–) powerfully combines a penetrating and mature intuition with the dewy aura of innocence. Portman was born in Jerusalem, Israel, but grew up in New York. After being "discovered" in a pizza parlor, she burst onto the cinema scene as a scared, emotionally scarred child who hires an assassin in *Léon: The Professional*. She was also a teenage standout in the ensemble film *Beautiful Girls* and added gravitas to the general goofiness of *Mars Attacks!*. During the making of the second *Star Wars* trilogy, Portman, who played feisty-yet-vulnerable Queen Amidala, admitted to some difficulty with the "blue screen" work—acting opposite non-existent creatures awaiting CGI treatment.

Happily, she regained her footing in the acclaimed weepers *Anywhere But Here* and *Where the Heart Is*. Portman again scored in 2004 as a charming eccentric in the indie hit, *Garden State*, and as a cynical prostitute in Mike Nichols' adult drama, *Closer*. 2005 saw the release of cult favorite *V for Vendetta* with Portman in the pivotal role of Evey.

Her interpretation of Nina, the neurotic, conflicted ballerina in the 2010 melodrama, *Black Swan*, was arguably the most compelling performance in a dancing role since Moira Shearer pirouetted in the *Red Shoes*. Portman, who took ballet as a child, trained for more than a year and was beautifully convincing as a prima ballerina. She went on to win a host of Best Actress awards including the Oscar, the Golden Globe and the BAFTA. Amy Wescott designed the film's costumes, while Rodarte created the tutus.

ABOVE
In 2009's *The Other Woman*, Portman, looking beautiful in a simple black cocktail dress, goes after her boss but ends up with something unexpected.

LEFT
Portman, in funky baby doll dress, plays a poker player who can't go home in 2007's *My Blueberry Nights*.

HOLLYWOOD FASHION | **THE NEW MILLENNIUM AND BEYOND**

ABOVE

Field managed to establish and maintain four distinct personas when designing for the quartet of friends in *Sex and the City*—uptown chic for demure Charlotte, preppy classics for lawyer Miranda, peek-a-boo outfits for cougar Samantha, and Boho separates for questing romantic Carrie.

The way you dress yourself is a form of self-expression, and a way of communicating to others who you are. But style is broader than just fashion—it's not only the way you dress, but how you decorate your home, the books you read. It all runs together. The more ways you can express yourself the better, because then you are communicating at a higher level.
PATRICIA FIELD

Fashion Legacy
- Ballet tutus as streetwear
- Field takes credit for introducing the modern legging to Europe in the 1970s
- Oversize flower pins
- Gold nameplate necklaces

222 2000s & BEYOND

THE NEW MILLENNIUM AND BEYOND | HOLLYWOOD FASHION

STYLE MAKER
PATRICIA FIELD

MOST FASHIONABLE DESIGNS
MIAMI RHAPSODY (1995)
THE DEVIL WEARS PRADA (2006)
SEX AND THE CITY (2008)

This high-octane costume designer and fashion pioneer manages to be totally today and amusingly retro all at the same time.

Movie and television designer Patricia Field (1941–) is often labeled a visionary for her ability to spot a style trend or take a tiny ripple in the fashion industry and turn it into a tsunami. The child of a Greek father and Armenian mother, she grew up in Astoria, Queens. Her career as a designer began with the opening of her Greenwich Village boutique in 1966, which for more than four decades would remain the fashion mecca for hip celebrities who wanted something quirky or memorable to wear. Field won her first Emmy in 1990 for *Shelley Duvall's Mother Goose Rock'n' Rhyme*, and was likewise honored for *Sex and the City*. She also won five Costume Designers Guild Awards, four for *Sex and the City* and one for *Ugly Betty*.

In 1995, while designing costumes for the film *Miami Rhapsody*, Field worked with actress Sarah Jessica Parker. It would prove to be a fortuitous meeting—Parker was impressed with Field's clothing collection and the two became friends. When Parker was cast as Carrie Bradshaw in HBO's *Sex and the City*, she turned to Field, a born and bred New Yorker, to give her heroine a distinctive "look." Field was soon designing or styling outfits for all the characters on the hit show; she became known for her ability to put together eclectic or vintage elements and make them contemporary and chic.

Nominated for an Oscar in 2006 for *The Devil Wears Prada*, Field admits that in this film she was more of a "style wrangler," putting together ensembles from couture designers rather than creating costumes from scratch.

With her signature bright red hair and outsized personality, the openly lesbian Field is a high-profile presence at many fashion events. She also appeared as the first guest judge during the inaugural year of Project Runway. She is currently working on U by Kotex to "ban the bland" and add color to feminine protection products. Field has also designed a line of inexpensive but fashionable shoes, boots, and bags for Payless.

LEFT

Field culled the best of the current couture collections for the fashions in 2006's *The Devil Wears Prada*. Here, magazine publisher Meryl Streep, in a classic trenchcoat, conveys her displeasure during a fashion preview as her art director, Stanley Tucci, pulsating with plaid, looks on.

HOLLYWOOD FASHION | THE NEW MILLENNIUM AND BEYOND

REESE WITHERSPOON

After paying her dues in character roles, this Southern belle moved to romantic leads—and proved brains and beauty were not mutually exclusive.

Reese Witherspoon (1976–) is known for playing upbeat, determined go-getters who aren't afraid of a fight. Born in New Orleans, Witherspoon made her film debut in the coming-of-age drama, *The Man in the Moon*, at fourteen. She was a standout in 1998's *Pleasantville* (looking delightful in retro sweater sets) and drew critical praise for the preppy, relentless Tracy Flick in 1999's *Election*.

The film that truly cemented her stardom (and made pink the new black!) was the 2001 smash hit, *Legally Blonde* (costumes by Sophie Carbonell). She followed with a rom-com about a fashion designer, *Sweet Home Alabama* (Sophie de Rakoff) and the 2004 historical film, *Vanity Fair* (costumes by Beatrix Aruna Pasztor).

Witherspoon did her own singing—and won the Best Actress Oscar—playing Johnny Cash's strong-willed wife, June Carter, in the 2005 biography, *Walk the Line* (costumes by Arianne Phillips).

In the 2011 period drama, *Water for Elephants*, based on the bestselling book, Witherspoon never looked lovelier in circus costumes and Jazz-age gowns by Jacqueline West.

MOST FASHIONABLE FILMS
LEGALLY BLONDE (2001)
VANITY FAIR (2004)
WATER FOR ELEPHANTS (2011)

Witherspoon Style
With her willowy figure, blue eyes, and honey-blonde hair, the actress does justice to clothing from any time period—but especially today's casual "rich-girl" choices.

Signature Look
- Ultrafeminine dresses and gowns
- Classy cardigan or pullover sweaters with high boots
- Big scarves over fitted jackets and blazers

ABOVE
Witherspoon raised her "adorable quotient" immeasurably by donning a variety of pink ensembles—including this honeysuckle leather suit, accessorized with pink shades and Bruiser the Chihuahua—in 2001's comic hit, *Legally Blonde*.

RIGHT
For references, *Water for Elephants* costume designer Jacqueline West used 1930s' films like *Polly of the Circus*, *Dinner at Eight*, and *Red Dust*, and a "fabulous" book by Edward J. Kelty called *Step Right This Way*, which documented circus life.

> It's funny that it all becomes about clothes. It's bizarre. You work your butt off and then you win an award and it's all about your dress. You can't get away from it.
>
> REESE WITHERSPOON

THE NEW MILLENNIUM AND BEYOND | HOLLYWOOD FASHION

ZOË SALDAÑA

Zoë Saldaña has starred in some of the most successful movie franchises—Marvel's heavy-hitters *Guardians of the Galaxy* and *The Avengers*, and the *Star Trek* reboot—and is about to re-enter the otherworldly universe of box-office champ *Avatar*.

Saldaña was born in 1978, in Passaic, New Jersey, to a Dominican father and a Puerto Rican mother. She was raised in Queens until age 10, when her family relocated to the Dominican Republic. There she nurtured an interest in performing by studying ballet and other forms of dance. Back in the U.S., she worked with Faces, a theater troupe that provided positive messages to at-risk teens. In 2000, her background led to a lead role in the dance film *Center Stage*.

Her athletic physique and exotic looks made her the go-to girl to play aliens and adventuresses (she even had a small part in the first *Pirates of the Caribbean*), and when James Cameron chose her for the pivotal role of Neytiri in *Avatar*, her future was assured. The film has remained the top box officer earner since its release. Saldaña went on to play Nyota Uhura in *Star Trek* (2009), and then was cast as Gamora, daughter of archvillain Thanos, in both the *Guardians of the Galaxy* and *Avengers* franchises. Meanwhile, Cameron has been filming two sequels to *Avatar*, in which Saldaña again portrays the powerful Na'vi warrior princess.

There may be an explanation in her past for her penchant for fierce female characters. "Growing up," Saldaña admits, "my dolls were doctors and on secret missions. I had Barbie Goes Rambo."

MOST FASHIONABLE FILMS

CENTER STAGE (2000)
AVATAR (2009)
STAR TREK (2009)
GUARDIANS OF THE GALAXY (2014)
NINA (2016)
LIVE BY NIGHT (2016)

Saldaña Style

An acknowledged style icon, Saldaña believes that she knows what looks best on her body type. For nights out she prefers pencil skirts or flirty mini skirts, and for the red carpet, she chooses form-fitting or mermaid-style gowns, typically in red, black, or white.

Signature Look

- Jeggings or leggings with short jackets
- High heels
- Long, wavy hair and smudged eyes

> **God as my witness, I am going to try to do everything I can to keep this ass together for as long as I possibly can—without going against nature.**
>
> ZOË SALDAÑA, ON PLASTIC SURGERY

ABOVE

In Ben Affleck's crime drama *Live By Night*, Saldaña plays gangster Affleck's Cuban wife; the film's 1920s period clothing was styled by designer Jacqueline West.

LEFT

On 2009's *Avatar*, Saldaña used performance capture to play CGI character Neytiri, a Na'vi warrior princess. The costumes by Mayes C. Rubeo and Deborah L. Scott endowed the Ne'ri with recognizable human qualities, including modesty.

225

HOLLYWOOD FASHION | THE NEW MILLENNIUM AND BEYOND

LUPITA NYONG'O

After she impressed filmgoers with her devastating potrayal of abused slave Patsey in *12 Years a Slave*, Lupita Nyong'o became a red carpet darling representing international designers.

The daughter of Kenyan parents, a college professor and a businesswoman, Nyong'o was born in Mexico City in 1983, but raised in Kenya. Soon after receiving her master's degree from Yale Drama School, she was chosen to play Patsey in *12 Years a Slave,* for which she won a Best Supporting Actress Academy Award. She then appeared in the action thriller *Non-stop*, Disney's *The Queen of Katwe*, did motion capture to portray Maz Kanata in *Star Wars: The Force Awakens*, and performed voiceover work for 2016's *The Jungle Book*.

2018 saw her cast as the romantic lead in the Marvel blockbuster *Black Panther*. Among other accolades, the film was notable for offering cinematic opportunities to black women. The four female leads consisted of Nyong'o, Danai Gurira from *The Walking Dead*, newcomer Letitia Wright, and Angela Bassett as the queen of Wakanda. Costume designer Ruth E. Carter and production designer Hannah Beachler both went on to win Oscars in their respective categories, the first black women to do so.

Nyong'o's 2019 thriller *Us*, directed by Jordan Peele, resulted in the best-ever opening for an original story horror film. Currently, Nyong'o is concentrating on numerous acting and producing projects and continues her charity work for women's rights and endangered elephants.

> **It's great to have something to dress up for…I spent three years in slacks at drama school, so now I like putting dresses on.**
> LUPITA NYONG'O

ABOVE
Nyong'o wears an African-style headwrap and gathered lilac gown by Elie Saab at the premiere of Disney's *The Queen of Katwe*.

RIGHT
In this scene from 2018's *Black Panther*, Nyong'o wears the uniform of the all-female Wakandan guard, the Dora Milaje. The blockbuster's costumes were designed by Ruth E. Carter, the first black woman to win an Oscar for Costume Design.

MOST FASHIONABLE FILMS
THE QUEEN OF KATWE (2016)
BLACK PANTHER (2018)
US (2019)

Nyong'o Style
The actress's taste ranges from classic looks like surplice dresses, to wide-leg dress pants, to African-influenced fashions. She doesn't shy away from bright colors or bold prints but also looks stunning in neutrals and pastels.

Signature Look
- Short, natural hair
- Trouser looks
- Ethnic prints and head wraps

THE NEW MILLENNIUM AND BEYOND | HOLLYWOOD FASHION

EMMA STONE

MOST FASHIONABLE FILMS

CRAZY STUPID LOVE (2011)
THE HELP (2011)
GANGSTER SQUAD (2013)
THE AMAZING SPIDER-MAN (2012
LA LA LAND (2014)
THE FAVOURITE (2018)

Stone Style

Emma's style both on and off the screen is classic, feminine, and sometimes flirty. It has sometimes been described as "accessible." Stone is a favorite on evening talk shows, where she displays crisp comic timing and a throaty laugh.

Signature Look
- Soft dressing
- Minimal make-up and sleek hair
- "Big" coats and jackets

With her gamine smile, wide-set doe eyes, and auburn hair, Emma Stone can evoke quirky humor, romantic wonder, plucky determination, or heartbreaking pathos, making her one of the most versatile actresses in Hollywood.

Emma Stone was born in 1988 in Scottsdale, Arizona, and is of Swedish, German, and British Isles descent. After performing with the Valley Youth Theater in Phoenix, she used a Power Point presentation to convince her parents to let her quit school and move to LA.

It was a providential decision. Early roles included a grifter fleeing the undead in *Zombieland*, a scheming student in *Easy A*, Steve Carell's dating-fatigued daughter in *Crazy Stupid Love*, and an earnest young journalist in *The Help*. In 2012 she played opposite Andrew Garfield in Marvel's *Amazing Spider-Man*, then handled the challenge of more serious material as Michael Keaton's reformed-addict daughter in 2014's *Birdman*. She even appeared on Broadway at the end of 2014 in a *Cabaret* revival.

She won hearts—and an Oscar—as an aspiring actress in *La La Land*, dancing across the Los Angeles skyline with her jazz musician beau, played by Ryan Gosling. The film's director, Damien Chazelle, had seen her in *Cabaret* and been impressed. In 2016 she again costarred with Carell, playing Billie Jean King to his Bobby Riggs in *Battle of the Sexes*. In 2017, she became part of a female power triumvirate, cast opposite Rachel Weisz and Olivia Coleman in the historical dark comedy, *The Favourite*. Stone and Weisz were both nominated for Best Supporting Oscars, while Coleman won for Best Actress.

> What sets you apart can sometimes feel like a burden and it's not. And a lot of the time, it's what makes you great.
> — EMMA STONE

ABOVE

Wearing a green and pink lace dress, Stone poses demurely for the press at the 2016 Venice Film Festival. A red carpet regular, she has modeled gowns by Louis Vuitton, Versace, Chanel, and Lanvin.

LEFT

Stone plays the scheming cousin of the Duchess of Marlborough in 2018's *The Favourite*. The film showcased lavish period costumes from the early eighteenth century from British designer Sandy Powell.

HOLLYWOOD FASHION | THE NEW MILLENNIUM AND BEYOND

MEN OF THE NEW MILLENNIUM
PIRATES, SUPERHEROES, AND REGULAR JOES

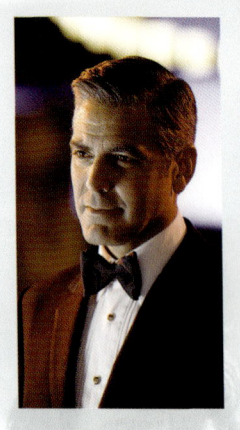

ABOVE

George Clooney remains Mr. Smooth in 2007's *Ocean's Thirteen*, the third installment of a film franchise featuring a gang of good-natured, "A-list" thieves.

TOP RIGHT

Christian Bale's Batman confronts Heath Ledger as the Joker in 2008's *The Dark Knight*. This film, as did earlier Batman productions, influenced everything from kid's pajamas and goth fashions to automotive design.

RIGHT

In his Oscar-winning portrayal of Ray Charles in 2004's *Ray*, Jamie Foxx deftly channeled the legendary R&B singer and even wore prosthetic lenses that made him blind for up to 14 hours a day. Here he is shown performing on stage wearing a beige tuxedo outlined with dark piping.

Johnny Depp owned the box office and the Seven Seas during the mid 2000s playing Captain Jack Sparrow in Disney's mega-successful *Pirates of the Caribbean* franchise. Depp not only created a unique on-screen character, he collaborated with costumer Penny Rose to create the now-iconic look of his pirate—coin-adorned dreadlocks, gold teeth, eyeliner, head wrap, and swashbuckling leather hat.

Not far behind Depp was Robert Downey, Jr., carrying two franchises—*Iron Man* and *Sherlock Holmes*. As *Iron Man*'s alter ego, Tony Stark, Downey wowed his boardroom with sleek power dressing (costumes by Rebecca Bentjen and Laura Jean Shannon); as Holmes (costumes by Jenny Beavan), he ushered in a return to nubby, more romantic fashions for both men and women—and inspired Steampunk fans everywhere.

As Daniel Radcliffe was growing up on camera during the *Harry Potter* series, he and his "schoolmates" continued to make the tweedy, preppy style of Hogwarts a popular trend on campuses everywhere.

Other screen superheroes of the new millennium included *Spiderman*, *Batman* (the Christian Bale incarnation), *Wolverine* and the *X-Men* brethren, and *Hellboy*. Their respective looks often influenced contemporary fashion—from *Wolverine*'s singlet undershirt to *Hellboy*'s Outback-style duster.

Making It Real

Film biographies reached new heights during this decade. *Walk the Line* featuring Joaquin Phoenix as Johnny Cash, "The Man in Black" (costumes by Arianne Phillips) and Jamie Foxx as R&B music legend Ray Charles in *Ray* (costumes by Sharen Davis)—were two standouts. Phoenix and Foxx were nominated for Academy Awards; Foxx went on to win the Oscar. Both films also showcased classic stage fashions from the 1950s and 1960s—country-and-western casual and rhythm-and-blues slick, respectively.

In 2008, Marvel Studios began its long box office reign with *Iron Man*, soon followed by franchises like *Thor*, *Captain America*, *The Avengers*, and *Guardians of the Galaxy*.

THE NEW MILLENNIUM AND BEYOND | HOLLYWOOD FASHION

Signature Menswear Looks of the 2000s
- Puffer jackets and tartan lumberjack shirts as outerwear
- Three-button sports coats
- Motocross jackets
- High-end sneakers (Converse All Stars, etc)
- Motorcycle boots

TOP LEFT

Johnny Depp, as Captain Jack Sparrow, balances on a ship's spar in the madly successful *Pirates of the Caribbean: The Curse of the Black Pearl*, the first of four related films that earned billions of dollars for Disney Studios.

BOTTOM LEFT

In 2018's *Aquaman*, action star Jason Momoa was outfitted by Kym Barrett as the half-human/half Atlantean superhero in the classic green and orange costume familiar to comics fans. Momoa says, "forget the swimming and stunts"...the hardest part of the role was removing the form-fitting costume to answer the call of nature.

BOTTOM RIGHT

Rupert Grint and Daniel Radcliffe, as Ron and Harry, confer in the library of Hogwarts in 2005's *Harry Potter and the Goblet of Fire*.

HOLLYWOOD FASHION | OSCARS FOR COSTUME DESIGN

OSCARS FOR COSTUME DESIGN

This award, voted on by the costume designers in the Academy of Motion Picture Arts and Sciences, did not always reflect the most influential or outstanding costuming, but rather the costumes that voters felt best served each film.

1948
B&W: *Hamlet*, Roger K. Furse
Color: *Joan of Arc*, Dorothy Jeakins, Barbara Karinska

1949
B&W: *The Heiress*, Edith Head, Gile Steele
Color: *Adventures of Don Juan*, Marjorie Best, Leah Rhodes, William Travilla

1950
B&W: *All About Eve*, Edith Head, Charles LeMaire
Color: *Samson and Delilah*, Edith Head, Charles LeMaire, Dorothy Jeakins, Elois Jennsen, Gile Steele, Gwen Wakeling

1951
B&W: *A Place in the Sun*, Edith Head
Color: *An American in Paris*, Orry-Kelly, Walter Plunkett, Irene Sharaff

1952
B&W: *The Bad and the Beautiful*, Helen Rose
Color: *Moulin Rouge*, Marcel Vertés

1953
B&W: *Roman Holiday*, Edith Head
Color: *The Robe*, Charles LeMaire, Emile Santiago

1954
B&W: *Sabrina*, Edith Head
Color: *Gate of Hell*, Sanzo Wada

1955
B&W: *I'll Cry Tomorrow*, Helen Rose
Color: *Love Is a Many-Splendored Thing*, Charles LeMaire

1956
B&W: *The Solid Gold Cadillac*, Jean Louis
Color: *The King and I*, Irene Sharaff

1957
Les Girls, Orry-Kelly

1958
Gigi, Cecil Beaton

1959
B&W: *Some Like it Hot*, Orry-Kelly
Color: *Ben-Hur*, Elizabeth Haffenden

1960
B&W: *The Facts of Life*, Edith Head, Edward Stevenson
Color: *Spartacus*, Arlington Valles

1961
B&W: *La Dolce Vita*, Piero Gherardi
Color: *West Side Story*, Irene Sharaff

1962
B&W: *What Ever Happened to Baby Jane?*, Norma Koch
Color: *The Wonderful World of the Brothers Grimm*, Mary Wills

1963
B&W: *8½*, Piero Gherardi
Color: *Cleopatra*, Renie Conley, Vittorio Nino Novarese, Irene Sharaff

1964
B&W: *The Night of the Iguana*, Dorothy Jeakins
Color: *My Fair Lady*, Cecil Beaton

1965
B&W: *Darling*, Julie Harris
Color: *Doctor Zhivago*, Phyllis Dalton

1966
B&W: *Who's Afraid of Virginia Woolf?*, Irene Sharaff
Color: *A Man for All Seasons*, Elizabeth Haffenden

1967
Camelot, John Truscott

1968
Romeo and Juliet, Danilo Donati

1969
Anne of the Thousand Days, Margaret Furse

1970
Cromwell, Vittorio Nino Novarese

1971
Nicholas and Alexandra, Yvonne Blake and Antonio Castillo

HOLLYWOOD FASHION | OSCARS FOR COSTUME DESIGN

1972
Travels with My Aunt, Anthony Powell

1973
The Sting, Edith Head

1974
The Great Gatsby, Theoni V. Aldredge

1975
Barry Lyndon, Milena Canonero and Ulla-Brit Soderlund

1976
Fellini's Casanova, Danilo Donati

1977
Star Wars, John Mollo

1978
Death on the Nile, Anthony Powell

1979
All That Jazz, Albert Wolsky

1980
Tess, Anthony Powell

1981
Chariots of Fire, Milena Canonero

1982
Gandhi, Bhanu Athaiya and John Mollo

1983
Fanny and Alexander, Marik Vos

1984
Amadeus, Theodor Pistek

1985
Ran, Emi Wada

1986
A Room with a View, Jenny Beavan and John Bright

1987
The Last Emperor, James Acheson

1988
Dangerous Liaisons, James Acheson

1989
Henry V, Phyllis Dalton

1990
Cyrano de Bergerac, Franca Squarciapino

1991
Bugsy, Albert Wolsky

1992
Bram Stoker's Dracula, Eiko Ishioka

1993
The Age of Innocence, Gabriella Pescucci

1994
The Adventures of Priscilla, Queen of the Desert, Tim Chappel and Lizzy Gardiner

1995
Restoration, James Acheson

1996
The English Patient, Ann Roth

1997
Titanic, Deborah Lynn Scott

1998
Shakespeare in Love, Sandy Powell

1999
Topsy-Turvy, Lindy Hemming

2000
Gladiator, Janty Yates

2001
Moulin Rouge!, Catherine Martin and Angus Strathie

2002
Chicago, Colleen Atwood

2003
Lord of the Rings: The Return of the King, Ngila Dickson and Richard Taylor

2004
The Aviator, Sandy Powell

2005
Memoirs of a Geisha, Colleen Atwood

2006
Marie Antoinette, Milena Canonero

2007
Elizabeth: The Golden Age, Alexandra Byrne

2008
The Duchess, Michael O'Connor

2009
The Young Victoria, Sandy Powell

2010
Alice in Wonderland, Colleen Atwood

2011
The Artist, Mark Bridges

2012
Anna Karenina, Jacqueline Durran

2013
The Great Gatsby, Catherine Martin

2014
The Grand Budapest Hotel, Milena Canonero

2015
Mad Max: Fury Road, Jenny Beavan

2016
Fantastic Beasts and Where to Find Them, Colleen Atwood

2017
Phantom Thread, Mark Bridges

2018
Black Panther, Ruth E. Carter

HOLLYWOOD FASHION | TIMELINE

TIMELINE

The following is a timeline of significant events, key inventions or innovations, and major milestones in both the world of cinema and the international fashion industry.

1839
While searching for a way to keep rubber from melting in hot weather, Charles Goodyear develops the vulcanization process. Vulcanization allows latex fibers to stretch and then contract, a new technique that paves the way for not only tires but also elastic fabrics and more comfortable corsets.

1850
Synthetic polymers are developed as an alternative to cotton, linen, wool, and silk fibers. They will ultimately supplant all natural textile bases as a source for manufacturing underwear.

1867
Harper's Bazaar magazine prints its first issue and assures readers that it will provide them with "the genuine Paris fashions simultaneously with Parisians themselves."

1886
Denim manufacturer Levi Strauss devises its "Two Horse Brand" leather patch, showing the jean being pulled between two horses to indicate its strength.

1889
William Kennedy Laurie Dickson, commissioned by Thomas Alva Edison, builds the first motion-picture camera and names it the Kinetograph.

1890
René de Réaumur uses synthetic resins to invent rayon. He dubs it "art silk."

1894
The Edison Corporation establishes the first motion-picture studio in West Orange, NJ, a Kinetograph production center nicknamed the Black Maria (slang for a police van).

1894
The first Kinetoscope parlor opens at 1155 Broadway in New York City. Spectators can watch films for 25 cents.

1895
In France, Auguste and Louis Lumiere, inventors of the Cinématograph, a combination camera and projector, hold the first private screening. The projected image of an oncoming train is said to have caused a stampede of frightened viewers.

1900
Harvey Wilcox, a Kansas transplant, buys 160 acres west of Los Angeles to found a conservative community. His wife Daeida meets a woman on a train who speaks of her summer home called Hollywood. Daeida convinces her husband to name their new community Hollywood, who wanted to name it Figwood.

1903
Edison Corporation mechanic Edwin S. Porter turns cameraman, director and producer to make *The Great Train Robbery*. With 14 shots cutting between simultaneous events, this 12-minute short establishes the shot as film's basic element and editing as a central narrative device. It is also the first Western.

1904
The American Charles R. De Bevoise Company selects "brassiere," a Norman French term, for its new product. Brassiere translates as a woman's bodice or a child's undervest. The product looks like a camisole with a few bones (or "stays") to maintain its shape.

1905
The first movie theater opens in Pittsburgh.

1905
Entertainment industry trade paper *Variety* starts, founded by Sime Silverman.

1908
French couturier Paul Poiret furthers a growing public disenchantment with the corset by designing "corsetless" dresses. Feminists had been criticizing the corset for years.

1909
The first permanent film studio in Los Angeles, the Selig Polyscope Company, relocates from Chicago. Their film, The Heart of a Race Tout, was the first movie completed entirely in California.

1909
The New York Times publishes the first movie review—on D.W. Griffith's *Pippa Passes*.

1910
Thomas Edison introduces his kinetophone, which makes talkies a reality.

1910
Hollywood officially becomes a part of Los Angeles in order to benefit from the water and sewage systems.

1910
Open-air automobiles require the donning of protective "dusters," hats with veils, and goggles.

1911
David Horsley purchases the Blondeau Tavern

232 TIMELINE

HOLLYWOOD FASHION | TIMELINE

on Sunset Boulevard and turns it into the Nestor Film Company, Hollywood's first film studio.

1911
The first feature film is released when the two reels of D.W. Griffith's *Enoch Arden* are screened together.

1912
Photoplay debuts as the first magazine for movie fans.

1914
The first feature-length film, The Squaw Man, is released. Its creators—Samuel Goldwyn, Cecil B. DeMille, and Jesse Lasky—made the film in a barn a block away from what is now the corner of Hollywood and Vine.

1914
Charlie Chaplin debuts the "Little Tramp" in *Kid Auto Races at Venice* after Mack Sennet tells him to "make himself up" prior to filming.

1914
World War I shortages affect skirt hems, which rise to well above the ankle.

1916
While filming *Intolerance*, director D.W. Griffith hires Clare West to be the first "studio designer" and craft costumes for the leads and the extras.

1919
The U.S. Navy introduces the precursor to the T-shirt, a "light undershirt" that includes an "elastic collarette on the neck opening."

1920
French designer Madeleine Vionnet introduces the bias cut to the world. Other designers of the decade include Patou, Molyneux, Chanel, Boue Souers, Louiseboulanger, and Augustabernard.

1921
The Sheik, directed by George Melford, debuts and establishes star Rudolph Valentino as cinema's best-known lover.

1923
German Shepherd Rin Tin Tin becomes film's first canine star.

1923
The Hollywood sign, which originally read "Hollywoodland," is put up as an advertisement for a housing development. After the ad campaign is over, the sign remains and becomes neglected.

1924
Walt Disney creates his first cartoon, *Alice's Wonderland*.

1927
Popular vaudevillian Al Jolson astounds audiences with his nightclub act in *The Jazz Singer*, the first feature-length talkie.

1927
Grauman's Chinese Theatre in Hollywood has its Grand Opening on May 18. The film shown that evening is Cecil B. DeMille's *The King of Kings*. A riot breaks out as onlookers try to see the stars entering the theater for the premiere.

1929
The first Academy Awards ceremony and banquet takes place on May 16 in the Blossom Room of the Hollywood Roosevelt Hotel.

1930
As head of the Motion Picture Producers and Distributors of America, William Hays establishes a code of decency that outlines what is acceptable in films.

1935
Zippers now replace hook-and-eye closures.

1935
Although a primitive, two-color process was first used in 1922, audiences weren't impressed by Technicolor until a three-color system appeared in *Becky Sharp*.

1936
Costume jewelry, popularized by Chanel's signature faux pearl strands, becomes an accessory staple.

1938
Small shoulder pads for women gain popularity.

1938
Surveys reveal that women clamor to look and dress like their screen idols, prompting some Hollywood designers to mass market their own retail labels in department stores.

1939
Glamour magazine prints its first issue. The editors assure readers that all women possess "potential glamour," which can be achieved with the help of the right accessories, hairstyle, cosmetics, deportment, and of course clothing.

1940
Surfers board shorts are born, probably in Southern California, as a response to skimpy men's bathing suits. Surfers needed more protection on their legs, as well as a firm closure in case of a wipeout. Surfboard maker Dale Velzy devises a prototype by cutting off white sailor pants just above the knee.

1940
The occupation of Paris by the Nazis proves a disaster for French haute couture, allowing the baton to be passed to the American fashion industry.

1940
With more women entering the workplace due to the war effort, slacks, once considered scandalous, gain popularity.

1940
Adrian's wide-shouldered, belted jackets, designed for Joan Crawford, become the rage, along with knee-length, fitted skirts and open-toed pumps.

1943
Norman Rockwell's painting of "Rosie the Riveter" is featured on the May 29 cover of the *Saturday Evening Post*, encouraging women to join the wartime work force.

1943
In June, a group of U.S. Navy sailors in Los Angeles, angered by confrontations with local Mexican-American youths, take weapons into nearby neighborhoods and target all those wearing oversized zoot suits. The "Zoot Suit Riots" demonstrated fashion's potential to function as a conflict-generating marker of the differences between various segments of society.

233

1944
"Shorter than a Capri and with a slightly wider leg," the "pedal pusher" is created by L.A. designer DeDe Johnson, who wants a garment that won't get caught in a bicycle chain. Teen idols Sandra Dee and Annette Funicello, and stars like Audrey Hepburn and Marilyn Monroe later make the look a 1950's fashion craze.

1946
Frederick Mellinger begins his risqué line of lingerie, Frederick's of Hollywood, with a racy catalog. Frederick's will eventually grow into a chain of over 175 stores.

1946
The Cannes Film Festival debuts in the south of France.

1947
French fashion designer Christian Dior debuts the Corolle line—dubbed "the New Look"—which features a cinched waist, rounded hips, and a long skirt. This popular style enshrines him as "the template for the designer as a celebrity," and places him on the cover of *Time* magazine.

1948
The Academy Awards honor Best Costume Design for the first time.

1949
The Hollywood Chamber of Commerce takes charge of the Hollywoodland sign, removing the word "land" and repairing the letters that now spell, simply, "Hollywood."

1950
This decade sees the birth of prêt-a-porter or ready-to-wear fashions from design houses.

1950
Middle-class women wear housedresses for "wifely" domestic roles and don cocktail dresses to entertain friends and neighbors.

1950
Hawaiian textiles and clothing become popular with both sexes.

1950
Teen films featuring rebellious girls and angry young men introduce black leather jackets, blue jeans, motorcycle boots, and white tee shirts.

1950
Balenciaga creates the shapeless sack dress and Yves Saint Laurent introduces the Trapeze dress, which morphs into the babydoll dress.

1952
Warner's introduces the Merry Widow corset. Its debut coincides with a movie of the same name, starring Lana Turner, in which she is filmed in a white long-line corset and high heels.

1953
To counteract the threat of television, Hollywood thinks big and develops wide-screen processes such as CinemaScope, first seen in *The Robe*.

1958
The Hollywood Walk of Fame is created.

1960
The first star is placed on the Hollywood Walk of Fame. The celebrity honored is Joanne Woodward.

1961
Chic First Lady Jacqueline Kennedy popularizes the sheath dress worn with a short jacket and pearls.

1960
The influence of teen fashion and the counterculture grows to include mini-skirts, colorful tent shifts, bell-bottoms, fur vests, space-age prints, and go-go boots.

1961
TWA starts regular in-flight movies with Lana Turner's By *Love Possessed*.

1967
The legendary Hollywood designer Edith Head bans mini-skirts from the Academy Awards because she feels they lack elegance.

1967
Balenciaga gives up his design house, declaring that "Fashion is dead."

1968
The motion picture rating system debuts with G, PG, R and X. In 1990, the X rating is changed to NC-17 (no children under 17).

1970
3000 people crowd MGM's sound stage 27 on May 2 for the greatest auction in Hollywood's history.

1977
Saturday Night Fever sparks the disco inferno as well as the popularity of movie soundtracks.

1995
Although CGI—Computer Generated Imaging—was first used in 1973's *Westworld*, it finally comes of age with Pixar's *Toy Story*. The hot new costume soon becomes the "motion capture suit" that allows a human to create movement and facial expressions for a CGI or digital character.

1995
James Cameron's period drama *Titanic* wins 11 Academy Awards, including Best Picture and Best Director. It goes on to become the highest grossing film in Hollywood's history and inspires fashion designers to make a return to classic elegance.

2001
The Kodak Theatre opens on Hollywood Boulevard in the location of the old Hollywood Hotel. Now called The Dolby Theatre, the building is the permanent home of the Academy Awards ceremony.

2010
James Cameron's science fiction epic *Avatar* becomes the highest grossing film in history, shifting Cameron's *Titanic* into second place. Blue becomes the new black.

Louise Brooks

Ginger Rogers

Gene Tierney

Sophia Loren

Ann-Margret

Liza Minnelli

Jamie Lee Curtis

Richard Gere & Julia Roberts

John Travolta & Uma Thurman

Kristin Davis, Cynthia Nixon, Kim Cattrall & Sarah Jessica Parker

NANCY J. HAJESKI

Award-winning author Nancy J. Hajeski has written a dozen historical romances for Penguin-Putnam as Nancy Butler. Her bestselling adaptation of Pride and Prejudice for Marvel Entertainment remained on the NY Time list for 13 weeks. Hajeski is also a recognized nonfiction author, writing in both the young adult and adult categories. Previous titles on celebrities include two acclaimed coffee table books—*Ali: The Official Portrait of the Greatest of All Time* and *The Beatles: Here, There and Everywhere*. She lives and works beside a world-renowned trout stream in New York's Catskill Mountains.

CREDITS

All images courtesy of PHOTOFEST
except pages:
COVER From original negative / Alamy Stock Photo
129 FULL PAGE: Pictorial Press Ltd / Alamy Stock Photo
190 BOTTOM RIGHT: Entertainment Pictures / Alamy Stock Photo
194 ABOVE: Allstar Picture Library / Alamy Stock Photo
212 RIGHT: AF archive / Alamy Stock Photo
215 LEFT: Image Press Agency / Alamy Stock Photo
225 ABOVE: AF archive / Alamy Stock Photo, LEFT: Moviestore collection Ltd / Alamy Stock Photo
226 ABOVE: Hyperstar / Alamy Stock Photo, RIGHT: Picturelux / The Hollywood Archive / Alamy Stock Photo
227 ABOVE: dpa picture alliance / Alamy Stock Photo, LEFT: Entertainment Pictures / Alamy Stock Photo
228 RIGHT: Moviestore collection Ltd / Alamy Stock Photo
229 BOTTOM RIGHT: Moviestore collection Ltd / Alamy Stock Photo